MARGINALISM AND DISCONTINUITY

Tools for the Crafts of Knowledge and Decision

Marginalism
and Discontinuity

Tools for the Crafts of Knowledge and Decision

MARTIN H. KRIEGER

Russell Sage Foundation   New York

The Russell Sage Foundation

Library of Congress Cataloging-in-Publication Data

Krieger, Martin H.
  Marginalism and discontinuity : tools for the crafts of knowledge and
    decision
  Martin H. Krieger.
    p. cm.
  Bibliography: p.
  Includes index.
  ISBN 0-87154-488-1
    1. Economics—Methodology. I. Title.
HB131.K75 1989
330'.072—dc20

HB
131
.K75
1989

64697

89-10047
CIP

For my son David

Contents

ety, goodness, value, and authority in perversion. Fetishes: their production (alienation, composition, destabilization, and stigmatization), and the appearance of anima (analysis, emergence, and discontinuity). Anxiety and revelation.

PART TWO: TOOLS AND SACRED PRACTICES

Setting up a model so that one sees what is true as true; a Husserlian phenomenology of the craft of mathematics. It "must" be true; it "must" go this way; models as Providence; the good example. Autonomy and fertility of the mathematical world. Learning to play with models; the rhetoric of proof. The horizon of meaning and application; the reasonable effectiveness of mathematics in its application.

Objective and situational tools in the craft of science. A linear world of separable modular objects. Physicists and their toolkit: mathematics, diagrammatic, rhetoric. The art of addressing nature—medium or genre, object or trope, interaction or plot, strategies of address, and commonplaces. The plenitude and modularity of nature. A linear, additive, smooth, dumb world.

The lessons of history in a scientific age; the apocalyptic and moral and the practical and particular. Plausible and probable stories of doom; Pascalian and worst-case scenarios; the limits of titration. Cooperation and survival; surprise and systematic ignorance and blindness; fluctuations and insurance. The storyteller and giving a warning; eschatologies.

Archetypes of place. Migration, insemination, and white people. Virginity, virility, and purity, and genocide in America. The East, the West, and the Turner thesis. A crossing of lines and a mixture of impurities. The fructiferousness of the Other.

The limits of toolishness. The good-enough mother; letting baby cry; Winnicottian problem solving.

Preface

MARGINALISM and discontinuity characterize a set of tools we need to get a handle onto the world.* These tools are the models we use for theorizing and acting. Their employment is a craft, a craft of knowledge and decision—a craft that is defined within specific historical traditions and concrete situations of practice. An account of "toolishness" is a demonstration of how we take the world in terms of specific tools and of how we recurrently draw analogies among the various models and their particular uses. Here "the world" is more or less defined by the tools we employ. And tools are understood as they are applied. Still, the world presents us with phenomena that defy whatever tools we do possess.

Marginalism makes for a world in which small increments or marginals are well defined, to be summed or to be balanced against each other, and in which all differences are small or a matter of a smooth gradation, with no sharp lines of division.† So, for example, on the title page of Alfred Marshall's *Principles of Economics* (1890) we find the Latin proverb *Natura non facit saltum,* Nature does not make jumps. Or, in *War and Peace* (Book III, Part III, Chapter 1), where Tolstoy says, "The progress of humanity, arising from an innumerable multitude of individual wills, is continuous in its motion. . . . Only by assuming an infinitesimally small unit for observation—a differential of history—that is, the homogeneous tendencies of men, and arriving at the integral calculus (that is, taking the sum of those infinitesimal quantities), can we hope to discover the laws of history."

Marginalism allows us to literally add up the world, piece by added-on piece, algorithmically. Namely, there is a process for identifying and enumerating the pieces, and that process is additive as well: As a consequence of enumeration it yields a sum. (This is a direct analogy to the discrete case: A child finds the number of toes on one foot by counting up—one, two, three, four, *five*. Of course, he also has to learn when to stop, and how to avoid double counting.)

Still, parts of the world are profoundly resistant to that additive

---

*Notes to the text, keyed to pages, begin on p. 141.
†For my purposes, differentiability, smoothness, continuity, and marginalism may be treated as being the same; discontinuity will be characterized by big jumps; and discreteness will be characterized by individuation. Also, again for my purposes, marginal changes may be smooth infinitesimals or small but discrete steps.

strategy. And so we shall encounter phenomena of path dependence, discontinuity, bigness, and stickiness, as well as fetishism, mixture, and perversion. Here history and artifact, archetype, and phenomenon are unavoidable, and leftovers and incommensurability are signs of the truth. And despite Tolstoy's wish, we cannot "leave aside kings, ministers, and generals," nor treat as secondary "the Revolution and Napoleon."

Once we take toolishness seriously, we shall find ourselves comfortably shifting between the marginal and the discontinuous, and as we shall see, between the mundane and the sacred. The models are provisional, each one to be tried on to see what work it can do, the success of one model not precluding the success of others in that same situation. In my descriptions I have deliberately alternated the language of the humanities and history and religion with that of science and mechanism. Here the world turns out to be both rhetorical and material, both sacred and mechanical. In Robert Venturi's phrase, this world is both-and rather than either-or.

Some lessons might be drawn from this description, demonstration, and analogy: Rather than asking what the world is really like, examine how we get ahold of it and so describe its phenomenology. Rather than asking why mathematics works in physics, describe how it works and how mathematics and physics are deliberately made to work together. Rather than asking whether the world is smooth or discrete or discontinuous, apply the various models and see how and when they are fruitful. Rather than being puritanical about fetishism, watch how we go about creating discrete objects and fetishes. And rather than choosing between methodological individualism or a solidaristic social vision, note how they depend on each other as aspects of an encompassing culture. For the solidary community is composed of individuals which are in effect animated, designed to do that solidaric work. And individualism requires an implicit social fabric if it is to be viable. Any story of parts and wholes is dialectical as well as mechanical.

In sum, our themes will be toolishness, marginalism, and discontinuity; our mode will be description and analogy; and our purpose will be to demonstrate a way of getting ahold of the world. And ideally, such a herbarium or bestiary of models allows us to recognize ourselves more generally, so unifying specific application and abstract theory.

In the first part I survey the phenomena of marginal change and of discontinuity, including the ironies consequent to adding up the world not so marginally, as in the market's Invisible Hand or in molecular accounts of discontinuous phase transitions. I am particularly concerned with the play of exchange and marginalism against incommensurability and discontinuity, the processes of fetishism or individuation that produce discreteness out of continua, and the transition from smoothness to stickiness to discontinuous jumps. Now within this realm of thought the calculus has a curious property of appearing everywhere. The calculus is the unique way of specifying and adding up the smooth, continuously changing parts of the world. That was what it was invented to do. And it has become a way of taming the discontinuous parts as well.

In the second part I work out some of the consequences of commitments to toolishness, marginalism, and discontinuity. I describe how mathematicians go about crafting, inventing, and discovering their world, developing tools that can do useful work. And I show how aspects of a physicist's practice may be described in terms of a specific toolkit, composed in part of those mathematical tools, in part of those methods of invention and discovery, and in part of models drawn from everyday life. The notion of tools and a toolkit can be used to make sense of an often-noted fact about natural science and other human endeavors: how a small number of ideas and methods keep reappearing and are applicable.

In the last two chapters I consider how discontinuity and transcendence play a central role in considering environmental issues. For these are issues which we endow with apocalyptic and millenarian fervor, and with rational and gradualist prudence. So they provide a good arena in which to watch the play of sacred practices and mundane contexts. Finally, in the epilog I suggest the limits of toolishness.

For most readers there will be literatures or technical points which are unfamiliar, but which I hope are still tempting. And there will be technical passages or detailed examples that might well be scanned, as I shall indicate.

One last point. Many of the problems I address might well be set within the canon of professional academic philosophy and social science. But I take my primary task to be verisimilitudinous and phenomenological description. Then we might begin to ask those philosophic questions.

Acknowledgments

I HAVE BEEN entranced for twenty years by questions concerning tools, marginalism, and discontinuity. Having been trained as a physicist and having spent my teaching career among planners, architects, humanists and social scientists, policy analysts, and engineers, I found the same problems reappearing in different guises.

Early on, I wrote an article ("What's Wrong with Plastic Trees?") pressing the point that what we take as nature is a historical, technological, and social artifact. Of course, this does not mean that what we may take as natural is arbitrary, nor that nature does not resist our wills and fantasies. But it does suggest that natural environments are subject to design and redesign. I was interested in how we consecrate our own inventiveness, but I was sometimes taken to be making sacrilegious assaults on reverential grounds. As a consequence, I became interested in the interplay of sacred and mundane processes. City planning, for example, is rife with such interplays, whether it be a concern with large-scale projects, transformative leadership, and moments of origin and creation, or with problems of decision, conversion, judgment, and evaluation. And the sacred is often expressed through urban form—think of Jerusalem, Rome, Medina, or the City of God.

A few years earlier, in the late 1960s, I did my first work concerning marginalism and discontinuity, a computer simulation model of rapid change in an urban area. The model was inspired by an analogy to phase transitions in matter, such as the spontaneous magnetization of a piece of iron or the freezing of a liquid. A large number of smooth, endogenous, microscopic interactions can yield discontinuous macroscopic effects. The simulation kept track of each individual separately, and it allowed the individuals to interact. A variety of outcomes appeared depending on the strength of interaction and on early fluctuations in the interaction processes. The model showed that big changes and a rigid orderliness may be a cumulative consequence of a not very large number of small changes—a few thousand, and surely much less than the number of atoms in a gram of matter, approximately 10^{23}. There is a special delight in such a mechanical and combinatorial example of emergence, as is as well evolution or the market with its Invisible Hand, the mechanisms being somewhat different for each case. And historically, explanations that produce qualitatively surprising consequences from comparatively simple, dumb, innocent components have been taken as a sign of Providence and of God's design of the universe.

Such simulation models also prove to be good ways for displaying situations which are not steady state, not in equilibrium, not optimal, and not well damped. Of course, one is tempted to find averaged properties by performing many runs of a simulation. But it may well be the case that many urban phenomena are in fact outliers, disequilibria, fluctuations, and transients.

A third influence is perhaps more parochial. When I was trained as a scientist I never asked why the calculus was used in physics (although I always did wonder why the signs of the positions and the momenta were different in the Hamiltonian formulation of classical mechanics—that is, $\partial H/\partial p = \partial q/\partial t$ but $\partial H/\partial q = -\partial p/\partial t$). Later on, however, I became curious about why the calculus had much to do with economics or why physical models were useful at all in social science. Straightforward answers—say an algebraic derivation of the Hamiltonian formulation from Newton's laws, or that the calculus is about optimization and hence marginalism, and so is economics—did not seem deep enough. For me, they neither provided satisfactory geometrical pictures nor justified the ontology, the natural units of these worlds. Now modern differential geometry provides a richer answer to the original question. And, for example, a study of nineteenth-century social thought shows how economy came to be formulated in marginalist terms, the so-called marginalist revolution. More generally, historical study shows how the identity of tool and world is contingent and a matter of their mutual adjustment.

I became curious about how we craft conceptual tools to do the work of natural and social science. Having been trained to think in terms of models and theoretical analogies, it seemed worthwhile to be able to describe scientific work in those terms. I was as well influenced by much of contemporary philosophy of science, which is also tool and craft oriented. My son David has made me think carefully about when none of these kinds of explanation apply, and so has led me to alternative literatures.

Several years ago, at the Massachusetts Institute of Technology, the Russell Sage Foundation gave me the chance to pursue these issues. And both at MIT and at the University of Southern California, the Exxon Education Foundation allowed me to consider them in the context of natural science. Exxon also supported the revisions for this book.

About half of this book has appeared in somewhat different form in scholarly journals. I am grateful for permission to reprint. The sources for chapters or parts of chapters are:

Chapter One: "Big Decisions and a Culture of Decisionmaking," *Journal of Policy Analysis and Management* 5, no. 4 (Summer 1986): 779–797.

Chapter Two: "Phenomenological and Many-Body Models in Natural Science and Social Research," *fundamenta scientiae* 2, nos. 3/4 (1981): 425–431; "The Culture of Decisionmaking," in M. Grauer, M. Thompson, and A. P. Wierzbicki, eds., *Plural Rationalities and Interactive Decision Processes,* Lecture Notes in Economics and Mathematical Systems no. 248 (Berlin: Springer Verlag, 1985), pp. 65–74.

Chapter Three: "Where Do Centers Come From?" *Environment and Planning A* 19 (1987): 1251–1260.

Chapter Five: "The Elementary Structures of Particles," *Social Studies of Science* 17 (1987): 749–752.

Chapter Six: "Essay Review of E. Livingston, *The Ethnomethodological Foundations of Mathematics,*" *Advances in Mathematics* 64 (1987): 326–332.

Chapter Seven: "The Physicist's Toolkit," *American Journal of Physics* 55, no. 11 (November 1987): 1033–1038.

Chapter Eight: "The Possibility of Doom," *Technology in Society* 9 (1987): 181–190.

Chapter Nine: "Ethnicity and the Frontier in Los Angeles," *Society and Space, Environment and Planning D* 4, no. 3 (1986): 385–389.

Epilog: "Research Policy and Review 11. New Tools for a Planner's Toolkit," *Environment and Planning A* 18 (1986): 1181–1187.

My personal debts are extensive and I am grateful for them. At Berkeley, Richard Meier, Dudley Burton, and Langdon Winner criticized a draft of Chapter 8; and a remark by Michael Teitz on big decisions made me realize how peculiar they really are. At the Center for Advanced Study in the Behavioral Sciences, I learned a great deal from Árpád Szabó, Robert Merton, and Chie Nakane. At the University of Minnesota, Jay Caplan led me to some of the literature on fetishism, Harvey Sarles and Barbara Noble asked poignant questions, John Brandl supported my work, and Leo Hurwicz made clear to me what sophisticated economists were up to. Hunter Dupree, at the National Humanities Center, reminded me of the richness of the implications of my scientific training, as did Peter and Trudi Riesenberg. Much of the initial work on toolkits was done while I was a visitor at the Van Leer Jerusalem Foundation at the invitation of Yehuda Elkana.

At MIT, Carl Kaysen supported my research and helped me find support for it. Chapter 1 is a consequence of a course on big decisions that I taught in the Department of Urban Studies and Planning

xvi   *Acknowledgments*

thanks to Larry Susskind. I had wonderful colleagues in the Program in Science, Technology, and Society, especially Michael Piore, Evelyn Keller, Sharon Traweek, and Sherry Turkle; and Charles Weiner, Leon Trilling, Larry Bucciarelli, and Roe Smith. Nat Kuhn cheerfully consulted on my mathematical confusions. Tom Kuhn and Sam Schweber offered me their wise judgment and counsel. I had helpful conversations with Thomas Schelling and Tim Kehoe. At the International Institute of Applied Systems Analysis, Michael Thompson and C. S. Hollings were gracious hosts. Michael led me to Brian Arthur at Stanford, whose concerns turned out to have a lovely resonance with some of my own.

More recently, at the University of Southern California, Michael Dear, Peter Gordon, Richard Peiser, and Gian-Carlo Rota asked me questions that led to some of these chapters. And the staff of the School of Urban and Regional Planning have created a warm environment for me. Our Dean, Alan Kreditor, challenges me in ways that inevitably prove fruitful.

Perhaps because it was a unique institution in its commitment to liberal education and to the training of physicists, my teachers at Columbia University twenty-five years ago continue to influence my work. I am more impressed than ever by their models of how to think and what are worthwhile problems, and by their standards for good work. Every once in a while I suspect that this sentiment is simply nostalgia or romanticism. But having taught at many other universities, I am more sure than ever that my gratefulness is appropriate.

Over the years my friends have encouraged me: Susan Krieger, Stephen Cool, John Hope and Aurelia Franklin, Judith Tendler, James March, Bruce Payne, Ann Douglas, Nell Painter, Tom Glanzman, Deborah Stone, Tom and Jehane Kuhn, Sarah Kuhn, Liza Kuhn, Karen Segal, Peter Crabb, Carol Jacklin, and Mimi Brien. Virtually no one writes a book without help in caring for his children, and I owe a very great deal to Maria Souza.

As I have indicated, this work could not have been done without support from philanthropic foundations. But even more valuably, that pecuniary support was accompanied by faith and appreciation. Peter de Janosi at Russell Sage and Robert Payton and Arnold Shore at Exxon represent what is best in that independent sector. Priscilla Lewis of Russell Sage has shepherded this book, and me, to press with grace and delight.

M. K.

Introduction

HERE I WANT to provide a fairly abstract epitome of the themes of toolishness, marginalism, and discontinuity. And then I want to look briefly at a countertheme, that of middles, mixtures, and transitionality.

Taking the World Toolishly. Toolishness is a vital theme in twentieth-century thought, transforming the Kantian transcendental categories concerned with perception and cognition into categories of action, intervention, and construction and repair. Tools are modular, they get around the subject-object dichotomy much as do the transcendental categories, and they are instantiated in vivid examples that "everyone knows." They provide a way of thinking about the task of constructing reality, acknowledging that the world is stubborn and resistant and not under our command.

We have a craft of knowledge. We get ahold of the world and we craft explanations by taking the world toolishly, the tools being archetypes, models, and mathematics. Surely those tools are things, but they are functions as well. For a tool lets me get at the world; it provides me with a handle onto it. The tool then disappears behind that world it allowed me to get a handle onto. For I am involved in the world, not with the tool as such. I only discover the tool as such when it does not work or when it breaks down, as Heidegger pointed out. I work within a concrete, practical situation, which is an example of that tool in its application.

Tools are usually employed automatically, without a second thought. So a description of tools and how they are used should strike practitioners as an "of course" and a "so what?"—as true to life but unremarkable. Methodology, how these tools are used as tools, is just what everyone knows. Craftspersons may recall the awkwardness of their apprenticeships, and even those times when they self-consciously or playfully or tentatively tried out a tool. But those are the exceptional moments.

Now the archetypes and models, as tools, never do address what the world is really like—except that it is subject to being taken toolishly, and by these tools. Still, we take their provision of the world as real enough, even if there is misfit and error, as there surely will be.

Toolishness allows us to make claims about how and whether the world can be repaired, tuck-pointed, or put together out of added-on bits and articulated pieces, rather than be started anew with virgin land, fresh plans, and new lumber. And phenomenological and methodological descriptive tasks supplant traditional dialectical oppositions such as that of smoothness and discontinuity, the profane and the sacred, or flow and discreteness. Consequently, the world's nature is often seen to be ironic. For marginal additions can add up, in the limit, to discontinuity; everyday mundane life can lead to transcendence; and flows can crystallize into discreteness.

The world as these particular tools tend to get ahold of it is characterized fully by its present properties. Those properties are congruent to the crucial features of the tool, whether it be a model, an archetype, or mathematics: The world is as we get ahold of it. And the world's history, how it got to this state, is in effect effaced and of no consequence. Such path independence or invariance is quite remarkable, for usually history matters unavoidably. When cooking or baking, for example, just how we combine ingredients is often critical to the outcome.

Taking the world toolishly is a condition for there to be explanations. For by their actual employment in constructing something, tools provide linked sets of actions that lead to what is to be explained. And so we have a sequentially cumulative account, an explanation. Tools also encourage well-defined notions of causality: mechanically, hit it and see what happens; archetypally, embark on a patterned transformation. We might give a history of natural science as the gradual ascendance of toolish answers over metaphysical ones to questions such as: How does the complex world exhibit local simple linear phenomena? How does an atomic world exhibit both smoothness and discontinuity? Of course, to answer these questions has required some remarkable inventions, such as the economist's Invisible Hand and the physicist's cooperative phenomenon.

Toolishness also encourages us to ask about what people actually do, their actual practice. Historical study of specific tools and applications will show just how these tools and applications are made to fit each other. In this context, if we ask why mathematics works, we are asking just how is it made to work. Now it turns out that the fit between tool and application is perhaps not so natural as it appears at first. Much has to be discarded if we are to have intellectual vestments that are wearable at all. Of course, one still might argue whether mathematical objects are discovered or invented, and still be amazed at the fit between mathematics and natural science. But now the question is set in a less fantastic light.

In describing what people actually do, I take what might be called a nominalist view of tools. Tools, models, and functions are known through their panoply of concrete interpretations within specific occasions, contexts, and situations. So a random walk is thought of as Brownian motion, or as a sequence of coin tosses, or as diffusion. And architects have a canon of specific buildings in mind when thinking of a church. In practice, I am likely to test out my ideas on a range of specific pictures and examples. Hence, a phenomenology of toolishness not only provides a description of how we encounter the world in terms of tools, but is an account of their application.

Tools are employed in subtly different ways in each context, yet a tool's versatility still tempts us to think it has an abstract quality or nature which is then to be applied to a situation. So drawing from particular cases, we may show which formal abstract features of the calculus, such as the Fundamenal Theorem, make it so widely applicable. Still, we come to appreciate the power and meaning of the Fundamental Theorem only when we keep in mind its application.

Any synthesis of the tools or models, a theory say, would be a curiosity without our immediately being able to visualize exemplary real fruit growing on this tree of organized knowledge. But sometimes the best one can do for a synthesis is a list of tools or a toolkit. For lists are a way of organizing incongruities and similarities, without insisting on their precise relationship.

For our purposes, a number of examples have proved to be seminal, and they reappear in a variety of guises and circumstances. There is the rite of passage represented by religious conversion; the phase transitions represented by iron becoming permanently magnetizable, by water freezing, and by the onset of epidemic or percolation; the marginal, additive, and invariant connection of parts to wholes represented by the Fundamental Theorem of the calculus; metastability as represented by the buckling of a beam; marginalism as represented in a market economy at equilibrium; the curious effects of combination as represented in perturbed random processes; and the creation of something from nothing represented by the entrepreneur.

Marginalism and Discontinuity.   Like most influential ideas, marginalism and discontinuity are meaningful within a historically developed set of dialectical tensions and within the set of situations in which they have been instantiated. The tensions, some of which we have already mentioned, include those between smoothness and discontinuity, flow and discreteness, the little-commensurable-additive and the big-incommensurable-unique, the gradual and the emergent, the profane and the sacred, the ordinary and the stigmatized, parts and wholes, the eternal and the historical, and the soul-less and the animated:

- Is each part of the world smoothly and gently connected to another part, marginally or incrementally different from it, the parts being mutually commensurable, perhaps on a linear gently gradated scale—the Great Chain of Being? Or are there abrupt jumps, discrete classes, distinct qualities?

  Is the material world accounted for by a story of flows and of added-on infinitesimals or small discrete parts, a matter of smoothness and marginalism? Or are its wholes emergent, discontinuously related to their putative atomic components? Are both stories true?
- Is history continuist, a matter of degree and small alterations? Or is it marked by breaks and by destruction, disruption, and invention? Are revolutions turnings or overturnings? Is it a Marshallian world, or a Schumpeterian one defined by "creative destruction"?
- Is our culture and toolkit one of partial derivatives, analyticity, locality, exchange, and independent parts? Or is it a culture and toolkit of fluctuation, taboo, preemptive moves, historical memory, emergence, and conversion? Either of these toolkits can be employed to construct the discrete individuals and fetishes which are meant to add up the world.

My main concerns here will be with how marginalism allows us to add up the world; how discontinuity is to be modeled as real and authentic, yet how it is also to be modeled as a limiting consequence of a sum of marginal influences; and how discreteness and animation are a product of our setting up the world in particular ways. Arithmetic addition is attractive as a mode of explanation or accounting because it is an algorithmic process—if you follow the rules you get to the sum. And marginalism and the calculus provide a prescription for defining the little pieces, one that ensures their adding up.

Our commitments to marginalism, discontinuity, and toolishness, and to their dialectical interaction, are in the best sense methodological prejudices—commitments that then allow us to get down to work. Each of those commitments is experienced phenomenologically as authentic and real. Yet we then may shift or transcend our commitments.

For example, in the scientific and humanistic traditions discontinuity and transcendence are taken to mark off what is beyond knowledge. But we then go on to getting ahold of what is beyond, the best we can. We teach ourselves to divide the world into mundane dumb parts—as discrete components or as marginals—that we may then put together or literally add up so as to recompose the world's discontinuities. And we learn to act out rites of passage, atone for violations of taboo, and taste what is beyond in conversionary moments of ecstasy, and so transcend absolute division and prohibition.

We go beyond "in the limit," so to speak. Molecular accounts lead to orderly equilibria as in markets and gasses, as well as to discontinuity as in freezing and spontaneous magnetization—in the limit of large numbers and volumes. Marginal accounts, as in the integral and differential calculus, add up or balance out the world—in the limit provided by smoothness and continuity. The conventions and rituals enacted in the mundane everyday world lead us to the sacred, the transcendent, and the archetypal—in the limit of faith, ritual and community, and grace. Of course, it is just these various limits which have defined the scientific and humanistic traditions—whether the limits be a matter of the Invisible Hand, random statistical processes, symmetry, scaling and the Great Chain of Being, infinitesimals and the calculus, or God.

As for the division of the world into dumb and discrete parts, the trick is to employ a mechanism that automatically does the work of classification, individuation, and aggregation. Then the world is set up to be dumb in the requisite way. In physics, economics, biological systematics, and kinship, the mechanisms are atomic interactions and phase transitions, market exchanges by rational economic individuals, reproduction and natural selection, and marriage. And those mechanisms lead to boundaries and interfaces that define discrete classes which organize a system and a culture and a society—of physical states or phases and particles, economic structures and institutions, species, and families. Those boundaries then define modes of interaction among the individuals, interactions which in their totality or plenitude confect the world as we have it. Similarly, fetishes, whether sexual or commodity or religious, are condensations onto putative discrete individuals of global or distributed features. These individuals then define forms of two-body interaction, whether literally corporeal, or as in billiard balls in collision, or in markets with buyers and sellers, or in rituals, which then in their totality reproduce a more complex system.

To create collective objects which act as individuals, out of interacting atomic objects, we set up conditions so that there are centers, such as cities or phases or an oeuvre, centers which may be spatial or conceptual. For example, if there is equilibrium and a proper range of temperature and pressure, there will be a stable separation of groups of atomic constituents into aggregates such as thermodynamic phases or elementary particles. We may then think of these centers as individuals. And often those individuals will interact smoothly with other such individuals, and be appropriately dumb and addable.

Ours is a story of analysis and diremption redeemed by synthesis and a sacred wholeness, and a story of the synthetic and sacralized dismembered or disenchanted by toolish manipulation and analytic thought.

Transitionality.   These various contrasts and tensions provide a powerful analytic framework. Were we perspectivalists we might say that from one point of view we see discontinuity and from another we see smoothness and marginalism—each point of view being legitimate. So, for example, atomically we see discreteness, while collectively and statistically we see smoothed and averaged quantities.

As indicated already, in the limit, and in actual life and work, these various contrasts and the historical dialectic they represent may be transcended. Much of everyday life is in between, "transitional" in D. W. Winnicott's phrase, not at all well understood in terms of division *or* wholeness, discontinuity *or* smoothness. Rather than either-or we have both-and: discontinuity and smoothness, the sacred and the mundane, the individuated and the homogeneous, apocalyptic doom and practical problem solving, playing and reality. The world is inseminated by ambiguity, complexity, contradiction, and polysemy.

Transitionality is perhaps most fully realized when we consider an infant and his mother or father. The dialectical tensions are not to be resolved perspectivally. (Here I follow Winnicott.) The breast or bottle is and is not under the infant's control, the parent is and is not other to the infant. There is a neutral area of experience between me and not-me, the thumb and the teddy bear, the subjective and the objective— experienced as in-between. In that area the breast *is* how it functions—and so it is both the baby's and the mother's. And the "good-enough" father or mother is available and responsive, objectively there but subjectively re-created each time by and for the infant. The parent actively adapts to the infant's needs, has an easy and unresentful preoccupation with him, is devoted to the infant. In that middle ground the parent is in touch with his child, paying attention to subtle details, the ones that say what is going on. Dependence and independence are not distinguished, nor need they be.

Such a middle ground is a rather more general phenomenon. Anthropologists and psychologists describe it as a margin between ordinary states, when contradictions are breached and categories are mixed, as in the middle of a rite-of-passage ritual. Historians and novelists describe periods of turning in their narratives, when what is happening is subject to the incommensurable interpretations of before and of after.*

Tools might be taken as transitional—determined by context and interpretation, subjective and objective, functions and things—and a toolkit might be taken as good-enough. And we may take our work as matters of craft and design. What the world is is what we can make of it, our actively adapting to its needs, being devoted to the work at hand. And the archetypes and models and tools feel as concrete and real as any breast or bottle ever felt.

Let us now turn to these tools and see how they do their work.

---

*I have given a variety of descriptions of that middle ground in a previous book, *Advice and Planning*.

PART ONE

Marginalism and Discontinuity

CHAPTER ONE

Big Decisions

Big and little, discontinuity and marginalism, and incommensurability and additivity are dialectical tensions within our culture. So, for example, much of modern natural and social science shows how "big" may be analyzed into "little," and more generally how discontinuity may be accounted for and so smoothed out by means of additive marginalist stories. Still, big decisions as understood by historians, novelists, critics, and political leaders resist such analysis. They possess their own integrity and their own archetypal form, and they are stubbornly discontinuous and historically specific. The dialectical tensions are in fact unavoidable. But also unavoidable is the insidious power of marginalist methods and the calculus.

A RECURRENT THEME IN modern thought and institutions has been the transformation of things big into sets, sums, or sequences of things little.* The aim is to be analytical and methodical: break something down into its presumed parts, and then properly and automatically recompose them all. Neoclassical economics relies on a "Principle of Continuity," as defined by Alfred Marshall in his *Principles of Economics* (1890), to assure the possibility of both analysis and recomposition through the calculus: ". . . that there is a continuous gradation" in preferences and time periods and ". . . that our observations of nature, . . . relate not so much to aggregate quantities, as to increments of quantities." And atomic theory, Darwinian evolution, and liberal de-

---

*Notes to the text, keyed to pages, begin on page 141.

mocracy are about the cumulative effect of putting together small discrete units—atoms, mutations, and votes.

In each case, what is needed is a means for adding things up or putting them together—whether it be an arithmetic, a mechanism, or an algorithm; whether it be deterministic or contingent, discrete or continuous. So, ideally, what we take to be a big decision would be a cumulation of little decisions, perhaps even something like a sum of signed numbers or vectors, the order of the additions not being critical.

Utilitarianism and its epigone have come to represent the marginal mode of analysis and addition—under a regime of optimization and equilibrium. For example, optimization is equivalent to marginalism if we are optimizing net returns, and so comparing something like marginal costs and marginal revenues: $d\,(A - B)/dx = 0 \leftrightarrow dA/dx = dB/dx$. What is crucial here is a means of comparison and exchange, as in a market, with perhaps a universal measure of value, such as money; a notion of what is not to be commanded or fully known, such as that of randomness and risk; and a justification for the alienation of the parts from each other, such as provided in individualist liberalism. Under a more generous notion of optimization, methods of satisficing and negotiation still allow for the titrational balancing of marginal increments.

In a marginalist analysis there is a comparatively fixed background structure, such as a market or an organization's hierarchy, onto which the addition of each of the steps is a small change. Yet often that structure itself is in no simple sense a marginal sum or an addition—think of a market or a crystalline solid—although it might well be composed of parts.

Still, we might build up a market person by person and exchange by exchange, as we might build up a crystal atom by atom. We know that eventually there emerges an orderliness, an orderliness that is not at all obvious as a prospect when we have just a few of the parts. And we might be able to tell a marginalist story of the emergence of that order as we build in more of the parts—the degree of order being a continuous parameter from some point of view. Or we may come to equilibrium or crystalline order through sequential processes of interaction among a large number of persons or atoms: Tâtonnement or haggling will find equilibrium slowly but surely if there are not too many peculiarities. And even crystalline order, which involves a phenomenologically sharp phase transition from a less orderly state such as a liquid, might be seen to be continuously emerging in terms of its extent and degree. Of course, many mechanisms cannot be so incrementally built up, and they show order only when all the parts are in their right places, as in a clockworks.

Whatever the mode of analysis, what tends to be effaced is actual history, and the particularity and residual obligation in our relationships with each other. But in actual fact not everything is for sale or exchange, and even if it were, there are leftovers and residues never to be cleared or paid back.

There are momentous arenas in which it is not clear that any addition or analysis could account for something like a big decision. Diplomatic initiatives and going to war are often viewed as major sea changes, even if they might be analyzed by means of a marginalist game theory. They seem discontinuous, abrupt, unique—big. And there are other cases, more heavenly and more mundane.

On the theological front, the rabbis' decision about the authenticity of Jesus of Nazareth is taken by Christians to be a big decision. Rather than being one more in a long line of Hebraic messianic claimants, perhaps to be assessed probabilistically as well as hermeneutically (for Christians), Jesus was the crucial one. Or consider Augustine, who describes his own conversion to Christianity as a big decision for him. It changed his life totally, at least in his eyes. (That such a decision deeply affected the history of Christianity is a secondary question, except for the obvious fact that we pay attention to Augustine's conversion because he became a historically significant figure.) Doomsday, although it is not a conventional decision point, is an example of a discontinuous unique moment. It is perhaps not one more event in a universe of possibilities. It is not a low-probability catastrophe to be avoided by means of investment and look-ahead strategies suitable for resource problems. And God's judgment on doomsday may or may not be a matter of adding things up, with plus and minus signs, and so balancing things out. For the orthodox, all of these decisions must be sharp turning points, not at all subdivisible—although in writing a secular history one might retell such stories analytically in terms of little decisions.

On a more mundane front, the Owens Valley California–Los Angeles water project, as presented in one recent history, is again something big, discontinuous from the past and treated as unique. Not only is there envisioned a very substantial change, but heroic effort is required to line up actors, commitment, and resources. This is true for many other public works projects, as well as for public policy initiatives. And political events, whether they be declarations of independence or new presidential administrations, are often taken as big changes or decisions. They are taken as transformative, revolutionary, or conversionary—total breaks with the past, discontinuous and abrupt, unique events in history.

In each of these cases there is an alternative story of small steps along a path. We drift into wars, the success of a messianic figure is seen to be a product of many rather inadvertent moves, a conversion turns out to take place over many years with much backsliding, and a project gets built through a long and perhaps incoherent bureaucratic process. But in the orthodox or canonical accounts such as the Gospels, Augustine's *Confessions,* or even mildly reverential national or project histories, the momentous decision has a primacy that is undeniable. What these canonical accounts do distinctively is to sacralize the decision; they justify the decision as a total break and as analytically irreducible. The account is a story of the initiation of a project, the gaining of commitment to it, and the transcendence of what seemed impossible.

Big decisions appear in a wide range of arenas—from personal decisions about how to lead one's life, to embarking on a unique civil engineering project such as a transcontinental railroad, to revolution and constitutions. Big decisions are qualitatively different from little ones—discontinuous rather than smooth, unique rather than one more of the same. Still, we often like to treat a big decision as a set of component or marginal decisions, decisions which we believe we can make more easily and systematically.

Yet the marginality of a little decision depends on a larger context; the perception of change as small depends on a framework set by larger transformations. So while there may seem to be a distinct culture of marginalism, as we shall see there is actually a more encompassing culture of decisionmaking, one that incorporates both little and big decisions, and smoothness and discontinuity.

In sum, big decisions are discontinuous, abrupt, and unique. Their consequent changes and transformations are big as well. Typically, they involve structural rather than marginal changes, radical alterations in the course of events, very substantial commitments of resources, and large impacts. Such a big decision might be described by a dramatic or historical narrative with a crucial turning point, or be modeled by the freezing of a liquid with a sharply defined transition temperature. Whether it be a matter of going to war, religious conversion, a large-scale water or highway project, or revolution—the change is a break with the past; it takes place over a comparatively short period of time; and the choice is often between incommensurable alternatives, the choice itself being taken as a once-in-a-lifetime event.

If big decisions are defined as discontinuous, abrupt, and unique, little decisions and their consequences are marginal and smooth, and

commensurable and additive. Decisions are big not because they involve large projects or overwhelming resources, although they usually do. Such decisions are big because they are discontinuous, and it is claimed that they cannot be reduced to the cumulation or the arithmetic sum of a sequence of commensurable little decisions. So they are generally seen as discontinuous with the past, and historically unique.

What may at first seem to be a little decision can have enormous consequences, tipping an unstable system or determining a country's future. And what may seem to be a big decision may have rather meager consequences. In the first case such a minor event may be retrospectively elevated to superordinate significance in order to justify the decision as big and unique. And in the second case the embarrassment of failure may lead us to downgrade the importance of the original decision. Indeed, as Whig history, this represents good historiographic practice. Still, there are some decisions in which the consequences seem to be roughly in proportion to the decision itself, and it is these that I shall concentrate on.

It may be useful to quote the economist Joseph Schumpeter at this point:

> Development in our sense is a distinct phenomenon, entirely foreign to what may be observed in the circular flow or in the tendency towards equilibrium. It is spontaneous and discontinuous change in the channels of the flow, disturbance of equilibrium, which forever alters and displaces the equilibrium state previously existing. . . . [It is] that kind of change arising from within the system *which so displaces its equilibrium point that the new one cannot be reached from the old one by infinitesimal steps.* Add successively as many mail coaches as you please, you will never get a railway thereby.

Two distinctions are crucial to what I have said so far: discontinuous versus marginal changes and marginal versus componential analysis. A discontinuous change is abrupt, unique, and incommensurable, and perhaps structural; while a marginal change is small, commensurable with other such changes, and may be added onto something much larger and presumably less changing. A marginal analysis takes a situation as given and then adds a bit more to it, while a radical componential analysis reconstructs something out of parts. Components may be atomic or discrete or mechanical, as are the individuals and exchanges in a market, the electrons in a crystal, the citizens in a democracy, or the gears in a clockworks. In general, reductionism is a claim that the world may be made marginal or componential.

Marginal parts are literally additive, while components are put together through processes of mutual interaction and exchange or by being fit together as in a mechanism. So marginal analysis in economics tells how an equilibrium system will respond incrementally if one of its parameters is changed, while a componential analysis shows how the equilibrium is put together out of individuals. Or marginal analysis shows how a crystal responds when it is tapped or when another atom is added to it, while componential analysis shows how the crystal was put together out of atoms. As we have seen, marginal methods may sometimes be employed to build something up from its components, piece by piece.

NARRATIVE STORIES AND CONVERSION EXPERIENCE

If big decisions are marked by discontinuity, abruptness, and uniqueness—what is even more impressive is the range of their precursors and consequences. Big decisions are not just made and done with; they must be developed and pushed and pursued. They are foci for the fear and anxiety and concentration intrinsic to large endeavors, and for the skill and luck we need to pursue them. Big decisions require a disturbance of what once may have been comfortable, and an eventual reestablishment of order and comfort and natural expectations. They deprecate the past and idealize the future. They are turning points in a narrative in which there is both sacrifice and redemption. To use Schumpeter's phrase, here we have "creative destruction."

It is the dramatic dialectic of precursors and consequences, and of prospect and retrospect, that invites treating a big decision as a conversion experience, as in a religious conversion. Although the archetype is perhaps Augustine, the most influential contemporary account of conversion is Thomas Kuhn's description of revolutionary scientific change and paradigm shift, both for individuals and for groups, and on the cognitive and the social structural levels. Here I shall follow Augustine.

For little decisions, one might justify what one wishes to do prospectively, in terms of past actions and events as well as expected consequences. But for a big decision, justification comes retrospectively. And in conversion, justification is in terms of a confession, a confession that is made after conversion.

A confession is a story that reinterprets the original prospect so that it now justifies and puts in proper place the way the world turns out. The story is rational, in that it carefully provides evidence and argument for a position, and it may well be laden with marginalist decision-theoretic apparatus. But what a confession does distinctively is to construct a history—showing how the prospect contingently but inevitably led to the consequences. Such a justification is neither arbitrary nor a cheap rationalization. For there is always enough complexity, defect, and failure that needs to be incorporated into such an account that constructing such a story is no mean task. Big decisions are historical and particular, marking time and stigmatizing the world. Their exact sequence and process matters, in detail, enormously.

Characteristic of confessional stories is a middle ground, neither before nor after the decision. The middle ground is in between, without a definite orientation about how things will turn out. It is a period of crisis: a sink for the past, a source for the future. Often it is not clear just how the decision was made during this period, although we may retrospectively designate a moment of decision and then provide a fable-like account of that moment.

Anthropologists have described the middle ground in some detail. For example, in giving an account of urban gentrification one scholar has called the middle ground "rubbish," such as in the decay of nice housing into a rubbish-slum, which then gets fixed up and becomes a revered preservation of the past. Rubbish is a middle ground connecting the past to the future. It is a seemingly arbitrary mixture, with no definite value, so it is worthless.

Also characteristic of these stories of big decisions is a sense that "after" is marked, stigmatized, and perhaps enlightened; that "before" was mistaken; and that "in the middle" there was redemptive sacrifice, such as the hard work called sweat equity, and not just pecuniary compensation. And so we are led to a grace-filled peace, such as a proper home, where things can be over and resolved, justified. Following Aristotle's description of dramatic progression, that middle is a transition from the state of the probable to the necessary, from what is possible to what actually eventuates.

Crucially, in big decisions values and probabilities are not given in terms of the "before" situation, then to be used for making a best choice. Rather, the values and probabilities are determined by the decision. For the decision sets in place a context of valuation and a world of choices. As a consequence of a big decision, comparative judgments are made and so values are changed, and commitments are made and so some developments become more likely.

Alternatively, one might view a big decision in mechanical terms rather than conversionary ones. It could be a tipping point of an unstable system, so that a small parametric change dramatically alters a whole structure. A beam may buckle after a small increase in pressure, or a nation might change its political alignments through a minor change in votes. Or the big decision, which appears as an abrupt irreversible change, is a result of a random walk or other such seemingly unbiased process. For a random walk can get someplace other than the average or origin, and stay there for a very long time. Such a walk may become an irreversible trend if there are economies of scale and agglomeration. And the outcome of such a process may well depend on early leadership of a particular style or trend. More generally, in a seemingly unbiased but highly unsettled nonequilibrium realm, the outcome will depend sensitively on the initial sequence of moves or choices or fluctuations. Those moves may well be preemptive, with the winner taking all.

Whether it be an account in terms of conversion or mechanism, this is a historiography of crucial moments. And mathematically, ordinary linear arithmetic won't produce the discontinuity and uniqueness characteristic of such a crucial moment. We shall need to employ nonlinearity, transients and fluctuations, and suitable limiting processes. And although the discontinuity of phase transitions, or of fracture and cracking, may be understood molecularly and sequentially, the suitable units for addition are not conventional molecules, and the mode of addition is not conventional arithmetic.

A CULTURE OF DECISIONMAKING

The play of big and little decisions takes place in an encompassing culture of decisionmaking. The culture consists of a set of decisionmaking practices, such as markets and systems of taboo. The practices must work together if each is to make sense; yet each is enacted as if it is the only one that is going on, in effect denying any other practice. Markets ignore but do not violate the taboos on what is to be traded; taboos ignore how markets may indirectly trade what is taken as sacred. And little and big decisions are made and seen as if the other kind were of negligible significance, if not ignorable.

Each practice employs a technology to organize and automate its operation; it possesses an ideology to justify itself; and it highlights particular phenomenological details of the world. For example, marginalism often uses the calculus as its technology; it takes the local nearby here-and-now features as the relevant ones; it is preoccupied with steering and marginal exchange; and it sees the world as modular, smooth, and objectively distant.

Besides marginalism, the practices of decisionmaking include taboo, as in the law, an account of division between the allowed and the forbidden, and of redemptive sacrifice; and the gap, as in a rite of passage, an account of transformation and discontinuity. There are as well three practices which concentrate on the role of an individual in decisionmaking: action, such as the hero, a story of the initiation of projects; judgment, as in the critic or referee, an account of rational argument and valuation; and entrepreneurship, a justification of risk and virtue.

Each practice plays against another practice, so that marginalism is opposed to taboo and action is opposed to judgment. Mediating in between are the gap and entrepreneurship, respectively. The oppositional structure of this culture is much like that used by anthropologists to describe other social phenomena.

To repeat, any single practice is incomplete. It is the set of practices that forms a culture: a system of action and meaning that encompasses the world and that accounts for itself, assigning roles and statuses and providing prescribed and proscribed ways of being. Within this culture of decisionmaking, such seeming poles as big and little or action and judgment are parts of a whole.

Let us examine each of the decisionmaking practices.

Marginalism. A prevalent model of decisionmaking is that of marginalism, a practice of small changes and of partial derivatives from equilibrium states; and an account of mostly uncorrelated and relatively independent events, and of probabilities in a universe of reasonable possibilities. In marginalism the world changes gently if not smoothly, and we can backtrack as well. At each point we figure out what to do next by looking nearby around us. And there are rules, such as those of the calculus and of probability theory, for doing that looking around so that the sum or net effect of our choices is best. We can be ignorant of the whole world, yet our local behavior, our local maximizing, leads to an optimum overall.

What is more remarkable is that this optimizing rule can work for the actors in a system, and then for the system itself. A marginal change in a component will make sense in terms of and be consistent with the whole. Markets and mechanics are the best-known examples of such marginal worlds.

A marginal world seems objective, ahistorical, rearrangeable, and manipulable. Yet a member or component or a consumer may be seen by outsiders, or may see itself, if the individual is a person, as reacting to conditions as set up by the external world. This is an individual who swims and steers in a sea not of the individual's own determination, but rather one to which the individual responds. For example, we often speak of electrical fields and prices as if they were externally fixed. And the world's subsequent response to each individual's actions seems local, a response to each individual alone. And so we may speak of individual properties or charges and of notions of ownership. But if a system is unstable, small changes can lead to discontinuous big and nonlocal effects. Hence the appeal of systems at equilibrium, which can provide for a marginal local world.

Taboo. A very different practice is needed if the world is not taken as smooth but as balkanized, broken up and divided, and marked by taboos and difficult-to-bridge separations. Such is the case in embarking on a new project, in separating pollution from purity, in testing a scientific theory, or in obeying the rules of kinship. For in each case there are sharp divisions: between waste and prudence, dirt and cleanliness, error and truth, and incest and allowed relationships. Here one has to master the law, namely, the structure of forbiddenness and allowedness, the structure of taboo and tradition. One also masters the means of sacrifice and redemption, the ways of restoring order when there is transgression. These ways may include financial compensation, purification ritual, or historical rewriting and memorialization.

Yet despite its division, this is a world that is whole, connected through its dialectical tensions. It is not plastic, rearrangeable, or arbitrary either, as the word seems to be in marginalism. Rather, the world is orderly and traditional, self-consciously bound by rules and historical precedents. Individuals are not alienated. They are an integral part of the world, a world which feels plain and ordinary, not subject to skeptical doubt. And while it is not to be controlled as in the marginal world, we might feel comfortable in it. One knowledgeably figures out how to live according to the law and how to deal with the inevitable violations.

Marginalism can make sense just because there are some things that are untouchable, that are not to be traded or exchanged. Mama or Papa are ontologically and morally different from the proverbially tradable guns or butter. If parents are to be given up, it is through processes of sacrifice or other transcendent ritual, not the mundane marketplace. In the practice of taboo one resolves problems and makes a peace rather than allocates resources. Of course, what is not subject to the order of taboo, what is not so protected, can then be made rational through marginalism or other modes of analysis.

The Gap. The world of taboo is stable, albeit multiply bifurcated by rules of classification. Now we might imagine that world violated but not reconciled, a world in the middle, on the margin: a world of the gap between relatively stable situations. (Here "margin" designates betweenness rather than an incremental add-on as in the practice of marginalism.) For example, say we are in the middle, as we might be in conversion, rather than before or after a big decision; or say we have a mixture of properties, rubbish rather than either pollution or purity. The mixture of the gap is arbitrary, often with values reversed, and with no well-defined ratios of the components. It is not simply a matter of an impurity that defines a pollution. In the gap we are not to be sure of which side we are on, or even to what extent. It is a world of mixture and crisis and tumult and flux.

Decisions are not so fully encompassed by the law as they are in the practice of taboo. Chance and fluctuation play a large role, and we cannot tell which influence will be crucial to the final outcome. Still, such a world has patterned modes of transition leading to reconciliation and stability—whether it be bank rescues, which take place on weekends; comedy and tragedy, which have a moment of revelation; or phase transitions, which are of a universal form. The practice of decisionmaking is a play between otherwise untempered chance and fluctuation, and patterns of ritual and transformation.

In general, changes have to be big if they are to lead to reconciliation and stability. We need new beginnings as ways of resolving the middle, and an emergent order to consolidate the resolution. It is perhaps not surprising that pregnancy and childbirth are recurrent images of the gap. And rather than a mastery of the calculus or the law, this practice requires a mastery of archetype, ritual, and storytelling.

Between marginalism's smoothness and taboo's divisions lies the gap's fluctuations and reversals. The gap's rearrangeability is global and entire, not so individual or local as in marginalism. The gap acknowledges the tabooed world's incommensurable divisions and polarizations, but the separation now is articulated and in effect made commensurable, for a path is provided through it. The gap is in between, in how it feels and in its location and meaning in the culture of decisionmaking.

So far, this culture of decisionmaking builds in some critical features of big decisions: that they violate what is untouchable and lead to sacrifice and redemption; and that they transit a mediating gap between a before and an after. Still missing from this culture is the person who makes a decision. For marginalism, taboo, and the gap are decisionmaking practices that address themselves to the world in which one finds oneself. But a person has a potentially separate decisionmaking role in such a world. One may simply follow the rules, whether those of the calculus or of the law or of the patterned transition, and so be circumscribed by those practices. But there are other practices, practices in which one's role is taken as transcending the world.

Action.   One may be an actor who expresses his will in an epical struggle with the world. Such an actor may be heroic, subject to tragedy, blind to the ultimate consequences of what he does. The actor initiates projects by inseminating the world with his power. Through his will he violates what has been otherwise taken as impossible, so the actor is said to "get things done." The actor is often presented in contrast to a manager or housekeeper or maintainer. But the actor's effectiveness depends on there being a managed world, a world to fulfill and work out his acts, a world where the garbage is removed and where peace and home are provided for. If there is Odysseus, there is as well Penelope and Telemachus.

The world of the actor is surely not marginal, but it is not taboo- or gap-like either. For although there is in this world violation and in-betweenness, they are not its central features. Rather, the world of the actor is a place that is given order through his will. That is just how Genesis describes God's acts of Creation.

Judgment.   Spectators or referees stand in opposition to, but are mutually dependent on actors. Such referees are engaged in the practice of judgment or criticism, whether in court or in the cultural arena. Disinterested, spectator-judges will still demand that others agree with their judgments—although the others may differ and offer judgments which demand agreement as well. What is crucial is that the demands are rational, articulated through evidence and argument. Disagreement leads to mutual appeals, which are attempts to convince others through such argument. An appeal is an appeal to the community's shared or common sense. So it is an appeal that intrinsically lays claim to others' potential allegiance.

Judgment is also justifying—putting things in order, and so making sense of the world. In aesthetic terms a justification is about the unity of a work of art; in religious terms it is a provision of God's grace; in legal terms it is the finding of truth and fair punishment. But there are limits to the claims that judgment may make; judgment is not rationalization. There is authentic resistance to our claims—empirical, rhetorical, conceptual. So we are circumscribed in the kinds of sense we can make and in the kinds of coherence we find satisfying.

Judgment is also practical. In making a judgment we take into account the power of will and the action we might muster. Yet judgment also alters that potential will and action. Judgment articulates and sets limits on the demands of actual life—which desires we take as needs, which materials we take as resources, which consequences we take as bearable.

If in their decisions actors make the world so, spectator-judges take it as something. Theirs is a world that is given order through acts of valuation.

Entrepreneurship.   Entrepreneurship is a meeting-ground of action and judgment. The entrepreneur both creates things and finds a market for them, and so makes them valuable. The entrepreneur's world is ordered through both heroic will and rational valuation, but that ordering is contingent. It is not determined ahead of time. And what is crucial is the nature of that contingency.

Entrepreneurs are often said to deserve their rewards because they take risks, and so evidence their skill in dealing with the chance unknown. As a consequence of their risk-taking, entrepreneurs may receive an extraordinary return on what we come to call their investments. Such a description of entrepreneurship is meant to justify these rewards or returns as fair and rational.

But imagine that the unknown were something like a biological sport, perhaps a random mutation, and the consequences a matter of natural selection. Here there is no deserved reward for survival other than survival itself, although entrepreneurs might well happen to receive something in addition. But it is not a desert. It is just what comes their way for being who they are in this situation.

Now imagine that the sport were taken to be a matter of Fortuna: an animate source of vicissitude, an agent of God, a wily woman, perhaps turning a wheel or picking a card from a deck. It is the entrepreneur's virtue which commands and molds Fortuna, making good out of what the entrepreneur is given, avoiding disaster and ruin. Virtue rights injustice, and it graces unending secular time with human historical action and dynamism and life.

Virtue is its own reward. That entrepreneurs act and make the world their own does not itself make for a world that they may literally own. An entrepreneur might even receive a prize for luck or exemplary virtue. But those gifts are not a matter of right; they are a matter of the grace of Fortuna. There is, so far, little here of the liberal notions of initiative, freedom, and will that go along with a notion of investment and its earnings. So if the unknown chancy world were a matter of sport or Fortuna, we would be hard put to justify reward as rightfully earned and so deserved.

To justify desert, chance-taking should be at the initiative of the entrepreneur. And the consequences of such chance-taking must be sufficiently well defined and isolated, so that we can mark off just what the entrepreneur has appropriated. Then we might even speak of a probabilistic notion of risk, where each outcome is independent of the others. And we might speak of marginal returns, which are the entrepreneur's as a consequence of that individual's actions. Unlike sport or Fortuna, here we have a game to be played. That an entrepreneur rises to the risk, takes it, and then succeeds marks the returns as rewards for that entrepreneur alone. Nothing else, whether it be Nature or Fortuna, can lay claim to share the rewards, for those rewards are now the entrepreneur's exclusive property.

If entrepreneurship is seen as risk-taking, then a rate of return may be assigned to it. It has become an act of investment. Entrepreneurial endeavor is now a matter for the alternative allocation of resources, and we may speak of expectation values associated with different strategies. Time is no longer biological, or the narrative time of story-telling, but objectified calendrical time. Time has become a commensurable realm in which comparable prospective projects can work themselves out.

Once projects are taken as investments, heroic action is tamed and becomes prudence, and critical judgment is no longer about quality and becomes financial. So heroism is identified with success rather than virtue; its reward is not eternal fame but transitory wealth. And virtue becomes skill, Fortuna becomes risk, and acts of appropriation become ownership. Entrepreneurs have made Fortuna their own. And in a perverse way, the entrepreneur's world comes to be a marginalist world.

Actually, the successful entrepreneur systematically links payoffs and probabilities. They are not to be independent. Expectation values are now nonlinearly dependent on payoffs, since if the payoffs are large the probabilities will be increased by deliberate planning and design. Careful control and anticipation of contingency are the mark of a good entrepreneur. And large investments will make it more likely that an outcome turns out as desired. So investments are strategic, altering the future probabilities as well as the payoffs. The entrepreneur acts most effectively as an entrepreneur in just those situations which are not marginal and not linear, when acts of entrepreneurship deliberately violate the limits of what was once thought impossible.

We close our consideration of the practices that compose the culture of decisionmaking by noting the rather different forms of command and control that inform each of the practices. Marginalism's changes are small and linear. So they may appear to be in response and in proportion to what one does, a straightforward control and mastery. In the world of taboo, one must be wily and hermeneutic, negotiating among the laws and their interpretations. And in the gap, command is a matter of mastering patterned but experientially unpredictable ritual. Similarly, action is directly commanding, judgment is often wily and wise, and in the middle is entrepreneurship as a play between pattern and invention.

Still, what is most remarkable is marginalism's pervasive and recurrent influence. In modern thought it has not only come to affect how we think of entrepreneurship, but the other practices as well (as we shall see further in chapter 5). In its own terms marginalism is a remarkably coherent practice. But big decisions are often better understood in terms of the other practices, especially in terms of models in which discontinuity is not just a compounded effect of small changes but has its own irreducible integrity.

Marginalism's power surely reflects its congruence with modern political economy. But I suspect that its alliance with mathematics, and the calculus in particular, is just as important. In the case of marginalism, the calculus not only plays a crucial role in defining marginal changes and how they are to be added; it plays a necessary role. For the calculus automatically provides for invariant modes of adding things up, where big can be a sum of little, with intermediate ups and downs canceling out—a restatement of the fact that Riemann sums possess unique limits and of the Fundamental Theorem of the calculus. That we may titrate differences to find equilibria, and climb hills to find optima, is provided for by continuity and the derivative. If we want these features, we shall have to resort to the calculus to do our addition. That we often seek to identify little (and even big) decisions with marginalism allows the calculus to be a dominant intellectual influence.

More generally, there is an unavoidable tension between unbridled contingency and rational predictability: between preemptive moves, Fortuna, and history, on the one hand, and smoothness and small fluctuations, risk and probability, and laws and rules, on the other. It will be useful to look more closely at the culture of the calculus, the various ways of adding things up, and at the role of discontinuity in challenging the smooth objective story that the calculus provides.

——————

CHAPTER TWO

Adding Up the World

As indicated in the preface, if we want to know how many toes we have on one foot, we have to be able to distinguish one toe from another, avoid double counting, and know when to stop counting. Then when we count up—one, two, three, four, five—the last number is the sum, no matter which order or grouping we happen to follow. This chapter might be seen to be an exegesis of this relationship between enumeration and measure—counting up leads to a sum—taking into account the special difficulties of defining the units of continua (the marginals) and of counting up to very large numbers.

We have seen how each practice in a culture of decisionmaking employs a technology that makes it automatic. Marginalism, for example, becomes natural and necessary when we employ the calculus. Such a technology, once developed to work on a limited aspect of the world, may then be used to channel, select, and command other parts of the world that are then taken as significant in its terms. And as the technology is used it is altered so that it becomes more effective and more applicable, and as a consequence it can be even more pervasively influential.

If additivity and commensurability play a central role in natural science, politics, and decisionmaking, mathematics as a technology can reaffirm those roles. It can model the world so that the world is manifestly additive: so that the addition is arithmetic, ahistorical or path independent, and a globally invariant sum of locally invariant steps. (Keep in mind counting up the toes.) Moreover, lots of the world may be presented as exemplary of the Fundamental Theorem of the calculus—either a story of invariant addition or of marginal changes in a sum.

MAKING THE WORLD ADDITIVE is a pervasive human theme. Can we find a scheme or algorithm which converts a series of steps into a process of arithmetic addition, their consequences into a sum? For the ancients there was arithmetic, mensuration, and harmonics. The modern mathematization of nature is a commitment to adding up the world as a way of putting together its presumed pieces, and an attempt to classify the cases, often about discontinuity, when that additive decomposition is not manifestly possible.

Here I want to explore the following claims:

1. Whatever else it is, mathematics is a tool. It is employed as a tool whether the mathematics has developed in concrete contexts, responding to specific applications, or has developed as a matter of what we call abstract thought, which is just the work done within mathematics. (In chapter 6 I describe how such a tool is made.)

2. As a tool, one of its functions is to add up the world, and to do so arithmetically if possible. The problem is to specify the little pieces that are to be added up and how to do the addition.

3. The integral and differential calculus ("the calculus") is the way of doing such arithmetic addition if the world is smoothly changing, or can be made sufficiently smooth. The calculus makes the world marginally additive by linearizing it—turning curves into tangents, arbitrary shapes into rectangles. It is difficult to add up curves, paths, and arbitrary shapes. It is much easier to add tangent vectors, velocities, and rectangles. So the calculus connects the marginal and the little to the total and the big. And it encourages us to make small changes—those linear marginal derivatives—often in a formulaic manner, as in a differential equation, and so steer our way through life. And if Leibnizian addition of differentials proves impossible, then a Newtonian approach that looks at marginal changes in sums is often fruitful.

4. The calculus has become such a pervasive tool that we are constantly adjusting the world—choosing what we take as interesting, setting up the conditions for experiments—so that changes are marginal and so that the calculus' mode of addition is applicable. There is, so to speak, a culture of the calculus.

5. But for some cases addition has to proceed by other methods, such as the probability calculus and combinatorics.

6. As for all tools, there is an intimate connection of the strategy of working and the structure of the world on which we work. Wonder at "the unreasonable effectiveness of mathematics in the natural sciences" is a standard trope of scientists and mathema-

ticians. That wonder is most remarkable if we ignore the technology's history of contingent early successes and the later mutual adaptations of technology and application.

Our main concern here is not reductionism, as such, how we try to understand the world in terms of simpler parts which compose it. Rather, how is that composition made literally arithmetic and additive? Often a reductionist strategy will lead to atomic components or parts of a mechanism such as a clockworks. But those parts are not to be added in any arithmetic sense. What is striking is how we then try to find new parts, or properties of those parts, and perhaps new modes of addition, so the adding up is arithmetic.

After examining the nature of little and big pieces (reviewing some of the material of the first chapter), we describe the arithmetic that the calculus provides and the culture that it encourages. We then examine alternative ways of adding up the world. We close with a discussion of how two tools—phase integrals and integration by parts—are made to fit the world: Strategy is made congruent with structure, and then the tools' employment can be both natural and ritualistic. This, of course, is how tools are employed by craftspersons more generally.

LITTLE AND BIG PIECES

The world may or may not present itself to us as composed of arithmetically addable pieces—where by arithmetic I mean that everyday arithmetic we learn in elementary school. But we then make the world additive or not—in part depending on our prejudices, in part depending on the phenomena we are accounting for. Now we cannot always get what we want; the world can be truly resistant to our desires. So when we do, perhaps having altered our desires along the way— having changed what we mean by addition, the pieces, or the world— we may well believe we have uncovered the truth. And because one of the most powerful forms of explanation, one of those few archetypal forms that define what we mean by an explanation, is showing how something is composed of other things, we have not only uncovered the truth, but at the same time explained it. But just how do we go about composing the world out of pieces? Here is one of many such accounts. Chapters 1, 3, and 5 provide some others.

The world may be thought of as a continuum in flow. But every once in a while we find we are able to isolate particular events or objects, isolable not only in principle but in practice too. For example, there are explicit decisions and sharply defined phase transitions, and there are atoms and solids. Each of these parts of the world is taken as unto itself, as individual. Yet because individuals still participate in the flow of a continuum, each individual is potentially a way of getting ahold of the whole world and affecting it. (In chapter 5 we shall call it a fetish and describe how it is isolated.)

In the first chapter, we have already met two kinds of isolable parts—little and big. In general, individual additive pieces are what I have called little, small compared with what they compose, whether the pieces be decisions or atoms, events or objects. To be arithmetically additive they have to be commensurable with and independent of each other. In such arithmetic addition, byways that reverse each other cancel out, just as $+X$ and $-X$ cancel in arithmetic. Such pieces include the economist's prices and quantities, or the physicist's masses, or the chemist's reacting molecules, but not the composer's notes, for which there is no such addition or cancellation. The generic analytic problem is to find nicely separable pieces and a reasonable mode of addition.

There are, of course, pieces which are incommensurable and unique, never meant to be added up. I have called them big, for often they are macroscopic, or roughly the same size as what they compose. In the physical realm they include phase transitions and the surfaces or boundaries of particles or solids. In a historical narrative such big pieces may be turning points—preemptive moves or events which preclude alternatives and which commit us to a way of life, and so they mark history.

The incommensurability characteristic of big pieces is often seen as discontinuity. Yet that apparent discontinuity may be a consequence of the particular way we slice up the world, and from a different point of view or topology there is smoothness rather than discontinuity. And, of course, big pieces may be analyzed into little ones. A secular biography of Augustine, or a dispassionate account of revolution, points out earlier failed attempts, Thermidors, regressions, historical rewriting, and the like. The piece is never quite so big and discontinuous as it is sometimes portrayed.

Conversely, little pieces are almost always constructed to go together correctly or to add up right. They are set up to do "big" work. Rational economic men are given just those properties needed for the general equilibrium market, and for marginalist analysis more generally. Electrons in crystal lattices are "little" individuals in the very special and varied senses needed to account for macroscopic crystal behavior. None of this denies the reality of little pieces. But they are subject to an account of how their alienation from each other, and their combinability and additivity, is an invention intended for purposes of explaining something big.

The usual question that is then asked is why and how can such jerry-built pieces be versatile, for they were originally made to add up right for just one purpose, yet they go on to be useful in many other realms. At one extreme, we might say: That is just what electrons do. It is our unwarranted presumption that just because we have to jerry-build some conception means that it is unnatural. Rather, electrons just are this versatile way. Electrons, of a given mass and charge, are the means of both conductivity and superconductivity. Surely they act differently in each case, in part because they make use of their crystalline environment in different ways. But that is what electrons do. The means of explanation and of adding up may well be qualitatively different for different phenomena.

Alternatively, versatility may be a consequence of our continually revising and altering the notion of the generic piece or object, such as an electron, so that it is useful in new as well as its former situations. We may ascribe to it properties that are more powerful, with a wider range of application. Also, we may redesign experimental conditions so that the experiment will now exhibit phenomena that are better explained in terms of the generic piece. Pieces that prove too specialized, that are not versatile, are abandoned for more versatile ones.

Both answers are true, although explorers might prefer the first one, and tinkerers might prefer the second. In any case, both encourage us to examine how we change our conceptions to fit the world, as a matter of actual discovery and of theory.

AN ARITHMETIC WORLD

In an arithmetically additive world the pieces add up in roughly the same way that integers do. Each piece must be independent of and uncorrelated with the others. For then the pieces may in effect be linearly superposed onto each other and so added up, as if they were rods or blocks. No matter how we do the addition, associatively and commutatively grouping the pieces, we get the same invariant result. And such addition will connect the local to the global. Stepping along in roughly the right direction we can get to any place, and there are local rules, such as "keep on adding units," for stepping and steering.

If the world is continuous and smoothly changing, the required arithmetic for addition is provided by the calculus. The calculus prescribes which are the appropriate pieces and how they are to be added.

And so we may find the length of a smooth curve, the area of a shape, or the average of a changing parameter such as a temperature. What we are told to do is to justify or rectify the world, linearizing it, turning curves into tangents, shapes into rectangles—where those tangents or rectangles are marginal differences "along" the curve or shape.

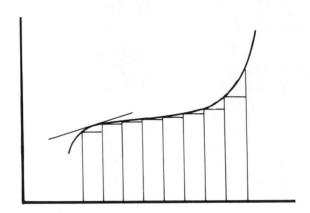

And then the adding up is invariant to how we do the addition (the integral) or how we construct the parts (the derivative). Insofar as we can linearize the world, we can add it up.

What is distinctive about linearization or marginalism as a way of analyzing something big into little is just that additivity, the prescription being that the linearization is simply the marginal change.

Technically, the Fundamental Theorem of the calculus puts it all together. Given continuity and smoothness, the Fundamental Theorem tells how to add things up between two points: Do an integral or do a Riemann sum of the little elements. And we will get to the right place or the correct sum—for example, the length of the curve—if we rectify or linearize the curve into tangent vectors and then add up those "derivative" or marginal elements: namely, $F(b) = F(a) + \int_a^b G$, where $G = dF/dx$, a marginal change in F, and $\int_a^b G \approx \Sigma_{\text{Riemann}} \, G(x_i)$. The manifest fact that the sum of marginals or differences, $\Sigma_i \, [F(x_{i+1}) - F(x_i)]$, $(\approx \int_a^b G)$, equals the difference of the end points, $F(b) - F(a)$, is just as true in the limit that $x_{i+1} - x_i$ is small and the number of sample points is large. Or put differently, if we just measure velocities, which are marginal changes in position, then in the limit of measuring many of them along the way, we can figure out exactly how far we have gone. Knowing the marginals tells us everything we need to know.

Note that this is an oriented addition, as in any accounting system. Minus a minus is a plus. As long as we keep track of the credits and debits separately, or of the direction in which we are going in a line integral, or of the ins and outs of surfaces—and this is what those oriented quantities such as cross products and curls help us do—ups and downs along the way will nicely cancel out. And it is just such an oriented addition that is needed for expressing conservation laws. And it is just the Fundamental Theorem or, equivalently, Stokes Theorem ($\int \vec{J} \cdot d\vec{S} = \int \mathrm{div}\, \vec{J}\, dV = -\int \dot{\rho}\, dV$, where $\vec{J}$ is a current and ρ is a density) that is needed to correctly relate flows to stocks and currents to charges.

Linearization is a self-consistent strategy. In this addition all we need use are the first order or linear pieces, the velocities or rectangles. Second and higher order pieces will be taken care of automatically, in the limit, never themselves to add up to something zeroth order.

A Riemann sum, for example, is such that it gives a unique answer independent of how we partition the interval $[a, b]$—"in the limit," just as $\Delta F/\Delta x$ is uniquely defined in the limit. And so $F(b)$ is well defined in the above formula. Second order pieces, those leftover triangular bits beyond the Riemann rectangles, can be ignored in the limit. And so we can just add up the rectangular parts, not worrying about the mode of partition, as if the rectangles had nothing to do with each other. (At first it might seem that all of what is left over could add up to something zeroth order, and also that what is left over in any one part might be significantly related to what is left over in others.)

The Right Pieces.   The calculus' linearization of a smoothly changing world may suggest and then ratify a natural way of dividing up that world. For example, once the calculus allows us to linearize motion into velocities and accelerations, we then might find a relationship between kinematic motion and dynamical forces, as in Newton's Second Law, $ma = F$. In this manner classical mechanics provides for a division of the world into masses, accelerations, and forces—each of which may be added arithmetically. The contingent fact of nature is that once we talk in terms of accelerations, then masses are well defined as F/a, and they are arithmetically additive. Other useful divisions of the world include the forces, charges, and fields of Maxwell's equations, or the linearly superposable states of quantum mechanics, or the prices and quantities of neoclassical economics. More generally, the calculus' instrument of making the world additive—linearization and so vectorial superposition—is a pervasive theme in much of modern science.

Whatever the technology we employ for addition, it works only if we add up the right pieces. And in practice we believe that we have found the right pieces if they can be added up nicely, namely, if arithmetic addition leads to good explanations. For example, in quantum mechanics and electromagnetic theory the right pieces might be transition amplitudes or electric field strengths rather than probabilities or energies, which are their squares.

Finding the right pieces is a practical as well as an analytical problem. Can we design an experimental setup in which our tweaking of the world induces the appearance of pieces (particles such as phonons, changes in productivity) that are independent, so not only will the pieces add up, but their sum will not depend on the order of addition? For example, if there is equilibrium and the tweaks are small, we may get nicely addable objects.

If we do not or cannot set things up so nicely, the arithmetic is not so straightforward. The order of addition may well matter, as in adding vectors on a sphere. In nonequilibrium systems, outcomes will depend on the sequence of the additions or moves. And the endpoint in unsettled oligopolistic competition will depend on who makes a first move, for that move may be preemptive and so there will be path dependence.

The Local and the Global.   The calculus makes use of continuity and smoothness to achieve linearity, additivity, and unique or invariant limits. It legitimates speaking of the world in terms of increments and differences, marginal changes that balance or cancel each other. And those increments or differences may well have global implications. Through that invariance of the derivative and the integral there can be accounting, steering, and titration: Small pieces add up to the whole, we can follow a rule to get to where we want to go, and every action allows for an equivalent counteraction. And not only is there accounting, steering, and titration; it is a local process. At every point things are conserved, we are on the right track, and there is balance.

As a consequence of these features, a large-scale goal might be expressed by a local and neutral rule. For example, hill climbing or the gradient will find optima; Newton's laws, or the Euler-Lagrange equations, will find a true path of a mechanical or an economic system. And a global extremalization rule, as in the calculus of variations ($\delta \int f \, ds = 0$), can lead to a local rule—action principles leading to Euler-Lagrange equations—because along an extremal path each step is extremal.

To repeat, the calculus presumes that small differences or differen-

tial quantities are well defined, that they may be added, that their sign
or orientation matters, and that the effects of a marginal change are
roughly in proportion to that change: $dy = F(x, y, dx)$, local and often
linear differential equations. Put differently, small changes have
small effects, the changes may be reversed or at least their effects
counteracted, and there is a local balancing of influences (and not only
a balancing of the global sum of the small changes).

Since the calculus is such a potent formal device, we are encouraged
to find ways of making the world smooth and optimal (that is, a consequence of an optimization principle). First, we smooth out discontinuities, say by averaging; or we classify and isolate them, keeping
track of the size of the discontinuous jumps so they can be added in
appropriately. Second, we try to define quantities such as energies,
total costs, potentials, and actions, such that their extremalization or
optimization leads to useful local marginal rules.

History and Invariance.   The length of a path should not depend on
how we measure it, and some properties of a state or a situation such as
its energy should not depend on how we set it up. More generally, there
are processes that efface historical information, producing the same
results no matter how we follow a path (invariance), or which path we
follow (independence). The calculus automatically provides for path
invariance along any single path, by the Fundamental Theorem. But
more stringent conditions are needed to achieve path independence.
For example, when we define energy in terms of a potential, so that energy is automatically conserved, we are providing for path independence.
(Technically, if Energy$(a) = \int_{\text{by some path }(0,a)} F\,dx$, and if $F = dV/dx$
so that F is defined by a potential function, then $E(a) = V(a) - V(0)$, a
path-independent quantity.) Practically, we may have to discover new
forms of energy, such as electrical or mechanical energy, or new kinds
of states, such as statistical averages, in order to achieve conservation
and path independence.

What if this conservative strategy does not work at first? In adding
up heat along an arbitrary thermodynamic process, as in adding up
vectors on a sphere, the order or path definitely does matter. To
achieve path independence we need a way of taking into account actual
path dependence, in effect extending our definition of marginal
changes and of what we should be adding up. Integrating factors, for
example, allow us to add up something that is otherwise not conserved.
So for heat, dQ, the integrating factor is the inverse temperature, $1/T$;
that is, what is "integrable" or what we add up path independently is
dQ/T, namely, the entropy. More generally, we employ curvatures,

connections, and covariant derivatives. To achieve arithmetic addition, we have defined new additive quantities such as entropy, or new modes of addition, such as using an integrating factor. These are ways of measuring and so compensating locally for path dependence.

Still, if we cannot efface historical processes, the alternative is to insist on them. In the calculus of variations, the crucial feature initially is that there is unavoidable path dependence in the integral. For example, the time it takes for light to go from A to B depends on the path followed. And there are potentially many paths from here to there. Classically, in many situations only one path is optimal or fastest, and that is the path we observe. And so we recover a unique answer despite possible path dependence.

Quantum mechanically there is a rather different account, now about a sum over all paths. But the rhetorical moves are not so different. Every possible path could contribute to the probability amplitude equally, but each contribution is of a different phase, $e^{i\theta}$, where θ might depend on the time of travel. (This is Feynman's path integral, democracy-of-histories formulation of quantum mechanics.) Near the classical path, the phases will differ only slightly for various alternative paths. For the time is minimal for that path, and so the first derivative in the time of travel is zero. Hence the phases of the alternative paths add coherently. Further away they cancel out. Again, one recovers a unique answer, despite path dependence.

Still, history and path dependence may be unavoidable. The symmetry direction of freezing ("broken symmetry") and the final state of a metastable system are quite path sensitive. Yet we may even then recover a path independence by taking suitable averages over all possible final states.

The calculus provides for a variety of invariance: the invariance of the derivative to how we find it, in the limit; the invariance of the integral or the sum to how we add up the pieces along the way, as long as the pieces are marginal or derivative, through the Fundamental Theorem; and the path independence given by conserved quantities and by integrating factors and curvatures. A countertheme is essential path dependence, as in action and path integrals and as in metastability. And a consequent counter-countertheme is how we then, through optimization and averaging, may seek to transcend those path dependencies.

The calculus provides or justifies the right pieces. They are marginally addable and they connect the local and the global. And they are the pieces we manipulate or see or hear—energy and entropy, prices, normal modes of a drumhead, the quasi-particles of a crystal, and curvatures. The real and measurable and the correction factors turn out to be the same. And on path-independent paths, such as geodesics or adiabatic transformations, sums are integrable, all is ahistorical, and there is reversibility.

ADDITION OF DISCRETE PIECES

So far, our story of addition has concentrated on smoothly connected pieces or their properties, a story of the integral and differential calculus. But if the pieces are discrete, lumpy, correlated, or parts of a mechanism, the world may not be smooth enough for the calculus to do its additive work.

If the pieces we are trying to add up are few and discrete, we might just add them or their properties, literally arithmetically. But usually other strategies are needed. If there is to be a doable arithmetic addition, we need ways of forming hierarchies of collected or summed objects.

If there are many discrete pieces, and they are loosely connected, we might be able to systematically count them using combinatorial and probabilistic methods, allowing even for a lack of independence among the pieces. Here I am thinking of Boltzmann and Planck, counting up the number of complexions of molecules in a gas or of modes of vibration in a blackbody corresponding to a particular macroscopic state. In practice, what makes these calculations doable is the fact that at equilibrium the modal distribution of molecular energies is vastly more likely than nearby distributions. And so various asymptotic approximations may be employed to get definite results.

If the discrete pieces can be ordered or grouped, we might be able to develop a "scaled" form of addition. For example, if we can figure out how to add things up in a small part of a gas, then by homogeneity and similarity, it is straightforward to scale up to the whole volume. If there is similarity but not homogeneity, as in a crystal or a pattern, adding up the properties of the pieces becomes a matter of finding a way of grouping these pieces so that similarity is honored, yet each collection or group of pieces may be treated as an individual piece itself. For example, we might form nested collections of pieces, or superimpose a sequence of increasingly larger sized grids onto the original crystalline order. We have in effect thinned out the degrees of freedom (to use Wilson's phrase), since the properties of individual pieces in a collection are surrogated for by the properties of the collection itself. This is not unlike a nested sequence of voting, as in a federal system or the Electoral College. With luck, the final result will be invariant to how we do the grouping, what is called a statistical continuum limit (Wilson). For, again, usually what we mean by a reproducible setup or observation is one that is characterized by unique path-independent quantities.

Now it might turn out that how we group the pieces will affect the final result, so that a sum is path dependent and not unique. As indicated earlier, a useful strategy for eliminating grouping effects is to define an average sum, over all the ways of groupings. So statistical physicists, probabilists, and insurance companies pool risks: Pooling will leave nothing out; all is averaged in; and there is just one answer. (Ergodicity, covering all possible cases, guarantees uniqueness.) To eliminate edge or surface effects, which often depend on how one groups the pieces, we go to an "infinite volume limit," and again get uniqueness. Pooling and infinite volume limits not only provide uniqueness; they also damp fluctuations of the macroscopic phenomena and provide for a more rigid and orderly world.

An entropy provides for the same sort of uniqueness as do pooling and infinite volume limits. For the quantity which was integrable and gave us path independence, entropy, is also a measure of the number of macroscopically equivalent microscopic states we have had to average over to get a stable unique state (Entropy = k log NumberOfStates). So in both thermodynamics and statistical physics, an entropy is what we need in order to get path independence and uniqueness.

The strategy of systematic counting adds up combinations of units; scaling adds up nested groupings by similarity; and averaging adds up the ways of nesting the groupings. Such addition is strongly ahistorical. After we have added things up, it does not matter how we did the addition. And so it proves impossible to infer or to go back to the original subparts, either structurally or literally historically.

However, as I have indicated, some of the time we live through particular sequences of events, such as a run in gambling, or the cracking or buckling of a beam, or the crystallization of a particular crystal. We live not an averaged ahistorical life, but an idiosyncratic one. In the pursuit of additivity we may have given up too much information on particular individual paths, their curvatures and histories, shapes and fluctuations. For there are patterns to nonuniqueness and path dependence. For example, the fluctuations may exhibit powerful patterns and correlations. Were one an arbitrageur or an entrepreneur, one might try to take advantage of such path dependence, disequilibrium, and nonuniqueness.

Finally, consider adding up the pieces that are parts of a mechanism. Here in fact there is rarely an actual formal arithmetic. Rather there are archetypes or patterns of design and organization, which prescribe how the pieces fit together. And a craftsperson masters these archetypes and their variations. More systematically, engineering shows how components may be combined, whether they be mechanisms, circuits, energy sources, algorithms, or communication processes. There are as well grammars, logics, and networks. And for so-called linear systems there may be actual cumulation and addition. But once we are in the nonlinear realm, and this is one of the charges of engineering, it is more difficult to achieve such an arithmetic.

Now for each of these various strategies of discrete addition, if we cannot use the calculus at the beginning, we often can at the end. Combining enough discrete pieces we may get something like a continuum. Or scaling and nested grouping lead to continuous similarity transformations (and statistical continuum limits and the renormalization group). And averaging creates stable smooth differentiable functions which may then change just a bit, such as the conventional thermodynamic potentials (dU, dS, where U and S are energy and entropy, respectively) or economic aggregates.

STRATEGY AND STRUCTURE

Invariance and linearization are our recurrent themes. In general, if there is an arithmetic, the pieces are to be added up in such a way that in the end it should not matter how we do the addition or how we define the pieces, at least within a wide range. And the Fundamental Theorem prescribes the generic strategies for good linearized addition. It restates the fact that sums and differences are the inverse of each other ($d/dx \int = 1$), to speak in Leibnizian terms; or that the sum can be recognized by the fact that its derivative at the margin is identical to what we are adding up (if $F(x) = \int_a^x f(t)\, dt$, then $F'(x) = f(x)$), in Newtonian terms.

So far we have considered mostly the Leibnizian strategy. However, the Newtonian strategy is both potent and influential. If we can guess the structure of a system were the pieces added up (what is sometimes called the ground state), we can test our guess by seeing if a marginal piece corresponds to the derivative of the guessed sum. Or we can compute changes in the structure, due to either small changes in state variables or harmonic excitations (lightly hitting or tapping the system)—by taking derivatives and then seeing if they correspond to tweaking nature a bit. The derivatives prescribe how a system interacts with the outside world.

Another linearization tactic is provided by the general story of perturbation theory, what has been called a "way of decomposing tough problems into an infinite number of relatively easy ones." One assumes that the tough problem is marginally different from an easier one, the latter defined often by its being a problem which we can solve or guess the answer to exactly. The answer to the tough problem may be expressed in terms of a small or linear change in the answer to the unperturbed or easy problem.

I suspect that we can and do keep returning to linearization strategies because the world may often be treated as hierarchized, walled off into regions, as a result of the very different strengths of the forces of interaction. At any single level of the hierarchy we can mostly ignore the others and pay attention only to small differential effects. Much stronger forces have presumably played out their role already, in setting up the hierarchy or the walls.

The calculus was meant to be an easily employed technology. Leibniz wanted to provide "a sensible and palpable medium to guide the mind," a language of dxs and $\int$s, a notational language which makes the technology transparent. We can much of the time safely add or cancel differentials; we interchange and cancel integrals and derivatives. Here mathematics is an instrument or a tool, its purpose being to add up the world.

More generally, there is a subtle connection between the tools we use and what we make with them. The tools are modified so that they can work on the materials we happen to have available; the proposed design of what is to be fabricated is modified to be more in accord with the capabilities of available tools; and our aims are modified so that tools and designs will work together.

The calculus is not only effective in adding up the world; it also suggests to us how we might reconceive the world so that the world is addable. The tool called the derivative identifies linear, well-defined, addable objects such as accelerations. But it is so familiar a tool that we may find it hard to think of it as such. So let us consider phase integrals and integration by parts, which are slightly less familiar, their use seemingly more arbitrary, and so their toolish qualities may be clearer.

Phase Integrals.   In a random walk or Brownian motion, in quantum mechanics, and in statistical physics the consequences of any single path or state—a walk, a transition process, a particular microscopic configuration—is taken as idiosyncratic. What is taken as physically interesting is an average or sum over all the relevant paths, as well as the distribution of their outcomes—stable observable quantities.

Often, the consequence of a single path is expressed as an exponential, $e^{if(z)}$, and what we are interested in is a sum or average of these exponentials or phase factors (formally, $\int e^{if(z)}\, dz$).*

Formal similarities in these integrals provide a unifying way of viewing what at first seem like disparate phenomena. The current view would have it that Brownian motion, which gives us diffusion or heat flow with their partial differential equations, is like the path integral formulation of quantum mechanics, which gives us the Schroedinger equation, an equation that is identical to the heat equation if we replace time, t, by an imaginary time, it. But historically, in each case rather different arguments were employed for justifying ending up with what we now take to be similar mathematical forms—a sum or integral of phase factors, and a partial differential equation of the form: $\partial^2 F/\partial x^2 + \partial^2 F/\partial y^2 = u\, \partial F/\partial t$. And to complete the analogy, both Brownian motion and quantum mechanics are like statistical mechanics and its partition function, if we take temperature to be an imaginary time. They are all sums over states.

Some of the time we may actually perform the integrals or solve the differential equations, albeit approximately. Coherent addition or positive interference of the phases may capture most of the contribution to the integral, the rest of the phase contributions mutually canceling out. Or, going from a real to an imaginary time, t to it, the damping provided by a real exponential (just as in statistical mechanics, $e^{-\beta E}$) allows us to do the integral.

Often, the capacity to actually do a calculation is associated with the capacity to define a physically interesting quantity. If we can add up the steps in a random walk, then we can define a diffusion constant which measures the mean square distance after N steps. Similarly, if we may add up the amplitudes for light propagation, we can define a direction of propagation; or if we can add up the number of macroscopically equivalent microscopic states, we can define a temperature

---

*Technically, the exponentials include: $e^{-W}/\sqrt{D}$, for the probability of a particular path, where W is the "conditional Wiener measure" of a path from a to b ($\approx \int_a^b (dx/dt)^2\, dt/D$, where $dx(t)$ is the step made at time t, and D is the diffusion constant); $e^{iS/h}$, for the transition amplitude in quantum mechanics, where S is the action ($= \int_a^b L\, dt$, where L is the Lagrangian, $m\,(dx/dt)^2/2 - V(x)$) associated with the transition); and, $e^{-\beta E}$, the statistical weight of a state of energy E ($\beta = 1/kT$, where T is the absolute temperature). The crucial quantities are the probability of a particular endpoint b, the total amplitude, and the partition function, respectively.

characterizing an equilibrium state. Physically, these are intensive variables that identify the bulk properties of a system, and they go along with an extensive variable such as time, space, or entropy.

Now when means and modes of distributions are not sharply identical—when fluctuations are high, or quantum effects are large, or there is instability—we may have neither conventional bulk properties nor integrals that are so easily finessed. The features which translate into the tractability of the integral, say most of its value being at a pole, are no longer present. And reproducible phenomena characterized by a diffusion constant or a temperature are also no longer observed. We might say that what is conventionally observable is observable for just the same reason that what is calculable is calculable.

More generally, observability and calculability share a tradition of mutual influence and invention. A new calculational technology might make it practical and so possible to consider different physical circumstances, or more efficiently study conventional ones. And the new circumstances might now become more experimentally interesting and more observable, the calculational technology pointing to new significant physical features. And, of course, new phenomena, rather than calculational advances, may initiate this process.

Integration by Parts.   Integration by parts—$\int F \, dG = \int d(FG) - \int G \, dF = I - II$—is used, even more than are phase integrals in a manifestly ritualistic fashion. Leibniz would have liked this, since he invented integration by parts as a technical means to do certain integrals—to convert quadratures to tangent problems.   The trick here is to make sure I or II vanishes.

Say that I vanishes, or the world is diddled with so that it does: One adjusts constraints, boundary conditions, functional forms, as need be. I may vanish because the integrand is a total differential, as in a gradient of a potential, and the integral is over a closed surface or path; or surface terms are zero, since there is screening and so fields fall off at infinity; or more generally, a well-behaved function falls off at the end points (as in a Fourier transform); or the variation vanishes at the end points.

For example, in doing the usual derivation of the Euler-Lagrange equations, one has within the integrand the variation parameter and its time derivative. To get a homogeneous expression under the integral, one does integration by parts to get variation in the parameter alone; and then because the end points are fixed, and so there is no variation there, a surface term also vanishes.

As Feynman, who spent a lifetime working with action integrals, puts it, "In fact, if the integrated part does not disappear, you restate the principle, adding conditions to make sure it does!"

If *I* does not vanish, *II* may vanish or at least it may be small. Again, *II* may be a surface integral that vanishes. More likely, *II* will be of second order. In a series expansion that is just what we might hope for: $f(x) = f(0) + \int_0^x f'(t)\, dt$ (by the Fundamental Theorem). Integrating by parts, $f(x) = f(0) + (t-x)f'(t)]_0^x - \int_0^x (t-x)f''(t)\, dt$, and we get a Taylor expansion. The last term is in the form of *II*, and it may often be shown to be small, vanishingly so. *II*'s vanishing linearizes the original problem.

Integration by parts converts a formal mode of addition into a practically doable one. It linearizes a problem ($II \approx 0$). Or it converts an apples-and-pears addition problem into an apples addition problem ($I \approx 0$); for there is an implicit connection between the apples and pears, as between the parameter and its time derivative. Feynman's point is that the tool is so attractive one assumes provisionally that the world may be made suited to it. But, just as important, we find that in making the world suited to the tool, we rediscover those linearities and those implicit connections. If the vanishing of *I* or *II* may reflect features of a linearized world, the everyday practices we use in employing integration by parts invoke those features automatically.

Integration by parts is, in fact, not only occasionally useful. It is a deep statement about the calculus as a mode of linearizing the world. The distinctive feature of the derivative as a linear operator turns out to be the product rule: $D(fg) = fDg + gDf$. Now the indefinite integral is D^{-1}. Applying it to the product rule, we get integration by parts.

The calculus is an instrument for linearizing the world and for adding it up—if the world is set up appropriately. Strategy and structure are to be made to work together, and what does not fit is for the moment forgotten and devalued. The ritualistic employment of integration by parts allows one "to forget the physics" for the moment and just follow the rules. Yet if we know about the physics, we can appreciate when such a ritual of integration by parts is likely to work. There's physics behind the formalism.

We might say that instruments and institutions become entrenched historically and conventionally. After contingent early successes, which often they were designed to achieve, they become established reference points around which people organize their lives. Once a workable technology developed for making smooth changes additive, one that could encompass many contemporary practical problems of seventeenth-century merchant capitalism, it then became the instrument or language to express new problems. What the calculus eventually offered economics, for example, was an ontology that gave primacy to differences (prices as marginal costs), smoothness (Marshall: *Natura non facit saltum*), and efficiency as optimization (and so tradeoffs at equilibrium).

Even if a technology might be influential, effective, and entrenched, developing in tune with a world in which it is supposed to work, such overdetermination is not determining. What in retrospect would seem like just-right and practical techniques are often not adopted, at least for some time. For natural science in the eighteenth century, for example, Leibnizian approaches to the calculus, centrally concerned with sums and differences and their relationship, with an arithmetic and algebraic adding up of the world, proved more fruitful than the Newtonian geometrical one, concerned with marginal rates of change. But it took until the beginning of the nineteenth century for the English to adopt those Continental ways.

Smoothness makes it possible for the calculus to add up the world, and in return the calculus justifies a culture of marginalism. Since the calculus was invented to solve certain problems concerning rates of change, tangents, maxima, and summation, it is not so surprising that these features of marginalism are intrinsic to the calculus' operation. What is remarkable is how well the tool hides its history and appears so autonomous.

More generally, making the world additive some way or another is a primary task of our culture. Almost always, one works to hide history and instability and to display eternity and simplicity. One wants to create a unique but contingent world, one that could have happened otherwise but turns out just this way. And last, every surprise of composition should have the silver lining of an additive explanation.

CHAPTER THREE

Where Do Centers Come From?

In these next chapters on centralization, stickiness, and fetishes, we shall see that while technology and world may be made to fit each other, a technology's meaning is never fully determined or exhausted. Even if we were restricted to a particular ideology, such as to marginalism, our capacities for invention and interpretation are still remarkable. Marginalism and discontinuity, toolishness, and additivity, whether they be expressed mechanistically, archetypally, or physically, are versatile and rich with application.

Centers allow us to answer scientific, historical, and transcendental questions. For a center provides a source or nexus around which causality, action, and meaning can do their work. As a marked point, a center is discrete, big, and discontinuous, and often a consequence of nonlinearity and path dependence. What is perhaps most curious is the belief that the centers we happen to have are inevitable and elected. Yet at best we may only be able to explain why there is a center, but not why it is at X. As we shall see, the mechanisms and histories of centralization prescribe the kinds of questions we may ask.

A CENTER IS A MARKED place in space, or in time, or in a collection of objects. Such a center could be a point, an orientation, or an asymmetry. It could be an author or a style, around which an oeuvre or a collection is organized, or a prime object, which defines all others as derivative or anticipatory of it. Surrounding a center is a structure that in effect supports it and points to it, and that structure is exhibited through inhomogeneity or pattern. So, for example, if there is falloff toward the boundary, or the periphery arises from the center and has its source there, we may recognize a center by the boundary or periphery surrounding it.

Science and scholarship are in the business of finding and justifying centers. Biologists want to find a center to explain differentiation, how a cell articulates into a complex multicellular organism. Physicists try to understand such centers as the freezing of a liquid, the spontaneous magnetization of a piece of iron, and other phase transitions in which there are marked points of transformation and marked directions of order and crystallization. And ecologists need to explain how niches come to exist and how localized ecosystems work themselves out.

For historians, there may be turning points or big decisions in their narratives. And causality might be a matter of agency, the actor as a center; or it may be the result of a complexion of structural, economic, and random factors, none of which are centralized themselves. Critics employ notions of an author and a style to organize the works of art they study, such an author or style being characterized either biographically or by its qualities and traits.

Islands provide archetypal cases of centralization. For ecologists, their comparatively well-defined boundaries make for idealized and simpler problems. For geologists, an island is an artifact—of erosion, uplift, and accretion. For writers, an island is a noplace, as in Shakespeare's *The Tempest*. Islands are lovely places of controlled experiment and simple organization. They are a product of chance, external forces, and fortune. And as we shall see, so are centers more generally.

How a center comes to be and why it exists are often related. Dynamics and history may be intimately connected to general conservation laws and global optimization principles—but not that intimately. Just because we can justify a center does not mean that it will actually exist, or will exist at X rather than Y, both roughly equally justified places. And just because we can tell a story of how a center came to exist does not mean that the center is efficient, or desirable, or even functional. For often centers are accidents that become facts—chance fluctuation, inhomogeneity, or arbitrary choice that then becomes entrenched through tradition, economies of scale, or global adjustments that make such a center stable and persisting.

In each case we are looking for marked points, from which and around which might evolve the complexity, discontinuity, hierarchy, and order in our world. Can we explain these phenomena in terms of processes of centralization? We may ask: Where do centers come from? Why is there centralization? Why is a center at a particular place? Why does it persist?

It is a curious aspect of the study of cities that such places are assumed to be centralized. Residents will claim that there is a down-town or a neighborhood or a city center, treat such a place as a pole around which their universe revolves, and scholars take those claims as manifest, needing only to be articulated. "Everyone knows" there are centers, and they are the sources or at least the aggregation points for urban development. And even if the center is not spatial, it exists in the social and cultural realms.

So the historian discovers a primitive act that defined a center, an act of founding. The engineer or biologist discovers a control center, as in a brain. The geographer might show how a place is more or less ideal locationally. The political economist points out how zoning, financial institutions, or planning set up a center, one that allows for oligopoly or comparative advantage. In each case, there is a center and the rest of development follows therefrom.

More complex accounts mix these various factors, so that an agricul-tural revolution leads to settlements, one of which becomes a central place—because of its more effective shrines or trade—in a system of place hierarchies organized for the convenience of capital. Or the his-tory may be a heroic narrative—namely, someone chose X. But X still has to be viable. It should have natural advantages, be locationally favored, or someone with great resources must be willing to absorb the costly premium needed to overcome its disadvantages. Each actual center might even be provided with a detailed and custom-made histor-ical account for its success.

Alternatively, centralization may be explained by a mechanism rather than a history, a mechanism that provides for optimization or dynamical interaction. For example, say that we are given a large number of interacting objects, with some reasonable constraints on their total energy. Let us now search for the most likely distribution of their energies or locations, the entropy here being maximized. We find that the most likely distribution features some sort of falloff, as in the Maxwell distribution in molecular dynamics or in gravity models in geography. And the distribution falls off from someplace, the center. Here the center is found by its symmetric location with respect to the falloff.

Still, despite our explanations, the set of centers we happen to have may not be historically so well motivated or optimal, although they are now resilient and viable. They may be a gift of fortune and grace, or be inadvertent consequences of failure, bumbling, and mistaken policy. And surely the effects of geographical and locational influences are not determinate; particular historical actions may reinterpret their manifest implications. A center might even be a collective effect of unintended actions, as in a market, or be a phenomenon accompanying a stochastic process, such as the fluctuations in a random walk. And the center's location might be arbitrary, its having been initiated at X being the result of a fluctuation. In every case, a center exists only because it is eventually developed around, development being the process that anoints a center as such. So in justifying the elected centers, we must allow for unfortunate contingencies as well. There are obvious centers that have failed, faded, or never developed.

PROCESSES OF CENTRALIZATION

Several exemplary models of centralization suggest answers to the question: Where do centers come from?

The *entrepreneur* or land developer comes to a place and marks it with an X, where such a place could be a specific mode of production or invention rather than a geographical location. Entrepreneurs then must convince others to go along with their designations. A successful entrepreneur creates so attractive a center that newcomers naturally reject all other places. But early on, things are not so sure. There are other contenders and entrepreneurs, and they may even offer what seem like natural comparative advantages. If the entrepreneur can get just a few newcomers to come aboard early on, for whatever reason or by whatever device, those moves may be sufficiently preemptive so as to discourage competitors and to offer as well an advantageous package of agglomeration economies. It will surely help entrepreneurs if they have deep pockets or have a backer who does, for then during periods of negative cash flow they can still stay alive, even pricing their goods well below marginal cost in order to gain monopoly power.

Of course, it is wise if entrepreneurs choose places with advantages others take as valuable or natural. But it may well be that a sister-in-law happens to own the plot of land or a patent, and an uncle is rich enough to take a lifetime perspective on an investment made as an avuncular loan.

It is not surprising that disequilibrium and exogenous effects play a role in this kind of explanation. In fact, they are crucial. Here the particular historical facts, which often represent disequilibrium and exogenous effects, are as important as the rational financial and locational factors. Those facts are not to be averaged out or treated as noise, at least if we want to have a powerful explanation of the process of entrepreneurship. Moreover, a center or an entrepreneurial success is overdetermined, with many facts and factors each being decisive, and none to be readily eliminated. Those particular historical facts contribute to that complex of overdetermination.

Despite these general features, accounts of a particular entrepreneur often assume that *this* entrepreneur is special, taking the entrepreneur's survival as a mark of election, and so explaining the entrepreneur's eventual domination. These explanations are not to be dismissed if they give due weight to the uncertainties, risks, and almost-disasters along the way, as well as to the miraculous recoveries and survivals. Correspondingly, failed entrepreneurs are often described in cautionary homilies, their being irretrievably defective or sinful and so not among the elect being the most appealing account in such a sermon. But just as successful entrepreneurs depend on good fortune, so failed ones may not have been so fortunate. The most subtle historical accounts of success and failure are about virtue—how we manage the slings of fortune.

In explaining the frequency of founding acts and entrepreneurial endeavors, one is less concerned with the idiosyncratic. Here we begin with an account of the richness of opportunities, the supply of entrepreneurs, the quality of natural resources, and the entrepreneurial character of a culture. Early fluctuations may be crucial, and so we need to characterize the spectrum of those fluctuations. How likely is it that one or two or three actors will come on board at one of the right times and save the day, so making way for what we now take as inevitable? Those early actors are likely to be influenced by forces usually exogenous to the main story—what is happening in their own investment climates, or religious persecution causing emigration from place Z, which is perhaps now declining. And so our explanations will have to be in terms of systems of centers.

The historiographical considerations of the last several paragraphs are traditional ones, and they are of practical as well as scholarly interest. For they deeply influence how entrepreneurs think of themselves and their deserts, as we have seen in chapter 1. Moreover, they indicate how subtle must be the connection between mechanism and history, between the potential and the actual, and between an account of generic centralization and an account of a particular center.

By the way, ecological niches share many of the features of entrepreneurial activity, although they may not depend on intentional choices. Can we survive and thrive long enough so that a stable ecosystem builds up around us? Or will competing organisms prevent our gaining a beachhead at a place? There are no preordained natural places, no analytically necessary arrangements—since there is a very wide range of ecological possibilities. No niche is naturally suited to its organisms, for "a species' ecological role is plastic."

DNA is a large molecule that codes the proteins needed for the development of an organism. In a suitable environment the code is read off by a hierarchical sequence of chemical reactions, eventually to produce these proteins, which through further sequences of chemical and biological reactions create complex differentiated organisms. Here the generalized center is a fully potent molecule that incorporates all the crucial information. The analytic problem is to decipher the code and figure out how it is read off, and then to describe the eventual interaction of the various products.

How the code is read depends in part on the chemical and physical environment. So the message is in fact not so centralized, for the environment or periphery influences the expression of the center, and it can alter the original code. Still, one assumes there is a center, that it is only mildly perturbed by the environment, and that the transmission is mostly one-way and in sequence.

But where does this center, DNA, come from? An initial answer is that it comes from earlier realizations, earlier decodings and the variation provided by reproduction, a story of Mendel and of Crick and Watson. So a center is a repetition of earlier archetypes. We might then ask how those archetypes have come to be. And for that we need either a creationary moment or an evolutionary process. If there is a creationary moment, then there was a center to start with—although it is incumbent on us to give an account of what happened at that moment. If there is evolution, then one has to account for the fact of centralized ordering we now have in DNA.

Consider a *random walker* on a line, unpredictably making a step to the right or to the left. Starting out at an origin, say the time and place when we first look, the walker will end up spending most of its time on one side of the line—as long as we look for times short compared to infinity, but long compared to say a hundred steps. (Over the very long run its average distance from the origin is zero, and it will spend equal times on each side of the origin.) Early on the walker may go back and forth, but within a short while it seems to have moved off in one direction and on one side, only to return to the other side in very long times. Its walk exhibits diffusion—its mean square distance from the origin is proportional to the number of steps ($\langle R^2 \rangle \approx N$). So once we are willing to mark the origin, we get a polarization or a center: the side the walker is on, its distance from the origin, and the direction of diffusion.

Now consider drifters, who once they are sent off in a certain direction persist in that direction, say at a fixed velocity. If we send off a sequence of such drifters randomly to the left or right, a center defined as the asymmetry, $N_{\text{left}} - N_{\text{right}}$, will diffusively move away from zero, in direct analogy with our previous example. It should be noted that the normalized value of the asymmetry, $(N_{\text{left}} - N_{\text{right}})/N_{\text{total}}$, will converge to zero. And over any middle-length run, there will more to the left than to the right, or vice versa.

Now imagine starting out by deliberately sending the first drifter off to the right and the second to the left. (Recall that each of these drifters continues in his chosen direction forever.) For the third and later candidates, probabilistically choose which direction to go off in, biasing the probability by the ratio of the number already to the right versus the total. In the very long run, we might expect a ratio $N_{\text{right}}/N_{\text{total}}$ to be one-half. But in fact, depending to some extent on what happens early on, any long-term ratio, from zero to one, is equally likely.

The center in this case is the long-term ratio, which is seemingly biased and not likely to be one-half. Such an asymmetry of N_{left} to N_{right} is obtained without any initial preference. Again, we get centralization without building it in. But if we ask why the ratio should be X, we cannot say—all we can give is the distribution of such ratios.

A last case, an Ising model. Imagine a crowd of forgetful and anxious men in an auditorium. Each one gets up and down from his seat fairly frequently. Being a good member of the audience each notices what his nearby neighbors are doing and tries to do the same. If the audience members are quite alert, then in fact after a while everybody in the auditorium will be sitting or everybody will be standing. They will be in phase. But if the audience is not so alert, then we expect around half will be sitting and half standing at any one time— although the fluctuations are substantial, and exactly the same as in the random walk. So even in the case of the not-so-alert members, the asymmetry defined by $N_{\text{seated}} - N_{\text{standing}}$ is likely to be substantial, although much smaller in absolute value than when they are in phase ($\sqrt{N} \ll N$). Now if we know their degree of alertness or interaction and their degree of nervousness, we can predict whether they will be roughly equally distributed between seated and standing or they will all be in phase, all up or all down. But we cannot predict, if they are in phase, which position they will all be in, seated or standing. Again, we may obtain what seems like a center—all seated or all standing—

although in fact each member is only acting locally and in his own interest, and there is surely no planned coordination.

More generally, in all of these cases centralization and large-scale order is consistent with the independence of the components and with their interactions being local and unprejudiced. We find orderly patterns because we look at the right phenomena and measures of them, and for the right duration. Fluctuations are in fact not fair in the short run, and balance is less likely than is imbalance. And especially when there is interaction among the components, a system is likely to be orderly and to be rigidly fixed in some direction, asymmetrical rather than symmetrical—our lack of predictive knowledge of just which direction being the surrogate for that absent symmetry.

Our last example is the unicellular organism *slime mold.* On a culture plate that is well supplied with nutrients, the organism will go along reproducing by means of division, slowly but surely covering the plate. Say that we starve the organisms, by crowding or by decreasing the quantity of nutrients. The organisms appear to aggregate and then differentiate into a multicellular organism, a slug. It seems natural to look for a coordinating cell (a "pacemaker") that guides this process and acts as a center, much as DNA supposedly guides development. But none has been found. Instead, it has been suggested that with a decrease in nutrients the system of independent organisms is less resilient and less stable, and eventually it becomes unstable. And then there are other modes of organization which are more viable.

One can model such a process nonlinearly, namely, as a process in which scale matters, here the scale being nutrients available per organism. At critical values of the scale parameter, the critical concentration depending on details of physical and biological dynamics, there will be instability and there will appear new solutions to the model and new modes of organization of the system.

What is needed for aggregation to actually begin is a fluctuation in concentration or spatial distribution, one that brings some starving cells into closer contact. Then the alternative state can begin to be explored, namely, some chemical reactions now become more likely, and so differentiation becomes possible. These fluctuations are always present owing to thermal effects. But they are effective in triggering transformation only when there is instability, when the cells are quite starved and they are fairly close to each other.

For these nonlinear processes one may be able to predict the conditions for centralization, the sharply defined tipping or instability points (measured by a scale parameter), and the spectrum of fluctuations. But one cannot say just where they will occur.

WHAT IS A CENTER?

A center is a marked place, whether it be a point in space or time, a trend or a direction, or a model or an archetype. A center is also a source from which all else flows. Phenomenologically, centers are the places around which there occurs that orderliness we call centralization. The examples suggest that centers are a product of history and mechanism, fortune and randomness, and instability and nonlinearity.

A particular center may have been chosen voluntaristically by an entrepreneur; or it may have been determined in varying degrees by history, God, or economic forces; or it may be a random fluctuation that happened to survive on its own. A center may be a preordained and explicit plan or be a consequence of a large number of interactions, the effect of an Invisible Hand. So centralization at X may have little directly to do with any mechanism's built-in and explicit central tendency, or with X, and a lot to do with consequences of combination and balancing. But once we see centralization at X, we often assume both central intention and the X location, and we provide a justification for that center that then becomes its legitimation.

Centers are not only overdetermined; but in seeming contradiction, no single cause is in general guaranteed to determine the exact outcome. There is a rather more complex story to be told. The task is to understand how what is contingent comes to be taken as necessary, how a potential center becomes actual and is taken as inevitable.

If we do treat a center as determined, necessary, and God-given, we need to recall that the ways of Providence include contingent historical processes and counterintuitive combinatorial ones, as well as the more straightforward if mysterious divine election and justified redemption. But if we assume that God may well even play dice, it still seems presumptuous to believe that God participates in our laws of chance.

Why might there be centers at all? We seem to need centers to characterize the phenomena we take as significant and to motivate the explanations we give of those phenomena. We mark the line and so can see the random walker staying on one side or the other; we organize an oeuvre in terms of styles and prime objects; we set up regimes of temperature and pressure so that phase transitions are apparent; we describe social changes as revolutionary. In a Kantian vein, we might say that a center is the transcendental condition for the kind of causality and interrelationship we take as natural: If there is a center, a single well-defined nexus, then we may engage in explanations that are causal and sequential. Here the answer to why might there be centers is an account of the kinds of phenomena and knowledge we might have.

A rather different answer is suggested if we say that Nature does not scale linearly, as we indicated in our discussion of slime mold. Having established a linear measurement scale reflecting values we take as goods—such as economic output in dollars or magnetization in gauss—phenomena accounted for in terms of that measure eventually become nonlinear. Small changes in inputs have quadratic and higher order or exponential effects. And a center marks that transition point as pecuniarily and symbolically valuable.

We might restate much of what I have said about centers in the even more technical terms of dynamical systems theory, the renormalization group, or broken symmetries. So, for example, the interesting scale variables are in effect order parameters that become significant at a phase transition, where order and pattern is equivalent to stable attractors or fixed points, and characteristic fluctuations are large at the phase transition. In various ways these technical accounts emphasize that under certain reasonable conditions—the kinds we might expect for equilibrium, for example—complex systems composed of many parts and variables collapse into only a few crucial variables such as temperature and pressure. And the systems may then exhibit sharp transition points in those variables.

Still, before writing equations, we might want to understand how things are set up so that those equations will apply. Hence my concern here has been phenomenological and historical.

The ethical issues are also crucial. There is an intimate connection between the ethics of value and the ontology and mechanism of centralization. For instance, we can create differentia of quality through advertising and art that then mark a place as locationally distinctive, say as rare and beautiful, and justified as optimal just because it possesses those created differentia. Those preferred qualities will justify the place's attractiveness and its eventually becoming a center. Similarly, accessibility and the scarcity of time—values often invoked in location theory to explain centralization—are a function of the tasks we set ourselves. In a different kind of culture, busyness need not be explanatorily useful, or availability of time the parameter where nonlinearity sets in.

This relationship of value to mechanism and centralization is even more explicit when God is the source or origin, as in Genesis, or when historical founding moments are taken to be sources, as for cities or political movements. Genesis is an origin story or center just because it justifies the social and political hierarchies of the Hebrews; the American Revolution as we now interpret it justifies or criticizes our current way of life.

If there might be centers, why might there be a center at X? If we know X ahead of time, we may supply a narrative account in terms of deliberate human intention, history and tradition, and chance and rational optimization. And if we have information on failed choices, Zs, ones that did not work out or were chosen and then rejected, we might tell a richer narrative, less deterministic, more ironic.

Given a set of Xs and Zs, we might find classification rules that say why X is successful and not Z. And as indicated earlier, we might try to account for the relative viability and resilience of different potential centers, and for the nature of the risk-taking or exploration that is required to achieve the given distribution of Xs and Zs—the creative destruction (Schumpeter) that attends capitalism's flourishing. It is most attractive to view the set of Xs and Zs as representing a set of random variables, for then we might employ the apparatus of probability and statistics in our explanation.

Evolutionary accounts of why there are centers such as species, and of the particular species we do have, are both narrative and classificatory. This kind of explanation assumes its endpoints or the Xs, the vestiges or the Ys, and the extinctions or the Zs. Its challenge is to incorporate the intermediate paleontological evidence (Ys and Zs), as well as what we may infer about earlier environments and about the modes of interaction of species.

Finally, we might be able to actually calculate the value of X, as we might calculate a freezing point or an optimal location. To do so we must employ a high degree of abstraction—which may or may not be an acceptable cost. In the case of entrepreneurship, such abstraction is likely to hide the crucial factors. Or, as we mentioned earlier, the abstraction will preclude our being able to predict features of a center, such as the direction of the symmetry axis of a frozen crystal, although we might be able to say that in a sample of crystals the distribution of such directions is isotropic.

To repeat, centers are products of history and mechanism, fortune and randomness, and instability and nonlinearity. And centers are not only points or places; they are global or contextual phenomena—for what is not the center points to it. So explanation of a center at X can readily justify global hierarchy, order, and domination. In the background is the fact that usually we first know about a center and then explain its existence. We much more rarely ask why are there no centers here, how could these failed centers have succeeded, or what is the order in this seemingly uncentralized place? More generally, explanations of centralization are provided within a context of value. Centers are cultural and ethical.

POLYCENTERS

Some of the time what we see are polycenters—a multiplicity or a sequence of centralizations. There may be several centers for a city (perhaps hierarchically arranged, although not necessarily concentric), or overlapping ecosystems with niches that function in more than one system. Historically, one of the most influential accounts of polycenters is Gibbs phase rule, which prescribes the number of different phases of materials that may be present in a mixture. For example, water and ice may be present over a range of temperatures and pressures, while water, ice, and vapor may be present together at only one temperature and pressure.

If there are polycenters, the naturalness of monocentricity is now called into question, its inevitability challenged by the facts of multiplicity. Of course, if we can put the centers into a concentric hierarchy, then monocentricity is reaffirmed. It is one of the attractions of the so-called Grand Unified Theories of elementary particles that they assume a single supercenter so as to account for various subcenterings at lower energies. But, in general, such a strategy might not work; the center may not hold.

If new entrepreneurs come along, and they succeed in establishing alternative centers, eventually perhaps replacing that of the initial successful entrepreneur, we need to understand why the preemptive move that established the original entrepreneur as dominant and robust may now be subverted. The structure of domination is no longer so stable. We might say that the environment had rich opportunities for development ignored by the original entrepreneur. Entrepreneurs are too busy with their own projects; there are limits to their individual control and knowledge; and scale diseconomies prevent a project from incorporating all opportunities within the entrepreneur's range. Or we might say that exogenous technological developments now make a new enterprise effective, the technology by happenstance being comparatively unusable by the well-entrenched original center or entrepreneur. Or, perhaps the original center produces environmental changes which then create new niches or new operative rules, and these just happen to be capitalized on by a new entrepreneur rather than the original one. (Note that "happenstance" and "scale diseconomies" are terms that surrogate for detailed historical and structural explanations, and for accounts of the nature of surprise and stubborn exogenousness. See chapter 8 for the practical consequences of these factors.)

In systemic terms, endogenous effects of growth, such as toxic detritus or changes in scale, or exogenous shocks may force a system to explore new ranges of its parameters, and so nonlinearities formerly missed come to the fore. Mechanisms that were until now unimportant may dominate over the original centralizing one. Of course, this kind of explanation typically discovers such alternatives and nonlinearities only after they have made their appearance. Polycenters are no more predictable than are monocenters themselves. But given such polycenters, they may well be justifiable.

Polycenters, or a system of centers, are perhaps more stable and efficient than the original monocenter. And the alternative of hierarchical centralization may in some cases be shown to be quite unlikely. Stability, efficiency, and probability may lead to organized inhomogeneity, as in a ferromagnet divided into domains or neighborhoods. And rather than the lovely homogeneity of a market, imagine dozens of submarkets with remarkably little mutual interaction (domain walls), the costs of perfect information being much too high. Large numbers of small independent parallel processors may sometimes be more efficient than a single large system, whether in computation or in economy.

Polycentralization may even be a processual phenomenon. Imagine a homogeneous liquid. It has a well-defined density, but no well-defined spatial center—if we might ignore its walls, which we are about not to do. When we change the environment exogenously and thereby heat up the liquid, the water will begin to convect and eventually to boil in one place or another, that place itself being a matter of imperfections and random influences we cannot know enough about ahead of time. We now have a monocenter in space, the boiling bubble, and a distribution in density. With more heat we get more boiling, polycenters within space, with a livelier distribution in density. Eventually we get a full boil throughout the fluid, a new kind of homogeneity. Such is the road to what is called turbulence and chaos, when spatial centers are everywhere and the distribution in density is roughly uniform. So the monocenter of a single boil, elected by imperfection—the nature of all such election, whether in religion, politics, myth, or nature and physics—becomes a democracy of homogeneity.

Sin is original because it provides an account of human nature, a sacred way of making peace with human imperfection. And even if there are seven deadly sins, just one of them—pride—is the crucial one. Centers are the way we make our mundane peace with imperfection, for a center provides a single source from which all else flows. And "Where do centers come from?" is about a great mystery, our capacity for knowledge of the world.

CHAPTER FOUR

Sticky Systems

In between the little and the big, the marginal and the discontinuous, the homogeneous and the centralized or individuated, and the smooth and the jumpy—lies the sticky and the conventional. Characteristically, sticky systems resist external forces, yet eventually and often then quite abruptly respond to them. Resistance and ratchetyness are fundamental features of society and nature. And exchanges are often incomplete or unbalanced. In general, even equilibrium may not settle in promptly. Solid iron will flow in response to gravity, as Marshall would approve— if we wait long enough, 10^{65} years.

The set of ideas and examples we have employed to model marginalism, discontinuity, and centralization may be reinterpreted to model stickiness. The models are either collective mechanisms or phenomenologies, and they involve either deterministic or stochastic processes. And as reinterpretations, they suggest that when the context is changed tools are subject to surprising and ironic application. This is most clear if we concentrate on a bestiary of detailed models rather than on generic mechanisms of stickiness.

In chapter 5 I shall describe just how we set up situations which are inhomogeneous, individuated, and centralized, and situations which are resistant, unbalanced, and sticky.

IF WE PUSH ON a part of the world, it may move smoothly enough in response, if not without a resistance. That resistance may be an inertia due to mass; or the viscous drag and friction of water, slime, or molasses; or the harmonic force of a spring or of an economy in equilibrium; or societal conservatism due to tradition, convention, and solidarity.

51

Such resistance may be proportional to the mass or drag of what we are pushing, its speed or its acceleration, and how hard we push. This resistance might even be termed marginal.

Yet the resistance is sometimes not so marginal. Turbulence may set in; price or wage levels may not change even if market conditions alter drastically; physical systems stay frozen even if we change external conditions; taboos seem absolute; and social and cultural conventions are not only traditional but atavistic, persisting well beyond their original apparent utility. In each case, the response to a push or an influence appears only after some delay, and often in an abrupt or discontinuous and catastrophic fashion, perhaps accompanied by fluctuation. And even then there will remain vestiges and leftovers. Such "sticky" systems could just be systems that respond very slowly to external forces. But what captures our imaginations is not only their lagged and viscous character, but their ratchetyness and their seemingly infinite if temporary resistance to change. Even if stickiness were shown to be a perverse effect of marginal smooth processes, an ironic effect of combination and interaction, the phenomena of stickiness and discontinuity, as such, remain most impressive.

Resistance makes sense as a term of description for the phenomenon we experience if we believe that there is a proper place, an equilibrium or a historical path, with which the system is not in accord—yet ought to be. So there is a contrast between bid prices and an imputed underlying real market value; or a contrast between a current state of a physical system and a more stable one, as in a supercooled fluid or a geological fault; or a contrast between a traditional practice and a perhaps more efficient modern one. We expect the system to settle down eventually to its proper place. Here in these examples the resistance is sticky, not marginal.

Now systems ordinarily exhibit a linear response to external influences, proportional to first derivatives, and so they are symmetrical. For example, if there is equilibrium, balance, and smoothness, harmonic or springlike forces ($F = - kx$) are symmetric; any resistance is again marginal. Here asymmetries based on nonlinearities and anharmonicities are in general small. But sticky systems are not only resistant; they may exhibit fundamental asymmetry in their response to external influences. Small shifts on the upside work differently than do those on the downside. Raising prices in an oligopoly or away from equilibrium, for example, may produce effects of a qualitatively different kind than does lowering them. And at a phase transition, as in freezing, adding a bit of heat may change the system in a different way than does removing some heat.

STICKINESS IN SOCIAL SCIENCE

Again recall that Alfred Marshall argued in his *Principles of Economics* (1890) for taking the world in terms of marginalism, continuity, smoothness, and equilibrium. Systems that appear to be sticky and unsmooth should be averaged over properly long-enough time scales, and mores and ethics are to be treated as general rules that affect preferences smoothly. Market fluctuations and long-term permanent structural changes are both to be treated in the same analytic fashion, their different time scales being all that distinguishes them.

While John Maynard Keynes (1936) was perhaps as committed to continuity as was Marshall, his task was to account for depressed markets, ones that did not equilibrate or clear. They exhibited long-term unemployment, a stickiness that should have been avoided by price and wage adjustments. His explanation made use of a combination of time lags, mechanisms that depended on the contrast between individually and socially appropriate responses to depressed conditions, and systemic sinks such as excess savings that prevented optimal equilibration. He suggested as well that the system of consumption and investment was damped (the "multiplier," and fixed effective demand). Hence, the feedback due to the Invisible Hand did not work effectively to balance the system. It was a hydraulics of viscous fluids, turbulence, transients, and leakage.

Joseph Schumpeter (1934) was also struck by the more general discontinuities, the stickinesses, and the ratcheting to new plateaus or equilibria, characteristic of political economies. Actual mature economies are remarkably resistant to external forces of transformation and must be shocked into change. As we noted in chapter 1, Schumpeter speaks of ". . . that kind of change . . . which so displaces its equilibrium point that the new one cannot be reached from the old one by infinitesimal [or marginal] steps." Qualitative novelty and custom play a large role in his analyses—as the means, respectively, to economic development and for social resistance to change. "In breaking down the precapitalist framework of society, capitalism thus broke not only the barriers that impeded its progress but also flying buttresses that prevented its collapse."

From Marshall to Keynes to Schumpeter we go from smoothness to discontinuity, a critical variable being the degree of stickiness that is taken as natural. There is a similar range in anthropological thought. In kinship, for example, there are systems of exchange that are in balance or are meant to be continually or smoothly balanced, just as markets are cleared. And there are systems of gift and exchange that always leave a residue of obligation, so that an exchange is never balanced and done with. That residue might be taken as a sign of stickiness, a stickiness that makes for solidarity. More generally, redemption, as in sacrifice and stigma, is never simply a matter of equivalence, or of an exchange that fully clears and so may be forgotten. Sacred ways of paying one's dues are biographical and historical.

Stickiness and ratchetyness are exemplified by rites-of-passage ritual and conversion experience. They are models of radically discontinuous processes, in which our retrospective accounts emphasize both the resistance to change and an eventual almost instantaneous response. Most committed believers account for their transformations in terms of a shock to their sticky systems. For it is through violating acts that then lead to a new orthodoxy that we may transform the boundaries or the stickinesses and change the taboos.

Collective, socially defined practices, such as custom, race, institutions, and moral considerations, stubbornly resist universalistic and formal rules, such as those of economy, that might allow for simple equivalence and marginal resistance. Particularistic practices segment societies and markets, institutionalize stickiness, and prevent full and free exchanges. Yet custom does set the stage for equilibrium and exchange, for it demarcates what is up for sale and what is beyond commerce, as we shall see in chapter 5. But custom's influence is then said to be excessive and problematic, preventing an ideal efficiency. But, again, if the world is discontinuous and segmented and sticky, then custom and the like are just what one must systematically describe and live with.

For example, what is most attractive about Thomas Kuhn's account of revolution is his justification of those who delay in going along, who refuse conversion at first, who exhibit stickiness. They are rational, sensibly committed to what may eventually be overturned. Their doctrine works rather well in its own terms.

A BESTIARY

The models and mechanisms employed earlier to discuss bigness, discontinuity, and centralization may be reinterpreted to provide a bestiary of stickiness. For even formal, precisely specified models allow for a diversity of interpretations. Still, we shall encounter just a few basic phenomenological models and a few mechanisms of interaction. The models of stickiness exhibit nonlinearity, metastability, fluctuation, asymmetric behavior, or classification and taboo. The mechanisms that produce stickiness employ stochastic processes, cooperative phenomena, and combinatorial sinks. Here our concern will be with just how these generic features are concretely embodied in vivid and poignant models. Let us embark on our tour of the bestiary.

First, there are some conventional accounts and explanations of sticky systems, as in ecology and in social science. A *lagged system of differential equations,* as in a Keynesian economy, perhaps nonlinear and subject to exogenous and stochastic shocks, will model just about anything, including metastability and stickiness. *Game theoretic sinks*—for example, the prisoners' dilemma—lead to less than optimal configurations which might be said to be stuck, a stuckness which can then be avoided or smoothed over either by centralized planning and coordination or by means of averaging, ignorance, and some random shaking. *Combinatorial sinks,* as in congestion-induced blockages or too-rapidly quenched annealing, are again less than optimal, and they often require a shock or some shaking in order to achieve more optimal configurations. And one may simply *assume segmentation* and ratchetyness, and then describe an equilibrium that jumps during transitional or punctuating periods to a new equilibrium state, with quasistatic changes otherwise. All these are models of situations that may well belie the Marshallian-like principle that behavior lies in equilibrium and balance, optimization, and the relaxation of transients.

Another strategy for accounting for stickiness is well represented in modern economic thought. One takes a smooth marginal model, such as the market, and adds some reasonable complicating features to its component individuals, and so there emerges collective stickiness. *Transaction costs,* such as those of information, search, collective action, and implicit contracts, prevent change to what are taken to be more efficient configurations, the latter being the ideal of universalistic and formal schemes such as neoclassical economics. *Aversion to risk* and problems of uncertainty lead to asymmetric attitudes toward change. And *feedback mechanisms* between individual and collective preferences lead to nonlinear equations which have multiple and distinct solutions, and hence to discontinuity and jumps. A contrary strategy shows how apparent smoothness hides stickiness, there being smooth unsticky equilibrated aggregates of sticky unequilibrated individuals.

In the context of an assumed ideal of equilibrium, sticky behavior may still be shown to be rational if we may invoke mechanisms such as risk aversion and feedback. Stickiness may serve everyone's interest since there are substantial benefits to a persistent, known, regular structure of economic activity, and substantial costs consequent to uncertainty and to obtaining complete knowledge. Rationality is limited or bounded. So there develop implicit contracts that maintain a conventional order. It pays to be sluggish and sticky, if we are unsure whether a momentary price signal is transient and temporary, or structural and permanent. And rather than smoothly changing preferences, it is through ratchets—in the form of market entry and exit—that actors display their economic behavior.

The putative imperfections usually invoked to account for stickiness—segmentation, differing attitudes toward risk, depth of pockets for absorbing downside costs and runs of losses, imperfect information or a lack of hedging and arbitrage, untempered fluctuations, and deliberate planning or conspiracy—are not casual or arbitrary facts about society, but rather are fundamentally constitutive of it. Similarly, environmental shocks, mutations, and vestiges are crucial to evolution, and entrepreneurship and sacrifice are often the engines of systemic development. Stickiness, tradition, speculation, and shock are to be expected in an imperfect real world.

Stickiness appears natural and necessary in a variety of phenomenological models. Analysis of kinship structure and of rites-of-passage ritual expresses stickiness as incest and *taboo,* the forbiddenness of specific ties and transformations. More generally, resistance or stickiness is needed to preserve *symmetry and order,* whether we think in group theoretic terms and of forbidden transitions, or we employ social structural categories that assume segmentation and pollution by race, class, or gender.

Phenomenological models of *phase transitions,* as in classical thermodynamics and in modern notions of self-similarity, scaling, and chaos, account both for discontinuities such as distinct phases and for resistance and eventual susceptibility to change such as melting. But for a physicist, on the sufficiently microscopic scale there is no stickiness. Surely there are forbidden transitions that would violate a conservation law; yet such violation is almost always permitted nonetheless, although it is less likely to occur than are allowed transitions. But fundamentally, all is smooth and local in space and in time, and resistance is at most marginal. Apparent stickiness and discontinuity are a product of thermodynamic or statistical or combinatorial effects—a consequence of well-defined exogenously provided thermal walls that separate systems from each other, and of the adding up of the collective influence of a very large number of atoms or steps or states.

If our expectations are that a system will smoothly track external influences, then discontinuous and aleatory responses are indeed models of stickiness. Such processes include friction, metastability, phase transitions, and random walks. Moreover, what appears as centralization from one point of view will seem merely sticky from another.

Friction itself is a smooth form of resistance. But a block on a slowly tilting inclined plane will eventually begin to slide, since static friction is different than moving friction. To become unstuck, such sticky systems just need to reach their tipping point and then be given a little shove.

More generally, systems may become *metastable,* exhibiting a critical point beyond which two or more rather different states are possible. Yet a system may well stay in one of its less stable states, resistant to small fluctuations, until a sufficiently large internal fluctuation shakes it up or an external influence shoves it a bit too much. For example, a new, more efficient mode of production might become possible. But if no one explores the new mode sufficiently, if there is no risk-taking or no fluctuations, the conventional one will persist. When the metastable system responds, the manner in which it does so can sometimes be understood as a process of fracture or as a shock wave. And the statistics and symmetry of fracture or turbulence, the morphology of cracks and eddies being self-similar at all scales, might be employed to describe how sticky systems fall into a more stable state.

As I have suggested, phase transitions provide a model of discontinuity that may also be interpreted as stickiness. Consider *first order phase transitions,* as in water melting. At the transition point there is a change from a crystalline solid to a liquid, a discontinuity in the density and symmetry, and a spike or jump in the specific heat. Phenomenologically, the system splits into two or more phases, here water and ice. A system fully makes a transition and then may begin to heat up only when sufficient energy is provided for the whole system's heat of transformation, melting it completely. Stickiness occurs here because the two states have different modes of organization, and before the temperature can begin to rise energy must be provided for the system to go from one mode to the other. Yet, of course, as energy is provided the material makes the melting transformation bit by bit.

Now consider such a system in its liquid state, and gently cool it below its freezing point so it is still liquid. It is now supercooled. And it is metastable. Since it is subject to thermal fluctuations—for example, in density—bits of the fluid will freeze. But if the size of a fluctuation is small, the frozen bit is likely to promptly melt again. The frozen state will be transient, and it will not spread throughout the fluid. The fluid will seem stuck in its supercooled state. Still, some of the fluctuations will be larger, large enough to survive and grow. As one is further on the downside from any such transition point, the system becomes less stable. Fluctuations of any given size are likely to spread and grow more rapidly rather than being damped as they would be closer to and above the transition point. A small fluctuation can more easily trigger a transformation. (This is the general picture of metastability subject to fluctuations.) One can increase the transition-encouraging effectiveness of the fluctuations by dirtying up the system. These extra "nucleation points" serve as growth centers, allowing smaller fluctuations to survive long enough to grow and become pervasively influential. There are now more paths available for the transformation, and so the system becomes much less sticky.

In *second order phase transitions,* as in iron becoming permanently magnetizable below the Curie point (about a thousand degrees Kelvin), the discontinuities are more subtle. There is no metastability, but there is a stickiness nonetheless. Near a critical or transition point, the system can be remarkably sensitive and responsive to external fields and shocks. Further above that point it is smoothly but weakly responsive to external fields, at least until it saturates. But much below that point, the system is comparatively insensitive and might be said to be sticky. Below the Curie point a magnet will remain magnetized—permanently oriented, frozen, stuck in its original direction; and it is difficult to change that orientation with an external magnetic field. (This resistance is measured by the shape of the hysteresis curve.) One accounts for the stickiness or rigidity below the Curie point in terms of the collective effect of many individuals (here, atomic spins) interacting locally and smoothly one on one with each other. Their local interaction is extended into the cooperative phenomenon of a systemic order over the whole collection, an order which is very difficult to change piece by little piece. Here the system can be sticky or marginal, depending on the temperature and on the strength of the interatomic interactions.

Percolation provides another model of stickiness. Given a two-dimensional square grid, imagine connecting adjacent vertices randomly, with a given probability. There is no path from one side of the grid to the other if the local connection probability is zero, and there are many such paths if the connection probability is close to one. As we lower the probability from one to zero, there is a point ($p = 0.5$, for this configuration) at which the likelihood of a completed path changes fairly sharply from yes to no—the degree of sharpness being more pronounced for larger grids. Once isolated small clusters of connected vertices are now very likely to be linked among each other and there is now a completed path. The system's "conductivity" can be sticky. Much above or below the transition point, small changes in connection probability do not affect conductivity. Yet near that point conductivity changes rapidly, jumping as we change the connection probability beyond its threshold.

Finally, one might model stickiness in terms of stochastic processes. As we have seen for centralization, *random walks* can stray far from their initial zero or starting point and stay far away for some time. If one has an expectation of short-term fairness, such a system might well seem sticky—stuck in a biased place, on one side of the line or the other, far from the origin. If the system happens to be N steps from the origin, it will take on the order of N^2 moves before it diffusively returns.

The fluctuation or randomness of molecular motions that is the source of the diffusion of a fluid also leads to its viscosity, dissipating the energy of external influences and slowing down flows. Were the viscosity sufficiently large, we might model stickiness in hydrodynamic terms. Viscosity is increased by congestion and by the availability of wayward diverting paths, each of which slows down a flow considerably.

Stickiness can also be viewed as a matter of conventionality, but now understood as a consequence of the increasing returns to scale of a widely shared convention, which then discourages shifts to another perhaps more long-run efficient convention. One can model the development of such stickiness, and presumably the possibility of giving up on it, as a *Polya urn* problem, as we did in chapter 3. For example: Place a red ball and a blue ball in an urn; blindly pick out a ball and opening your eyes replace that ball by two balls of the same color; continue this process of picking-out and replacement. Depending mostly on what happens early on, often in the first few dozen or hundred tries—the final ratio of red balls to the total can be from zero to one, with every value equally likely. What looks like a necessary convention—as in the typewriter keyboard—may well be a product of an initially unbiased random process. We become stuck with a particular convention. Such processes exhibit nonoptimality or inefficiency, so that we may be stuck with a less than best option; sensitivity to initial conditions or nonergodicity, so that early moves preempt some outcomes; inflexibility, locking in an outcome, so we are stuck; and nonpredictability of their final locked-in state, as Brian Arthur has pointed out.

We might epitomize our tour of the bestiary by classifying the animals:

	Deterministic	*Stochastic*
Collective Mechanisms	game theory combinatorial sink transaction costs feedback	risk aversion phase transition percolation random walk Polya urn
Phenomenological Models	lags in time and space segmentation classification rules phase transition friction	metastability

What might we conclude more generally? What is curious about sticky systems is our notion that some states are stuck, and that they will be dislodged or need to be dislodged and so fall back in line. And stickiness is often used to represent waste, disequilibrium, and defect. Yet those pollutions may be efficient given the costs of perfection, and they may be rational considering the costs of disruption. Stickiness is structurally constitutive for societies, in that it provides for coherent and stable organization and for solidarity, persistence, and commitment. Resistance to change is a way of making a world we can live in, safely protected from what appear as arbitrary external forces, whether of economy or of politics or of nature. Now these forces might in the long run push us in directions best for all of us. But in the short run, our lifetimes, they are likely to disturb our homes and hearths and our modes of production and consumption. And custom is perhaps as effective as pecuniary incentive in making sure people are committed to each other and to their jobs and work. Solidarity and stickiness are the foundation for liberal society. They set up the possibility of playing the economic games of exchange and equilibrium.

The ways we choose to make sense of the world, the models and the mechanisms, build in tacit presuppositions about what is natural and appropriate. Is stickiness to be understood and appreciated as fundamental and natural, or is it to be explained away as secondary and derivative? Of course, this choice will not only be a matter of our preferences and commitments. In the end, what will count at least as much is the power and effectiveness of a particular way of thinking about the world. One of the most powerful contemporary ways is economy, a story of smoothness and absolute fungibility. Yet since the world is surely sticky, economy has been concerned with modeling stickiness. In the next chapter we shall explore the play of economic exchange and sticky resistance.

CHAPTER FIVE

Economy, Perversion, and Fetishes

Incommensurability and individuation are cousins of discontinuity. If there is incommensurability, trades cannot balance and the world may not add up. And if there is individuation, discreteness may be sufficiently insistent that it cannot be smoothed over into continuity. Perversion is a model of incommensurability; like stickiness, it is in between marginalism and discontinuity. Fetishism is a model of individuation; and like centralization, it is in between alienation and solidarity. (Here perversion is defined by mixture, not by incompleteness as conventional sexual morality sometimes suggests.)

Fetishism turns a perverted world into an economic one. For the perverted world then becomes both individuated and commensurable, the individuals having properties that may be balanced against each other. Still, there will be leftovers, signs of perversion's presence, that belie economy's hegemony. So even if we may treat the world as if it possessed handles we might pull and twist—as if it were toolish and handleable—we'll still discover memory, residues, and sidelinkages that remind us how our handles are incomplete and awkward. Modern marginalist economic theory does provide ingenious modes of accounting for perversion, hierarchy, structure, stickiness, and waste. But as phenomena, economy feels rather different than perversion, as marginalism feels different than discontinuity.

What we need to keep in mind is that just because we can show that something is a setup does not mean that it is arbitrary. Fetishes are setups, but only certain parts of the world will act individually. And just because we can explain something does not mean that it will be explained away. Despite our explanations, economy, perversion, and fetishes are primordial and persisting. And just because we might condemn a practice does not mean that it is separable from what we approve. As we shall see, perversion is inextricably bound up with the rules of properness, whether they be sexual or economical.

61

ECONOMY IS A STORY of exchange and property, a story that appears in commerce, kinship, and natural science. Conventionally, an economy is a means for allocating and valuing goods and resources through processes of comparison and exchange. It may employ monetary intermediates, and the prices assigned to goods treated as commodities tell how valuable they are in relation to each other. In market economies the prices are also signals indicating where we might make our investments and purchases, valuing alternative opportunities. Economy also provides a justification for alienation. Individuals, as alienated, achieve their best in a market economy. For it is just their alienation, combined with the workings of the Invisible Hand, that leads to the market's efficiency.

Marginalism in market economy is a story of prices as marginal costs, decisionmaking as local steering or optimizing "at the margin," the recruitment of agents such as labor and entrepreneurs in terms of marginal returns, and of ownership accruing to those who make the incremental or marginal or local changes—given that the system is at equilibrium. It is also a story of the calculus, of first and second derivatives, of fungibility or the connectedness of the various parts of the world to each other, and of equilibrium, optimality, and smoothness.

Still, actual economies are imperfect—segmented, disequilibrated, and sticky, and many goods defy their mechanisms. Such imperfections may be transient flaws subject to repair, or intrinsic perversions which upend economy on its fictions.

In perversion, exchanges are incommensurable, stickiness is necessary, and imperfection is unavoidable. Perversion is characterized by mixture, pollution, and "impropriety," when properties never fully encompass our relationship to things. Yet in order to actually work, economy depends on perversion, much as marginalism and free exchange depend on discontinuity and stickiness. The link between perversion and economy is provided by fetishes. Fetishes are constructed so that they are potent, namely, possessing the properties needed to do economy's work. Yet they are also taken to epitomize perversion's impropriety. And I shall argue that it is just through fetishes that we do get an authentic handle onto the world, including a handle onto other persons like ourselves.

ECONOMY

Modern economy was perhaps a good solution to the eventual inadequacy of ancient and feudal ascribed orders. As described by Moses Finley, those orders regulated life in such a way that places and activities were controlled by convention and tradition. The operative notion was not the most efficient use of materials and people, all to be treated as fungible resources, as would occur in a market economy. Finley shows how "irrationally" large sums were spent by those of high status for personally sponsored public works so as to signify their status. Farmers acted not as capitalists, but as landowners whose land itself was what counted. In commercial life, much more profitable trade arrangements could have been set up, but only by violating the traditional way of doing things. Of course, in actual fact changes took place, and they were in part in response to market or economic forces. We might even show how all such changes could be explained in these terms. But no matter what our explanations, the reasons offered in ancient times were often not economic, and the actual power of the orders was quite real and substantial.

A mode of orders can continue to regulate people's behavior as long as it provides the means they need to continue in their way of life. But say that the mode no longer provided those means. Perhaps the exogenous system of trade changed, and pecuniary returns were no longer sufficient to maintain the mode of orders. Tributes might not be paid; servants might be let go. Allegiance to the orders might well decline, although that decline may take some time and be a sticky process. Modern economy, featuring self-interest, profit, and capital accumulation, might become the new order. Economic achievement replaces ordered ascription. All now is a reflection or metaphor of a single value, perhaps denominated by money, and all is commensurable with respect to it. There is no independent order of Nature or Aristocracy beyond the economy. Of course, in actual economies privilege is often "protected" from economic encroachment. Some aspects, such as racial and generic hierarchy and family structure, are erected as *icons*, relatively insulated from commercial or market transactions.

Domination, once expressed by a position in an order, would now be expressed by relative valuation, such as through prices. And if there were no orders independent of the economy, those (monetary) valuations would completely describe and so exhaust the relationship between people. The community is fully expressed in the economy. The universalistic character of the economy, a single value scale to which all pay allegiance rather than the many independent orders, is said to lead to an alienation of people from each other. They share nothing else.

Economy's characteristic feature is the process of *exchange* and the employment of a universal means of comparison. The price mechanism is fully capable of valuing things and of signaling intentions and directions for action. Actual economies have residual unpriced aspects, the icons, which appear immune to changing relative prices—except in extreme cases or over very long times. So these economies are in effect *protected.*

In an ordered society we follow tradition. But in an economy anything goes, as long as it is profitable and efficient: valuable along the monetary scale and more valuable than alternative activities. A protected economy moderates a swashbuckling economy by some gentlemanly rules. Imagine then removing the protections, but with a vengeance—so that there are now many scales of value, and not everything is commensurably encompassed even if we employed all the scales. Such will be our second story, that of perversion. But first we shall examine some features of economies, protected or not.

In an unprotected economy a thing is known by its valuable properties. It has no hidden essence. All is commensurable in terms of price, and I can buy out your land, your title, your status. There is no essential residue, one that is untouched by economy's processes, whether they be markets or plans, as there is in hierarchical orders. Even God's placement of us in this world would be played out by economy's rules.

We can know everything about others through their properties, through exchanges that touch upon and define them. Nothing is privileged. That you own private property through purchase, and it no longer has a relationship to its past owners, means as well that your privacy, too, may now be invaded by other purchasers. To treat all there is as knowable by its properties is to take commodifiability and to give it the magical power of representing all that is significant. Commodities are now fetishes, a part or an aspect fully representing a whole. (Of course, commodifiability may represent everything that is significant, and fetishes may be just the way the world is, the only means we have to get ahold of it.)

We change our roles by exchanging properties. Exchange is always possible, since all properties are commensurable. Now it might turn out that not all properties are exchangeable at any one time, if the economy is a protected one. But practically, those protections often do not appear to be significant restrictions, even if they actually are. So it seems that there may be nothing immune to exchange, and it is only by chance that there is a gentle preservation of goods. Here buy-outs, bankruptcies, and growth are more likely to upturn tradition than is political revolution. This is a Schumpeterian/Hegelian world, a businesslike yet bacchanalian revel of invention, competition, and liquidation. There seems to be no core around which the properties might organize a coherent history or memory, no natural kinds to define and prevent monstrosity.

The organization of the world is merely a by-product of the exhaustive iteration of the formal processes of exchange, following through on the rules. It is not formally planned or prescribed. Yet one of the triumphs of economic theory is to show that by following a rule of free exchange, the organization of the world turns out to be an efficient and roughly stable market.

The consequences of exchangeable, economizable property are rather different than those of a system of orders. Once something becomes a matter of property and commodity, it can be smoothly and continuously changed into something else, through exchange and through recombination of the means of production. Similarly, pecuniary earnings affect social position. And land becomes an efficiently usable resource rather than a marker of one's position in life. The old orders are loosened, and development need not suggest breakdown in a fixed system—since there is no fixed system. Finally, economy's means of cleansing pollutions is through buying up to a higher more clean status. This is perhaps more flexible, although less satisfying, than is sacred or political purification ritual. And in economy we alter the boundaries and taboos through exchanges rather than through ritual violations of the conventional rules.

The process of exchange is quite general. As I have mentioned, economists often show how what is conventionally taken to be an order-like system, such as marriage or law, may be understood in terms of prices, transactions, and effective markets. Anthropologists show how such systems may be understood in terms of more or less fair exchanges, with some exchanges being forbidden. They are, however, perhaps less concerned with efficiency and more concerned with solidarity.

For example, kinship structures may be shown to be the consequence of the exchange of women between families, and such exchange is as well the process of marriage. An exchange is usually symmetric and fair, conserving value, each family receiving its due. Exchanges completely define society, and so exchange is equivalent to society in this mode of analysis. The process of exogamy provides for social solidarity, since it links once disjoint families into a complex network. And everything in the society is known by its kinship or marriage relationship to everything else. Processes of change and transformation are to be taken as matters of exchange and marriage.

There is a precise analogy with chemistry or particle physics. For, again, interaction is a process of exchange, but now of electrons, atoms, and other elementary particles, where such exchanges conserve value of various sorts, such as energy and angular momentum. And the natural world is composed through those exchanges and interactions.

We make extraordinary demands on a classification structure such as kinship, the periodic table of the elements, or the symmetry groups, such as SU(3), of particle physics. The dynamics of interaction or exchange between families and the modes of classification of individuals into families are "the same," reflecting just one structure. Classification predicts interaction; interactions are used to infer classification schemes; and everything that is not forbidden or tabooed will exist or happen. In each realm one wants to find a current or currency which is conserved, so that the system or market clears.

If something is known through *properties* that are to epitomize its nature, it is both ahistorical and subject to gentle transformation. It is ahistorical and is disconnected from its past in that its properties almost always are about its current status and refer to separable disjoint qualities. So there is no memory, and there need be no canonical order into which the properties must fit. Hence, without memory or archetype, tradition cannot be prescriptive in an economy. Yet, curiously, property provides for continuity, because we can change a particular property possessed by something without destroying its essential quality—it has no fixed essence. And a small change in one property will usually have marginal effects. We might say that property is something we own, and it may be ascribed to us; yet it is separable from us, and it may be de-ascribed. If it can be ours, then it may enter the world of commerce.

Still, there will be protected icons, supposedly immune to market forces. When an economy replaces a system of orders, some of that system re-emerges as iconic, as still immune to the economy, and is even supported by it. So families are sacred, and some of the aristocracies are not only wealthy, but become the mercantile and financial powers. Yet economy's insinuating powers are eventually to challenge each icon.

Iconic economies privilege some properties, giving them absolute value. So an icon might be an untouchable center of commerce, not being for sale itself. But as a consequence the icon has no justified place in the economy, unlike the well-defined places in the orders of old. There can be no internal ideology that supports an isolated icon as an icon, for all should be subject to exchange or sale according to economy. And if there is such an external supporting ideology, then economy's hegemony is challenged.

Maleness and whiteness are conventionally thought of as icons which denominate value in an economy. As icons they are incommensurable with presumably lesser values such as femaleness and blackness. Not only do the icons lack a justified place in the economy; they can be polluted if they are touched by the lesser values: Femininity destroys maleness; miscegenation destroys whiteness. For these icons are taken as pure, and any foreign influence is an infiltration. Hence, as Hegel pointed out, the iconic master is subject to the economic slave. Now ordinary economical relations allow for any sort of mixture with marginal consequences. Any pollution of an economy could be cleaned up by being bought out. But here any mixture is insinuating and devastating, discontinuous rather than marginal in its effect.

We might model the iconic aspect of a protected economy as follows: There is, let us say, a single standard of value, A, representing maleness or whiteness, for example. Everything else, let us call one of them Z, depends on A. A dominates Z, is more valuable, more real, more enduring. Z is a pale reflection of A; Z is a weak metaphor of A. And A is independent or exclusive of Z and does not share its degraded quality.

Z's deficiency depends on there being a reasonably simple notion of wholeness, completeness, and truth: A's iconicity. If defect were ever-present and original as sin, and there were leftover parts everywhere, A would be no more whole than is Z.

PERVERSION

Perversion is literally a turning away, from the true and proper to the false and incomplete. Or so we are told by puritans. But we have just seen how tenuous and dependent are the true and the proper. In practice, perversion is a mixture of the proper and the improper, of the sacred and the profane. The icons might well be up for sale. Most generally, perversion is characterized by a multiplicity of independent goods or ways of living, none of which, even in combination, can claim dominance or authority or hegemony. And no icon is fully protected. There is no single controlling universal good.

If there is A, B, C, . . . , then A is not dominant over and determinate of the others. And there is no stable hierarchy. B is not even a version of A. No function exists such that B is a formulaic combination of A, C, D, . . . There is as well no way to divide the world into Male/Female or White/Black, As and Zs, since the world is multi-polar, not bi-polar. There is difference along many dimensions, not a split along one, and the dimensions may not form a single mathematical space.

From the point of view of economy, perversion is about incommensurables. Conversely, from the perspective of perversion, economy's single scale of value and universal mode of exchange is a presumptuous fetishism, giving a magical value to prices—a value that may be useful in some places but is surely not universal.

A geographical analogy might be helpful. In a complicated terrain or manifold we can put down a more or less square grid over an area and use it to plat out the land. We might be able to put down little grids everywhere and then provide rules for changing from one platting to another. Now it turns out there will also be discontinuities, places where adjacent mappings cannot easily be compared. Perversion is about the times we spend at the boundaries of those grids. Economy is a Cartesian truth, great on a four-lane freeway, but we need perversion, a Jeep or a horse, in rough terrain.

If there are borders we cannot cross smoothly, and so there are goods which are not definable or commensurable with respect to the others— what is to prevent one of these isolated goods from setting up its own duchy, and then claiming dominion over the rest and declaring as rubbish what is left over or incommensurable? But, of course, all such goods may set up their own duchies. Then they can attempt to inseminate each other along their shared borders. There is also likely to be a black market, more concerned with profit than dominion. As a consequence of the mutual claims of dominion and of the subversions by the black market, the isolated duchies might well make a peace among themselves, as do cartels, establishing trade and currency exchanges, all in a quite provisional way. So it begins to look as if each good may be defined in terms of the others, economically, and there will be mathematical functional relationships among them. Still, the peace is not complete, in that the borders remain discontinuous. Each good retains its own residual quality. But even that quality, which is supposed to lead to a distinctive identity, is not fixed. Technology may radically alter the contours of the terrain. The goods influence or flow into each other, devastating the conventional boundaries.

Consider a set of trading countries where each has a unique raw material that is an essential but perhaps small part of its trade. A copper country or a high-technology country seems set in its position, having an impermeable identity. But internal transformations, and inventions or discoveries made by any of the countries, will change the supply or demand for these unique materials, sometimes in quite uncontrollable and unpredictable ways. So the stability of each country's identity, the value of its unique resource, is challenged.

We might say: For the moment, $B = g_B(A, C, D, \ldots)$ " $+$ " ϵ_B, $\epsilon \ll g$, where g is something like a function, ϵ is a residue or leftover, and the symbols of equality and inequality might refer to dominance rather than size or quantity. Now in perversion not only is ϵ perhaps not addable to g, but ϵ could eventually be larger than or dominant over g. There are, of course, (g, ϵ) for A, C, D, $\ldots$, too. Functional relationships define a provisional system of exchange. But the residues can disturb that provision—as a system of interconnection, as such—and not just the particular equilibrium settled upon. The system depends on what it provisionally ignores.

Each country has its own view of the others, and no country is universally dominant. And each country possesses something the others cannot do without. Yet even if I travel from one to the next, visiting all of them, buying up adequate supplies of their distinctive resources; when I get back home from my odyssey the world has changed; and I'll need to go off again, since we now need new things. What is perhaps remarkable is how far we may still go in assuming there is a stable system of exchange and a stable structure of production—how much perversion is economical. But this is perhaps no more remarkable than mathematics' utility in physical science—a story both of mutual adjustment of tool and world and of tools or situations abandoned for lack of such congruence.

Mixture. A perverted world is not metaphoric, since the residues are nonzero and incommensurable, so substitution never quite works. It is not conservative, since when we return home we find that home has changed. It is not dominant, since no icon will universally denominate all else, and an icon may well be influenced by its subjects. And perversion is inherently multiple, since there is no preeminent icon. In comparison, the ideals of economy might be said to be metaphor or substitutability and conservation or balanced accounting; and for protected economies the ideals are a robust iconicity and hierarchic domination.

Perversion mocks economy's ideals. There is no market in which, after an exchange, we fully own something. There is no set of properties or fetishes that exhaust the meaning of a thing. Iconic hierarchies will surely be infiltrated, since influence is everywhere and protection may be breached. The goods can become unstable in their formulaic relationship to each other, since the residues might go wild and become large and significant. What we thought of as more or less commensurable no longer may be seen as such.

After a while the goods settle down again into recognizable, function-like configurations. Even monsters—when the residues are large—may eventually become normal. So we cannot treat monsters as if their stigma or residue is intrinsic or necessary to them. The perverted world can still possess a normative force, as we shall see. But it is without either the absoluteness or the utilitarian balancing we usually associate with an ethical norm.

> There might be new g' and ϵ', such that $\epsilon' \ll g'$, or new A', B', such that $g(A', C', D'. \ldots) \gg \epsilon$. One might think of a matrix whose elements are changing. A diagonalization ($\epsilon \ll g$) will eventually fall apart ($g \cong \epsilon$), and after a while a new one may be possible ($\epsilon' \ll g'$). This is, of course, a general problem in classification and systematics.

Perversion makes for mixture, impropriety, provisionality, resilient ultimates, and deference.

In perversion I choose *mixed* and incomplete ways of being: the extravagant and the frugal, the wasteful and the efficient. There is no way to surely identify excess, waste, and excreta as opposed to the enough, the frugal, and the pure and necessary. There are leakages, voids, and incoherent combinations. This is a dis-economy, an unending expenditure and dissemination, a mixture of savings and waste for which there is no formal accounting.

Here purity is a curious notion, since all and everything is polluted. (And so pollution makes no conventional sense either.) Qualities, such as the genders or races, surely influence and flow into each other. And there will be potentially unbounded and monstrous consequences of such mixing—or merely marginal ones.

Naturally, a protected economy is scared of perversion. For if there is perversion, we give up the normative force of a unique icon and a pollution taboo. Purity is now an idiosyncratic preference, an unlikely choice among a very rich set of equally valued alternatives.

Mixed and polluted, the perverted world is *improper* as well. There is no way property may be owned free and clear, no way of paying it off, no title insurance. For things are not fully characterized by their ownable properties. And lacunae in loan agreements and deeds, which we now ignore or protect ourselves against, may become monstrous in time.

There can be no rational title insurers. Title insurance makes up for vagaries of history such as disputed title claims, so that market-defined property can be fully cleared, bought and sold in a transaction.

But the residues of history may be substantial. Perhaps all the property will be reclaimed by the aboriginal peoples because the treaties have been violated. The insurer could not accurately assess its risk on the down side if the world were truly perverted.

Planning does not work, either. The residues are invisible debts which may become known to us only when they are due, and they may be much larger than what we had thought to be our potential exposure. So we cannot prudently plan, or treat these obligations actuarially. In the long run there may not be an accounting which balances. Or there may not be a sufficient independence of events to give one a law of large numbers and a central limit theorem. So the conventional probability distributions are not at all Gaussian, the tails perhaps large, lingering, and asymmetric.

The possibility of arbitrary expropriation makes investors demand substantial short-run returns and material guarantees for security. But if there are no alternatives to these kinds of uncertain enterprise, not even hoarding (for, again, the world is improper), none of the opportunities need offer a premium for uncertainty and high risk. It then makes sense to invest broadly, hoping that no coherent revolution will invert the value of all the properties. But it might, and there is not much to do about that.

Property, rationality, insurance, and investment are poor models of how we should manage our resources, except in the special and rare situation of an economy. If there is perversion, fortune, or protection, then what might work better is an articulated solidarity which allows others who have special skills and resources to come to our aid because we need them. There may well be overload, and that is managed by a tacit triage, doing the best we can. This arrangement perhaps gives "too much" help to those beyond repair. It is called community.

When there is leakage and dissipation, the economical or mechanistic strategy of pinpointing the source of trouble and impropriety, and so finding the knob to turn or the policy to follow, will in perversion reinforce the experience of disconnection and radical expropriation. The leaks are at least multiple, much as they must have been on that ship in *The Tempest*, reflecting how whole lives had gone awry. Since there is no single source of leakage, as such, plugging up one hole may well increase the flows through others, as well as change the functional structure of their relationship.

Conversely, being nonchalant about leakage won't help either. Some projects will be destroyed by incontinence and a lack of discipline. Now if we can stay afloat, we need not demand perfection or complete control. We could even transfer to different boats, one after the other. This strategy is reminiscent of Otto Neurath's image of scientific theory as being a ship at sea, to be repaired a plank at a time, and so being able to stay afloat. Both maritime strategies describe the provisional character of a way of being in the world. But if there is a sense of progress and craftsmanship in Neurath, they are only sometimes artifacts in a perverted world.

Still, we find that a perverted world works reliably and predictably much of the time, even without economy's universalistic normative regime. Subverting elements, residues, contractual ambiguities, gender- and category-crossings, and questions about title are not always devastating. Rather, we work within a local and traditional regime which provisionally puts aside the subverting elements, and then offers both set rules and modes of interpretation for dealing with subverting elements when they cannot be avoided. So law, contracts, and promises are honored; we usually agree how to argue when they are breached. We have modes of transferring what we call private property that are remarkably uncontested. And we all learn, by the time we are adults, the conventions of when gift, sale, or bequest processes are over, and ownership is reestablished.

Perversion has little necessarily to do with decadence or disorder. Rather, it is a fact we are made to live with. For life is a matter of taking care and being sensible—and we do well enough most of the time. Yet insofar as we claim that we live in an economy, ignoring perversion's presence, we are to be tempted by fetishes and haunted by illusions of perfection.

The economical languages of accounting, prudent investment, hydraulic conservation, and growth imply that the sinful alternatives are bankruptcy, irrationality, waste, and decay. But it is how we live with sin that is our test, much as we are judged by how our virtue commands Fortuna. Now we may note that bankruptcy depends on how long others are willing to carry our debts; that rationality in investment is based upon a probabilistic notion of risk; and that conservation and growth often assume there is just one efficient combination of resources and means of production. But in perversion, impropriety is the normative regime. The world is roomy enough for a range of choices—if we do not demand complete command over it. A going concern is ongoing by grace of its creditors; risk is entrepreneurial and fortunate; and it is the choice of a social organization of the economy, and that there always is such a choice, that then sets the stage for a regime of conservation and optimization. Again, it is how we live with these choices that is our test.

Goodness. In traditional society, *development* takes place along a fixed path of orders and places. In economy or evolution, development is marked by the growth of a value measure such as money, or more generally by movement on a scale of denomination such as wealth or "intelligence." But it is not clear ahead of time what the developmental path will be or what should count as wealth or intelligence. All we know are the rules of play. For in a market economy, or in a Darwinian evolutionary process, there is no substantive hierarchy, no teleology, no structure built into the rules of interaction. Rather, what the processes of exchange and natural selection yield as a matter of course is what we call development, our problem being to discern a scale of value or a hierarchy of denomination so that there is what we take to be growth and improvement.

In perversion, development must be understood without such a scale of value. While the goods might have a local ordering, that ordering is not expected to endure over time or over all regimes.

Perverted development occurs under a multiplicity of incommensurable values and at best provisional hierarchies. Yet if there is historical and cultural continuity, then at the overlaps incommensurabilities or continuity problems must be practically resolved. Traditionally, these overlaps have been ritual transformations such as weddings and funerals and elections and revolutions, transitions that explicitly acknowledge and resolve the incommensurabilities without denying discontinuity. They are what we have earlier called "big."

Perverted development requires that there be improvement without hierarchy, coherent growth with multiple alternatives, and criterial standards that may be sometimes violated. An ultimate value, let us say $U(A, B, C, \ldots)$ "$+$" $\epsilon = 0$, needs to be authoritative and resilient, meaningful even if subverting elements are at work. The value is ultimate in that it is definitive rather than hegemonic or universal. For example, the family and the law of conservation of energy are often treated as ultimates. But we revise what we take to be the exact composition of the family, or what we consider to be energy, in part to make sure that the ultimate is preserved. After saying that the family is necessary, we still have to say what, and how, and why. And what we say, including why the ultimate is necessarily of this particular form, will depend on local history and culture. Here ultimates are generic modes for organizing life and for talking about how life ought to be conducted.

Alternatively, we might call a particular social arrangement a representative of an ultimate: This particular case is a family. We legitimate it by connecting it with past representatives, saying that they are all in the same line. They share certain qualities or grow out of each other, that sharing or growth being something we discern retrospectively. And each new arrangement, insofar as it is justified and put in the same line, is testimony to the definitiveness and persistence of the institution. If the sameness is articulated as development from one form to the next, as is often the case, then we may describe hierarchies of precedence and excellence. But development could be an exploration over an interesting terrain, discovering all the various natural forms and marveling at each of them. Each locale is as just right as the others, good in its own way, as complete as any other.

Ironically, we might try to encompass an ultimate value by an explicit list of its properties or functions. A set of rituals would define transcendent election in a religion; children and a lawn might define a family. If that set of properties were thought to completely encompass the ultimate, then the ultimate value could be replaced by a collection of institutions that each individually fulfilled one of the various functions. We might then have The Saintly Path, Inc., or Family, Inc. Each institution could purvey its services in the market, and so the ultimate is then purchasable as a set of commodified properties or functions. As a purchasable set of properties, the ultimate is now parceled out into disjoint, independent units, or perhaps it may be treated as a team with a joint production function. It is broken away from the social nexus, such as church, community, and home, in which the ultimate value originally made sense. We can now pick and choose from among the properties to put together a new version of the ultimate.

Under economy, this ironic strategy may be governed by the market, and perhaps by a protected icon. The price mechanism disciplines our picking and choosing. In perversion, there may be no such governance. Yet if the residues persist, and they must in perversion, the irony will turn back on itself. For the ultimates never will be fully and stably surrogated for by a corporate entity. The chosen combinations are actually mixtures, not commensurable and titrated balancings. And they signify something more than the sum of their parts, as do our everyday notions of the family or of a saint. We might say that there is meaning or quality to be discerned in a particular combination, a significance that is in addition to its corporate functionality. A mode of production is as well a means of social organization, for example. And it is that significance which governs perversion. Here it is culture that disciplines our picking and choosing.

Goodness, in perversion, is a matter of virtue, excellence, and wholeness. Such a goodness is neither unitary nor free from defect nor eternal in its particular form.

More generally, one picks and chooses from among the possibilities to form a deferent whole. That whole defers and pays homage to the conventions, but in its own way, and that ownness is what is crucial to the meaning we discern. Not only is such a whole a mixture, in perhaps nonaliquot ratios, but it will selectively and deliberately leave out what are conventionally taken as the most important parts, or insert extraneous and contradictory double-crossing material. Imagine a three-year-old deliberately putting together an ideal meal. It is such a cuisine that exemplifies perversion.

Still, one might well choose the conventional combinations. But we will have to answer for that choice as much as any other. Nor will any general principles or laws protect us from monstrosity or insulate us from surprise and delight. We cannot know for sure what will work and how, although we may have a good idea.

The *authority* of perverted values comes from our owning up to those values and to perversion itself, rather than from their being dominant or perfect or exclusive. We allow and assert, "The world could be otherwise." And even if the world could be otherwise, we say, "It shall be this way." So we make the world ours.

Although it could be otherwise, the ways "it could be" are mostly bearable. Wild scenes happen but rarely, and there is no cure for them. We are better prepared for "them," the really wild and other ones, if we do not treat them as other to ourselves. They are part of our world.

The perverted world, while not sloppy or neglectful, is surely not pristine. There is bound to be dirt and rough spots. In perversion, the authority of a foundation such as God or science depends not on its being dogmatically accountable for all of what there is, but on its resilience and flexibility, its ability to handle challenges and dirt and putative pollutions.

So we say, "It is all the same—both 'them' and 'us.' " There is no way of excising and throwing out a part of the world so that it is safely separated from us. And, "There is no other place." There is no other world, a world that might certify the truth of this one. The authority of perversion depends on our generously taking the world as our own, all of it, not rejecting parts as other or different.

In sum, perversion is ownness expressed through processes of reinterpretation and repetition: It could be otherwise; it shall be this way. It is all the same; there is no other place. It is our own; it has always been ours.

The difference between economy and perversion is epitomized by the stories they tell of economy's putative imperfections. Economy identifies those flaws, such as market failure and irrational plans, that protect us from the economic ideal of exchange. Perversion analytically describes our wayward paths, taking those flaws as constitutive of our being, as are the vices and sins.

Violation of an economy's rules leads to a waste and inefficiency beyond friction and transaction costs. But perversion is roomy, and we are not much bothered or destroyed by sin or errancy. A recurrent fantasy of modernism is that eventually economy will do itself in and be inadvertently crushed and danced over by perversion. But, in fact, the next morning everyone goes back to work. Economic rationality remains one of the powerful modes of persuasionary discourse, even if it is not always a good guide to quality. And since protection is practical and icons are solidaristic, no one listens too closely to economy's catechistic admonitions, even while repeating them.

In an economy, rational and prudential considerations presumably guide our actions. Marx argued that Jewish persons in civil society exemplified this economic role. Such persons, for Marx, are defined by the extensive net-like lattice of commerce. Their traditional monotheism is replaced by a polytheism of economic needs. Jews now fit in, yet they are contingent, dependent not on elected Israel but on the economy. The net of commodified life opens up so much to those Jews that they realize only much later, in a most poignant way, the vulnerable space they are placed within.

Perversion never denies the traditional and the orthodox, nor does it incorporate them. Its world is heterogeneous, and the mixtures, while contradictory in principle, have a quite functional if provisional *modus vivendi*. Every once in a while the world gets out of hand, and it seems without a handle. No one knows how to control it, or even seems to care. Rather, we get along with perversion and with economy, both.

FETISHES

As I have indicated, often we may ignore perversion's temptations and act as if the world were economical, composed of well-separated, nicely propertied parts. Even if things, animals, and persons are woven into a seamless fabric, we do notice them as distinguishable objects. They just might be treated as if they were isolable individuals, each fully characterized by some properties, properties which turn out to be signs of its potency. And then it could be a fetish. A religious fetish, such as a voodoo doll, possesses seemingly unto itself esoteric properties and powers, which may be activated in order to affect the world. A commodity such as an automobile possesses desirable properties and value, seemingly intrinsic to its nature, which then may be acquired by purchasing it. A particle such as an electron has properties (mass, charge, flavor), properties which are supposed to define its nature, and which then account for its coupling to the world. A sexual fetish, such as a foot, is desirable of itself and independent of its owner, and if we interact with it appropriately we may obtain satisfaction. Here, a fetish is an extraordinarily potent individual—a relic, an automobile, an electron, a penis or breast, or another person; and it is potent through those properties that fully characterize it. Such fetishes are means to action and satisfaction, to salvation, control, knowledge, and pleasure.

Tools may be considered as fetishes. They are objective isolated instruments which possess a remarkable power over the world through their properties. They are taken to be dumb, subject to our wills. Yet, of course, they are to resist us, to force us to use them properly. Moreover, as fetishes tools are one way we authentically get involved with the world.

Now a fetish is rather intimately connected with the world from which it has been abstracted. And that connection is the source of the fetish's potency. So let us think of a fetish as a handle onto the world, whether it be about passion, knowledge, force, or possession. The fetish's potency is a matter of how the handle is attached and the subtlety and intensity of our grips.

The fetish's qualities—such as desirability, value, autonomy, power, and anima or soul—are purportedly confined or embodied locally in that individual object. But the phallus, the commodity, or the physical particle can be potent and thereby exhibit its qualities only in a particular situation, a situation that we have set up. For example, our setup of an experiment allows a particle to show its attractiveness. How do we do such setting up?

To set up the individual objects, we *alienate, compose, destabilize,* and *stigmatize* the world. We discover those realms of action and experience in which it is possible to pull out a part from the world, alienating it, so that it can be comparatively unto itself. Think of a single musical note, given the context of Western music. We also discover ways of putting together those parts into coherent forms, composing them, those forms then having their own unity. Again, think of notes which become a piece of music, or blocks which become a building. We also find or create highly unstable situations which then lend themselves to our own capacities for organization, and so we find individuation in that instability. Here think of the order we find in Steve Reich's repetitive and rhythmic work or in John Cage's use of a multiplicity of "random" radio programs. And, last, we are able to mark out space and time, stigmatize it, so making it geographic and historical and compositional. A piece of music may be given a beginning and an ending.

To repeat, we practice alienation, composition, destabilization, and stigmatization. We make the most of abstraction and independence. We deliberately delimit our range of experience in order to attend to its particularities and organization. We live off chance interactions and fluctuations. And we make preemptive stigmatizing moves, forcing a situation into boundedness.

Individuation leads to potency. As a by-product of the acts of individuation we have set up a situation in which the object itself is powerful. Material or intellectual abstraction produces handles (the object) that are as well still connected to the world. Our problem is to figure out how to get ahold of them. (A physicist would say that a condensed state is characterized by a small number of parameters which couple to the world, such as the temperature and magnetization of a ferromagnet.) Once we do get ahold of these individuals, we are almost surprised by their potency and fruitfulness. They do more than we could ever have expected of individuals. And so we allow them what we allow to our children—soul or anima. Having been born, abstracted from their natural home, they retain a connection to that source of their animation. Potency and anima may be notionally located in the core of an elementary particle, the (erection of a) penis, or the internal mechanical properties of an object. Phenomenologically, anima is a manifestation that alienation is never total, never settled. A thing will have a life of its own just because it still depends on its home. And anima is that archetypal mother or source.

The distinguished biologist Barbara McClintock suggests: "Organisms can do all types of things; they do fantastic things. They do everything that we do, and they do it better, more efficiently, more marvelously." They will do what they must in order to survive. "Anything you can think of they will do." Now this inventiveness of living organisms is also characteristic of many of the supposedly inanimate objects and tools we employ, at least when they are in our hands. Atoms will do what they must in order to produce nature (as will mathematics or physics or chemistry). We originally designed atoms to do that work, and they do it remarkably well. They have to, so to speak. Nothing else will produce nature, at least for many scientists. More generally, parts seem to have an interest in their ultimate compositional role, as we have seen in chapters 1 and 2. Of course, we know them as parts through the compositional work they are in actual fact made to do.

Still, we take the parts' fruitfulness and invention, and even the parts' limitations, as signs of anima and of their being real.

Naturally, anima appears after birth or conception, although maturation is often needed as well. But it is the mechanical story of anima's appearance, as a sequence of *analysis, emergence,* and *discontinuity,* that has captured modern imaginations.

We analyze some thing, break it down into its constituent parts, those parts then going together to make it up. The appropriate analysis, and parts, and going together will depend on what we are interested in explaining about that thing. The parts are parts teleologically. And so is the mechanism for putting them together teleological. But, of course, the mechanism may then account for a multiplicity of effects, many of them unanticipated.

Emergence becomes the mode of anima's appearance. To say that something is emergent is to claim that it is made up of parts, none of which possess those properties that distinctively characterize the emergent whole thing: a solid made up of molecules, a market made of rational individuals, a thinking creature made of cells, a home made of lumber and nails, a computer program made of instructions. These parts are chosen to do synthetic work—to make up that home or that program. And they are deliberately chosen to be dumb—that is, not possessing the emergent properties and, of course, not aware of what they are to compose. That is what a part is. The dumbness of the parts makes for the surprise of emergence, so setting the stage for animation.

A demonstration of emergence requires that we convince ourselves both that the parts are dumb and that the parts can do the necessary compositional work. Ideally, the mechanism of composition accounts for the emergence, showing just how it happens—although it is at this point that argument begins about what would be such an adequate account. And at the end of the demonstration we have to believe that the parts are dumb still. For to then discover that the parts are not so dumb is to enchant the world in frightening ways.

Emergence may be based on predecessors, evolution, and history rather than on parts, composition, and structure. The great setup here is to view the various organisms as parts of a single system—organized by Genesis or by evolution, and their various features as in a rough hierarchy of sophistication, what I have earlier called a scale of value. And then there can be the wonder at systemic and historical emergence: how a substantially more sophisticated thing emerges from a less sophisticated thing.

More generally, we animate the world by creating separations and discontinuities in the continuum, again as I have described in earlier chapters. In order to do so, we may employ conventional but not arbitrary restrictions of our range of concern and our point of view—such as a range of temperature and pressure so that there is a phase transition, as in freezing. The restrictions make the world interesting for us, in that they allow us to safely pay attention to its specific features and to work on it, and to be surprised by some phenomena. Under a different thermodynamic regime there might be mixture and fluctuation and turbulence rather than a nice separation of phases of matter, and the number of properties or degrees of freedom might be too numerous to manage yet too few to average over. Residues, sidelinkages, and leftovers would take over. But it is a fact for us, given our world and how we live, that fluctuations are small enough so that ice forms in winter.

Things really are these restricted and interesting ways for us. A perspectivalist or historical attack, one that supposedly reveals how dependent we are on our models or paradigms, rarely if ever convinces us to give them up. The contingent purposes we are up to, our interests and restrictions, are no mean purposes. They set up a world of natural units and objects that we may then take as real.

The mechanisms for producing fetishes (alienation, composition, destabilization, and stigmatization) and the modes of anima's appearance (analysis, emergence, and discontinuity) make for a fetish that is self-contained and potent. And they allow the fetish to be an animated object, provocatively appealing and insidious in its effect. Subsequently, we may forget these mechanisms and modes, and we treat parts, restrictions, and dumbness as just the way things are. So the fetishes we invent will seem objective and disembodied, unconnected and ahistorical.

A boundary is supposed to separate the not-alive from the alive, the soul-less from the animate, the simple from the complex, the smooth from the discontinuous, the mundane from the sacred, the knowable from the unknowable. There is to be nothing in between, nothing transitional. Such demarcation lines may mark off a world of dumb objective parts which gently interact with each other.

Fetishes are a relief from anxiety and fluctuation. For if we set up conditions properly, the dumb parts are condensed out from instability, in both a Freudian and a thermodynamic sense. Leftovers and interactions may be considered small—even if there once were correlations, interconnections, and residual linkages, and even if development is historical and so preemptive moves have foreordained the outcomes.

Still, the leftovers are significant. The fetish that is a consequence of condensation and alienation provides a handle onto some thing—for example, wage labor for persons or an electrical charge for a particle. The handle then allows us to reincorporate the thing into a more encompassing whole, such as an economy or a solid. But getting ahold of something just by its handle is not quite what we have gotten. There are surprises and discoveries still. There is a play between recognition, in choosing a handle, and reconciliation, in figuring out how it must do its work. The fetishist's practices are constitutive of the ways in which we make and know something. And fetishes, dumb that we might skeptically take them to be, lead to authentic involvement with the world—animation itself.

Explanation, no matter how dumb its material, is tempted to produce a meaningful world, namely, to account for the dumb world as not only fruitful and surprising, but uniquely so. That account may be structural or historical, a matter of a unique mathematical solution or of mythic and scriptural marking. The latter include acts of initiation as in Creation, of stigma as in the Israelites' election, and of contingency as in Exodus. The world could have happened otherwise, but it happened *this* way. Following theological usage, let us call such a uniqueness "revelation." Revelation is not dumb. It speaks and demands to be heard. That demand is embodied in its mysteries, riddles, and contradictions. Perhaps the most wondrous of these uniqueness rules in the sciences are variational principles ($\delta \int L = 0$), which are often known for their mysterious and subtle workings.

Fetishism was a powerful theme in late nineteenth-century thought, bringing together atomism, economy, sexuality, and anthropology. The triumph of economy and modern marginalist methods was to take fetishes as natural, but then to devalorize the perversion that allowed for fetishes in the first place. Perversion's revenge is to insist on itself, reveling in animation and in the ineradicable residues. The dialectic of marginalism and discontinuity, and of economy and perversion, is mediated by objects which are both-and or transitional, and it is their appearance that is a sign that something more is going on.

PART TWO

Tools and Sacred Practices

CHAPTER SIX

The Horizon of Mathematics

Mathematical technology and physical models enjoy remarkable esteem in the natural and social sciences. Yet mathematics and physics are often vilified for distorting the modes of conceptualization in the various fields of inquiry, as if those purported distortions were not desired by the borrowers of those technologies. There is a tradition of such polar estimations of the influence of mathematics and physics, whether it be about the value of formalism and abstraction, or about the ideas—say about smoothness and additivity or about fluctuation and symmetry— implicitly fostered and given concrete meaning by these approaches.

We shall now examine, in two rather different ways, how mathematicians and physicists do their work. The lessons to be drawn will echo those of earlier chapters: how tools, which we take as abstract and inevitable, have developed in the concrete context of specific needs; how their use is a matter of subtle invention and of supple adaptability of tool and world; and how linearity, addition, and marginalism—that the world can be manipulated just a bit, and slowly but surely fixed—are pervasive themes in this kind of work.

Mathematics, which is often treated as a dominating juggernaut and a natural truth, is actually quite contingent in its development and application and plastic and dialectic in its consequences. And what we might take as abstract mathematics is also a matter of concrete invention and adjustment. For lying within the horizon of mathematics are the panoply of pictures, tools, models, examples, and cases the mathematician uses to figure out what "must" be true about the world—what naturally follows, what ought be the case if other features are to make sense. Tools play a twofold role in this work. The mathematician employs them to do mathematics, and so is like any other craftsperson. But that mathematics is eventually employed as a tool by other crafts, and so the mathematician is a toolmaker as well as a tool user.

The effort here and in the next chapter is not so much philosophic as descriptive: This is how some people go about doing their work. In one case I provide a phenomenology, in the other a toolkit and a set of skills for employing it. In each case, the scientist's task is to confect a model and a notation with which one might get ahold of the world, and from which one can "read off" the truth about it. And then we may begin to explore the horizon of what is not so well understood or handled. More generally, tools allow both for conventional work and for speculative elaborations on those conventions.

Now surely there are other ways of doing mathematics or physics than the ones I describe here. But in providing a verisimilitudinous description, one need not claim universality or exclusivity or hegemony. Still, ideally, to many a mathematician or physicist my description should ring true. It should be an "of course" and a "that's right, so what?" And if I have succeeded, I have also shown how those scientific practices are much like other crafts.

MATHEMATICIANS KNOW THAT A rigorous proof is only one aspect of actually doing mathematics. The challenge is to find a theorem, a mode of stating what must be the case, that is worth proving. And for that we must understand what is really going on. Then we can begin to construct a proof for the theorem, although at that point we will surely discover even more about what is really going on, modifying both proof and theorem. Sometimes a proof is crucial, in that our blindness is epitomized by the proof's flaws or by a problematic passage. The pride of insight is shown up. But the lacuna lies not so much in the proof as in our understanding of the world.

The order and rhetoric of actual proofs is very far from the logician's dream. And although a proof must eventually be provided, it is just one way, an often clumsy one to be sure, of convincing other mathematicians. The mathematician at one point or another can say "I know it's true" with a well-founded confidence—which we are willing to allow could be misplaced—well before the rigorous proof is achieved. The logic of the mathematician's practice is based on seeing through to what is actually going on in the world, and then showing others how to see.

Actual practice depends on the mathematician's education and natural expectations: what is to be seen clearly and manifestly, and what is to be discerned just at and over the horizon. That horizon is multiply meaningful, waiting to be interpreted and become of interest and application, ready to participate in our fantasies. The objects that the mathematician deals with, whether they be groups or topological spaces, have an autonomy of their own, and in their productivity and fruitfulness they can be quite fertile. The mathematician's problem is to set up a world of objects so that what is true is seen clearly *as* true: a world in which the deeper truths about itself are evident, or at least they are empirically discoverable by exploring appropriate concrete examples. The great achievement is to set up not only those worlds but also moments of revelation, whether they be particular examples or in elegant proofs, when what might or might not be the case is seen to be obviously and necessarily the case. Put differently, the problem is to create a potent and fruitful artificial world which then has a life of its own, and in our watching it we discover what is true about our world. And in so seeing, mathematics is not only true and ready to be rigorously proven, but is applied and applicable and useful.

"IT MUST BE TRUE"

If you are educated you have appropriate expectations, intuitions, and inklings about the world. When you say "it must be true," you are usually right; and you can give good reasons based on archetype, example, experience, and explanation. Now, your intuitions could fail you. But other educated persons will appreciate why you might have believed that your insight was valid. Your failure is indicative not of carelessness or idiosyncratic commitments, but of more general errors shared by others. When you say "this *must* be true" about the mathematical world and "the proof *must* goes as follows," your claim is based on the same kind of understanding you have employed in many successful past experiences where you have been right about what is true. And then you need to figure out just how to go about convincing others who are not so sure or insightful about your claim.

When you tell yourself that the answer is of a certain sort, you have a someplace from which to go to work. That particular set of someplaces or prejudices is what makes you a mathematician. It is that set of models, pictures, and cases, successful past practices and techniques—parts of a toolkit, a craft, and a culture—that provides you with a mathematical world, and a way of getting along in it. What is inchoate and schematic defines who you are; it is not at all arbitrary.

Just because you see something does not mean you see it clearly or whole. So you may have a formalism, but not appreciate its meaning. You have seen a few aspects of the formalism realized in some models, but you do not have a good idea of what a full model would look like. You might even be able to use the formalism to organize lots of particular observations, but still not be sure what it is you have gotten ahold of. You might say you have a notation, but no picture. Or that you have seen two sides of what must be a many-sided object and have no idea what it is. For you know something more is there; you are sure of it. The horizon is open and beckoning. And on that horizon there are many possible pictures—that is what it means to possess a horizon— pictures you have already encountered. So eventually you might find a picture that fits, especially if you know how to piece together and otherwise alter pictures you already know well. Now you have an idea of what that something looks like.

When you are sure what it is you have a hold onto, you believe you see why the various aspects appeared to you as they once did, and you appreciate why they now hold together and belong together. You literally see what is true, just as you do ordinarily every day.

Of course, the picture here may not be an image, but be a formal model. Yet the visual analogy is employed nonetheless. Still, we might want to manipulate the world, or employ a mathematical object as a tool. And so a kinesthetic and technical analogy replaces the visual one. We want to get ahold of the world. I am not arguing here whether or not this is a warranted way of discovering mathematical truth, or whether truth is visual or technical, but rather that this is what many mathematicians actually do.

Mathematicians employ a variety of tools and tactics. For example, an experienced mathematician knows that if one goes to a "co"-space, something might be clearer or easier to prove. Typically, you have a repertoire of transformation rules and test examples which you casually invoke, not needing to be sure they will apply, make perfect sense, or will always work. But they have before, and they just might now.

If you are stuck, if your intuitions and inklings fail you, if you do not know where to go next, you may try one of these transformations and tricks and see if it helps. Of course, with more experience you have a better feel for which ones are likely to be fruitful. And you are as well likely to be biased against others, so that if they are the right ones this time you will miss them—and someone perhaps of a younger generation will make a discovery.

Education and experience provide you with a rich horizon of interesting problems and useful ideas and intuitions. You have mastered the tools, and even when you are stuck you have an idea of what to try next. The horizon of mathematics is open and beckoning. And as we shall see, it is also autonomous and fertile.

AUTONOMY AND FERTILITY

To a practicing mathematician the world of mathematical objects is surely something given form to by the mathematician. But that world then presents itself as a defiant challenge: having its own will, its own structure, its own truth—much as the material or medium in craftwork has its own way of being, its own integrity. If it is an invented or crafted world, it seems to come alive and have its own way with us. We need to acknowledge that autonomy and animation, and we need to pay attention to just how the world resists our initial intuitions, inventions, and discoveries. Just because a particular mathematical space is supposed to have certain properties does not mean it will possess them. And just what it does not possess will tell us a great deal about how we have to revise our intuitions and eventually the construction of that mathematical space or object.

Moreover, if we treat mathematical objects as real and independent of us, if we take our craftings and inventions as discoveries, we then seem to have the right attitude for attacking mathematical problems and mysteries. Surely, we want to have a feel for these objects, and in that sense be in sympathy or at home with them. But it is a feel for something that has its own being and will, something that will resist us as it will. Such a realism is not so much a philosophical or metaphysical commitment as a practical one.

Another attestation to the autonomy of the mathematical world is that it defies our generic practices. Say we know how to do a series expansion following a general rule, such as in a Taylor expansion. We might come to believe that such general rules produce series that converge in some nice way. We then, in what we have come to call divergent or asymptotic expansions, apply another general but still seemingly innocuous rule to produce a series. But in fact that series blows up after a certain number of terms. Our disappointment, and the world's resistance, lies not only in that divergence, but also in the failure of that general rule to work all the way down the line. Here the generic practice fails as a generic practice, even if it often does produce fine approximations.

Once we have a notation that works, or a formalism that is effective, there is likely to be a regime in which that notation and formalism is not only true, but is manifestly true. We can actually see, typically in a model, a picture of how the world works. We take that existence of a model as a sign of the reality of mathematical objects. Resistance has now yielded to verisimilitude. Our formal confections, if they are true, are actually realized in nature, apparently autonomously.

That autonomy of the mathematical world extends to its possessing its own modes of unity and composition. So a mathematician is often surprised by the generic character and the productivity of a mathematical object. One designs objects and spaces and then discovers that they are just like predecessor objects. Or perhaps objects can be readily transformed into each other by formal rules such as converting indices into exponents. Now in part this unity might be attributed to mathematics being a description of an objective world, and so seemingly different objects might be merely different perspectives on the same object. Or the unity might be attributed to a mathematician's patterned modes of working; or that mathematics itself exhausts the variety of patterns, so that design, invention, and discovery are within well-worn paths and forms. So naturally the objects just work out to be the same. But often those similarities are not at all straightforward, and substantial apparatus and argument are required in order to justify them. Usually it is eventually possible to show that the formal unity is in fact manifestly obvious and necessary. And in fact without it being so possible, it is not likely that the substantial apparatus and argument will be believed with conviction. But it was not so obvious at first.

The mathematical world is also fertile—fruitful, playful, and involving, and its mathematical objects are animated. They do things that they were not set up to do, and they are applicable in surprising places. A structure created for one motive becomes productive in what initially may seem like a rather different context. Unexplained fruitfulness is usually disturbing. So at this point one shows how disparate areas are actually the same, or surprising capacities are simply a matter of our not having appreciated how much potency we have already built into our seemingly dumb objects. Our anxieties become domesticated: Aspectival variations are now attached to a well-defined object, an object that does everything we could possibly imagine. Fertility becomes mundane reality.

Still, what remains are some phenomenological facts of mathematical life—the world is fertile, it is more unified than we first could expect, and objects in that world seem to have a potency of their own. It is a world of surprise, closure, and invention. These phenomenological facts deeply influence everyday practice. For one expects in doing mathematical work that there will be both fertility and unity. And the phenomenological facts also inspire speculation on the nature of the mathematical world, on the causes of fertility and unity. Those reasons or causes are perhaps best seen as justifications for a faith, rather than as ontological investigations of the mathematical world. For autonomy and fruitfulness are characteristic of tools in general, and the features of fertility, unity, and potency may well appear in other worlds of craftsmanship.

The fertility of mathematical objects is often a matter of how pictures, symbols, or icons grab us and lead us to new insights. Carefully constructed, they will play harmoniously on our imaginations. If we write derivatives as quotients *(dy/dx),* following Leibniz's deliberate intention and guidance, and then treat such quotients as ordinary fractions, all sorts of nice rules are immediately suggested—and often they are true. Now if we play around with such notational or formal objects, become familiar with them by looking closely at specific examples and cases, and are willing to pay attention to their particularity and idiosyncrasy, they give us back further insights. These details, specifics, parts, and pieces are taken as significant of the whole, and they act very much as fetishes. A peculiar feature charms us; it is a mystery that arouses our interest and leads us into a deeper relationship with the world. Although mathematicians aim for generality and universality, understanding just how that is possible may well require being involved with a particular case, a peculiar problem, or an exception to what one has taken as the rule.

Having been grabbed by a picture or an icon, or by a suggestive formal intuition, we are still left unsatisfied, wondering just what about it we find attractive. Working for years with an inchoate problem, we build up a catalog of special cases, partially understood aspects, false starts. We are hungry for new leads, and we are on the lookout for and so recognize promising ones when they come along. They fit terrain we have already worked over in many ways and from many angles.

Such playing is productive. For those who know how to play, improvisatory moves are replays of well-practiced schemas that have worked in the past. Trial-and-error is effective because in actuality it is not arbitrary but conventional and patterned. Like most secular people, mathematicians believe that the form of the truth will be much like predecessor forms, and one is encouraged when one comes close to having such a form. That the truth may have turned out to have revolutionized the field, that retrospective fact, tells us little about how to play.

Eventually, in working out lots of particular examples, we may be able to find or invent a rich and capacious model that embodies everything that we know about this part of the world, what I earlier called a picture that fits. We then work on this model hoping that the more general truth will emerge from it, that the model is exemplary. So we may discover the crucial features of a mathematical object or space through empirical work on an exemplary model and on various concrete examples, employing test cases to exercise the model. And our claim then becomes what might be called hopeful induction: It is true in this situation—for these models and cases which are either representative or exhaustive of all the possibilities—and so "it must be true" and "it must go this way" more generally.

Some of the test cases are part of the standard repertoire of a mathematician in a subfield; others are idiosyncratic and even private, and perhaps shared with students. These test cases cannot be publicly claimed to be fiducial, for they will surely fail sometime. But for the moment they are rather powerful guides and tests.

Although he was not a professional mathematician, it is instructive and I think not exceptional to quote the theoretical physicist Richard Feynman:

> "Good. Give me one example." That was for me: I can't understand anything in general unless I'm carrying along in my mind a specific example and watching it go. Some people think in the beginning that I'm kind of slow and I don't understand the problem, because I ask a lot of these "dumb" questions: Is a cathode plus or minus? Is an ion this way, or that way?
>
> But later, when the guy's in the middle of a bunch of equations, he'll say something and I'll say, "Wait a minute! There's an error! That can't be right!"
>
> The guy looks at his equations, and sure enough, after a while, he finds the mistake and wonders, "How the hell did this guy, who hardly understood at the beginning, find that mistake in the mess of all these equations?"
>
> He thinks I'm following the steps mathematically, but that's not what I'm doing. I have the specific, physical example of what he's trying to analyze, and I know from instinct and experience the properties of the thing. So when the equation says it should behave so-and-so, and I know that's the wrong way around, I jump up and say, "Wait! There's a mistake!"

A good example instantiates the world faithfully enough so that we can infer general consequences by properly reading them off the example. The general consequences are manifest. And in this sense a good notation is perspicuous, in that what is true is true merely by the form of the notation and the set of natural operations that goes along with it. What is true is manifestly true.

What still needs detailed accounting is how one learns to properly "read off" and to make the "natural" set of notational moves, an account of mathematical education. For in being educated one is taught the conventional modes of reading and moving, modes which have worked in the past and which might even have been justified within mathematics.

Once we have some good models and examples, and a notation through which we can read off what must be the case, we begin to see through to what is really going on. But this is only a beginning, for what is then needed is a more general vision, a greater variety of examples, and a theory with proofs, to articulate and back up our insight and to assure ourselves that we have seen it all. Technically, after revelation comes doctrine and theology.

Yet rationality, rigor, and orderly proof are ultimately justified by what is true being manifest and obvious. Just because we can formally prove something does not make it believable. For while a proof may give us a feel for the world, it just might not do so. And, of course, proofs are regularly found to be in error, especially at first provings.

Expositions, including proofs, are historically located events. They take into account the expectations of the community of mathematicians, and the alternatives, the examples, and the counterexamples they might naturally consider. What is required is a staged sequence of moves and setups, so that the proving is educating and rhetorically effective, so that what is displayed is set up for seeing.

THE HORIZON

Early on in the development of a field, there will be a period when there is much wallowing. There may be perspicuous examples, some of which show what must be the case; and others which are not quite right, but not quite right in interesting and tantalizing and problematic ways. The latter will eventually need explaining. Of course, some of our original insights do not work out as planned. Still they are almost always recycled along the way. After a while a halting, inelegant, but valid theory and proof is found, one that makes us believe even more strongly in our model examples but does not quite tell us what is really going on. In time, new concepts and definitions are created, new notations are imported and invented, and we can say what is true in a more compact fashion. Perhaps a new model which embodies the truths of the definitions and notation can be confected. Then a theoretical structure and a proof come along in which what once was a formal curiosity follows naturally and obviously, maybe even in one line. Along the way, "this is true" or "this is it" is no longer a matter of logic or example, but becomes a manifest part of reality, eventually to be freed from its rhetorical and historical invention, to be seen as just there, as just a fact and an object of nature.

When rough interpretation eventually yields to understanding, we then possess deeper insights and powerful modes of proof. And we have models and pictures of the world, from which we may read off what is true about it. Mathematics' applications lie within this horizon. For mathematics has application by showing how the world is to be taken in its terms, in terms of its tools and models. And in the process of reading off we implicitly point to application: showing how the world is to be taken, referring to a concrete worldly context of everyday objects, exhibiting the paradigms of application. If invention is taken in the sense of rhetoric, as the act of modeling, and justification is taken in the sense of theology, as providence, then we may say that theory invents practical needs in order to justify itself. The theory is then meaningful.

Our design of the mathematical world is not a matter of putting together a tinkertoy set of alienated objects. We work with objects that we have already encountered, here mathematical objects quite laden with our practical experience. They are a part of the world, and they refer immediately and everywhere to application. So they are quite alive; they are animated. This is why we can work with them in the first place. They participate in our fantasies and stories at first hand. The trick in doing mathematics is to learn how to acknowledge the objects' life and richness, figuring out what questions to ask of them that they can answer for us. For we may design a mathematical world, but it turns out to be vastly more potent than we could have imagined ahead of time.

The rhetoric of mathematics is quite specific and professionally prescribed. Notational form and the symbols one uses cannot be arbitrary—if the work of proving is to be perspicuously understood. Order of proof and use of example are crucial. If it is the moves that mathematicians make at the blackboard or in research papers which allow them to convince others of the truth and meaning of their findings, they have to be moves of the right and mostly conventional sort.

Proving is demonstrative and educating. A proof's apparatus works if it convinces others and oneself of the meaning and truth of the theorem. A formal derivation is never enough. Proving is a revealing, showing what is true as true.

None of these features of the actual doing of mathematics will be surprising to the working mathematician. If you are educated and develop appropriate horizons and expectations, if you respect the autonomy and fertility of mathematical objects, if you play with such an empirical world in order to find out more about its most pervasive properties, and if you work at setting up a display of what you have come to understand so that others can see it as clearly as you do—then you are a mathematician. In sum, the horizon of mathematics is toolish and concrete, and abstract and open. But, of course, none of these features would be surprising to any journeyman craftsperson. My claim in providing a phenomenological description of mathematical work is that such a description is remarkably generic. It epitomizes the actual experience of doing toolish work on the world.

CHAPTER SEVEN

The Physicist's Toolkit

Here I try to provide a systematic description of how some people go about doing their work, a description that may strike a chord of recognition in its practitioners. It is a story of tool and craft; of adding up the world, and of finding good individuals with which to do so; and of the way models allow us to get ahold of the world. If in the previous chapter there are the beginnings of a Husserlian logic of doing mathematics, in this chapter there is a rhetoric of doing physics. I have been fairly specific and detailed, for the essence of any claim of toolishness is to provide a toolkit and its practice. Consequently, there will be technical passages and specialist examples which might be skipped by some readers.

NATURAL SCIENCE IS OFTEN described in sacred terms, whether it be a search for the truth or an uncovering of Nature's secrets. Yet the everyday life of scientists is surely mundane. They do their work mostly between breakfast and supper, within a complex bureaucratic system, they themselves being well trained in their field but are otherwise rather more ordinary people. We have already discussed some of the connections between mundane and sacred practice, how we set things up so that we may appreciate the wonders of nature. Still, everyday practice remains veiled to outsiders, perhaps because it is mystified by descriptions of the sacred. Yet physicists, for example, are wont to describe their own work, at least to themselves, in the very concrete terms of tools and toolkits. After examining how tools are more generally understood, let us try to make sense of some of what a physicist is up to.

TOOLS

Tools may be thought of as things we use for doing our work. Like a hammer, a tool is both standardized and multifunctional, generic and concretely applied and meaningful, and archetypal and polysemous. Rather than being material, a tool can be notional as in a model or a paradigm. And objects may be tools, so elementary particles themselves may be probes which cause well-defined effects. (As Ian Hacking puts it, "Long-lived theoretical entities, which don't end up being manipulated, commonly turn out to have been wonderful mistakes.")

Tools feel objective and are literally shareable, while the skills needed for using those tools are personal and are often learned from other skilled persons through imitation. A toolkit of seemingly abstracted or objective tools comes along with a specific and concrete practice of tool-using—how to work and how the work is organized, and a larger sense of what it is that the craftsperson is up to. Carpenters' toolkits surely have hammers and chisels. But carpenters also use nails and work with wood, they know how to swing a hammer, they may work during regular hours along with other crafts, and they are in the business of making something much like what they have previously made. The toolkit's contents and its associated practices depend on the historical time, where the work is being performed, the kinds of material being worked on (wood, metal, atoms, or generic condensed matter such as liquids and solids), and what is being constructed. There are standard tools, as well as personal modifications and gadgets, and jerry-built devices. The term "toolkit" suggests a small number of versatile tools meant to work together.

Tools may be complex articulated instruments, such as telescopes and particle accelerators. Then the particular features of those instruments, and of the mode of interpreting what the instruments produce, what is called data, may be shown to play a crucial role in the making of science, organizing its culture and production. The instrument sets up what we might know and how we might know it. Scientists often encourage national commitments to the material instruments vital to their work, such as accelerators, and to extending the instruments' capacities. They present their research as being driven by tools rather than by people or ideas.

Tools have been described objectively and situationally. In the objective tradition a tool is a thing, such as a hammer or a microscope, possessing certain manifest capacities. A trained person picks up the tool and uses it to do something. Such a tool may be made by a toolmaker, and when it is done it is then available for use. In modern times, making and use are for the most part separated, although as I have indicated craftspersons will modify a tool for particular uses or to suit their own idiosyncrasies. And they may well uncover capacities that others had not conceived before. Still, in this tradition a tool is passive, objective, and modular.

Skills are capabilities for using tools. One becomes more adept through practice, say by doing many integrals. And one may become more versatile in employing a toolkit, by working on many problems and by mastering a variety of paradigmatic cases. One might even solve the same problem in a variety of ways, say solving the equations of motion of a harmonic oscillator using every formulation of classical mechanics. Different users of what we take as the same tool may have different purposes and skills, and this will affect how a tool is employed. Crystallographers and elementary particle physicists use group theory, but in different ways. Still it may be taken as roughly the same tool.

Eventually skills come to be automatic and so unnoticed, and apprenticeship is perhaps over. Masters of a craft employ tools in more inventive and subtle fashions and produce finer than usual objects. Their products are masterpieces, but not so distinctive or difficult that they cannot eventually be produced by others. For it is the production of a masterpiece that signifies one's entry into the guild.

> Those of us who were fortunate enough to watch Enrico Fermi at work marveled at the speed and ease with which he could produce a solution to almost any problem in physics brought to his attention. When he had heard enough to know what the problem was, he proceeded to the blackboard and let the solution flow out of his chalk. He kept in trim by doing a lot of problems, either for the courses he taught, the talks he gave, or the papers he wrote. Most frequently, he worked out his own solutions to problems he heard about, in seminars, or in discussion with those who came to talk physics with him. Fermi's solutions were almost always simpler and easier to understand than the ones obtained by the person who raised the question in the first place.

Fermi's style and methods were appreciated, imitated, and then taught to several generations of physicists. His lecture notes became texts, his approach repeated by his students to their own.

In the situational tradition tools are functional. A tool is defined in terms of the work to be done rather than by what it looks like. Different instruments might perform the same function, and in effect be the same tool. Not only is a tool known by what it does; the craftsperson's skill is essential in defining the functionality of a tool. For a tool makes sense only in its context of practice. Here tools are ways of getting ahold of the world and manipulating it, taming its many degrees of freedom. Now we discover tools as such, as abstract objective things, when they do not work. We notice the hammer when its head flies off, or we have to pay attention to an asymptotic expansion when it blows up. In this tradition a world is known by how it is handled; tools exist in practice; practice is learned and commanded in specific environments and for specific tasks.

The objective and situational descriptions are complementary, and each inherits a complementary problem. The objective description must give an account of how tools are used and are versatile, an account of what might be called play. The situational description must account for how tools come to be seen as objective, separable and disengaged from their original contexts, and as universal, available to all. And both descriptions must account for how the world we discover and make is intimately related to the tools we use.

Much of professional work, including doing science, may be seen as a craft practiced within a guild. Its journeymen and masters employ a toolkit, furnished with a small number of tools, whose use may be mastered through apprenticeship. The guild members carefully choose and formulate their problems so that they can work on them using their kit of tools. It is within a context of tool and craft that a practice is orderly, clear, natural, and simple. And it is in terms of tool and craft that a personal style is realized.

A guild, a craft, and a toolkit are successful if there is important work they can do and a market for their products. Of course, they will try to convince others of the value of their work. But there are authentic difficulties and resistances to this strategy. For example, in a history of contemporary particle physics, field theorists are described as having an interest in exploiting their tools and expertise. But at that particular moment they are mechanics without useful tools. They knew how to calculate high-energy phenomena of quantum chromodynamics, but what was needed were low-energy calculations which could be compared to the well-known particle properties. Then along came high-energy experimental findings that were both problematic and suited to their tools. Now they could go to work.

Partly out of tradition and partly because it has been so successful a strategy, physicists persist in picking out smoothly changing or at least linearizable situations, so that they can add up the world. And they invent good ways of hiding the nonlinearities. For example, by finding appropriate symmetries that define a ground state or a vacuum, they may otherwise ignore the nonlinear processes that made up the ground state. (In this context, a vacuum is an emptiness taken as a lack of energetic excitation. It is not restricted to a literal absence of matter.) In effect, a shield of ignorance is provided by such a ground state. Physicists explain their capacity to encompass nature by giving an account of the hierarchy of forces or the monotonicity of a temperature scale, and hence of well-separated phases of matter, and an account of the stability of matter in its various phases. Then their linearizing, perturbative approach should be effective, since at each level in the hierarchy or at each phase transition one has a stable base from which to work.

In sum, taking the world toolishly provides us with a powerful way of understanding what craftspersons do. We may describe just what is in their toolkit, and the skills and judgment needed for effective practice. We might account for how a scientific theory or a professional ideology is effective, in that it provides the right tools for doing the work and justifies that work as the appropriate work to be done. Tools that do not do the work are abandoned and forgotten, perhaps to be revived at another time; tools that may be made to suit the task are eventually taken as natural and necessary. Insofar as a tool may be selectively borrowed to suit the craftsperson's needs, and carefully recrafted to be even more effective, the tool will again seem natural and necessary. Of course, in making any such assessment we rarely consider the possible tools that are never borrowed or recall the recraftings that do not work out.

The notion of a toolkit is attractive because it gets around the conventional separation of theory, hypothesis, and idea versus experiment, testing, and instruments. All of these might be taken in terms of tools. The traditional questions about scientific truth, knowledge, or belief do not disappear, but they now allow for a rather more concrete approach.

PHYSICISTS AND THEIR TOOLKIT

Many physicists like to think of themselves as possessing a set of tools and as being capable of employing them in a craftsmanlike way. Perhaps that is why Fermi gained notoriety for approaching problems in a simple fashion, using a small number of models such as electromagnetism and adapting them as need be. Back-of-the-envelope calculations and order-of-magnitude estimates are part of the legends of physics. A study of Einstein begins with a one-sentence scientific biography: "Better than anyone before or after him, he knew how to invent invariance principles and make use of statistical fluctuations." Lev D. Landau's course on theoretical physics, "the theoretical minimum," is well known, in part because of the series of seminal texts it engendered. On his fiftieth birthday, Landau's students gave him a talisman and an emblem: a stone engraved with his "Ten Commandments," his most useful formulae and models. Richard Feynman's diagrammatic methods are explicitly tools for expressing the relevant physics. At the same time they provide the algorithmic means for doing the consequent calculational work, although in fact much facility is required above and beyond those algorithms for actually completing the calculations. More recently, Kenneth Wilson has described a new set of tools based on computation and computer science, and a formulation of quantum chromodynamics (lattice gauge theory), that have proven to be effective instruments for working on the low-energy problem referred to earlier.

Physicists also readily offer coaching advice about choosing a problem to work on, the right level of difficulty to start out with, or where to search for new laws: Freeman Dyson suggests, "Don't try to revive past glories. Don't do things just because they are fashionable. Don't be afraid of the scorn of theoreticians." As means of guidance and caution, Rudolph Peierls describes surprises in theoretical physics, surprises in that initial intuitions and approaches proved incorrect. And an advanced text in quantum mechanics by A. B. Migdal aims to expose the student to how-to-do-it qualitatively, like a real pro. And it is explicitly written as a toolkit. I summarize some of its guidance in the chart under "Commonplaces."

The Physicist's Toolkit

  I. Mathematical Tools
    A. Counting and approximation: combinatorics, statistics, asymptotics
    B. Pattern: geometry, symmetry, conservation laws
    C. Linearity and limits: calculus, optimization procedures
 II. Diagrammatic Tools
    A. Geometric and spatial: vectors and graphs
    B. Algebraic and symbolically patterned expressions: canonical forms
III. Rhetoric
    A. Tools
       1. Media: spacetime vacuum, hydrogen atom, crystal, continuous elastic medium, fluid, gas
       2. Objects: particles and excitations, oscillators, fields and waves; linear operators including differential equations and groups; correlations; translation operators

3. Interactions: objects with objects and with media (potentials, particle exchange, force field, scattering), interaction Lagrangian, response functions

B. Approaches

1. Strategies: good vacuum or ground state, equilibrium, conservative potentials; analogy and heuristic, homology of equations and solutions; $N \log N$ vs. N^2

2. Commonplaces: qualitative methods: become friendly with nitty gritty material like Coulomb wave functions; look for big contributions, the physics lies in the poles; use a classical picture, supplemented by quantum rules; things fall off, but asymptotics are important; know about potential wells, oscillators, one-particle transitions, polarizable media, . . .

A physicist's toolkit might be divided into three parts: mathematical or calculating, diagrammatic or picturing, and rhetorical or describing. The trivium of mathematics, "diagrammatic," and rhetoric corresponds roughly to structure and number, pattern and image, and argument and language. As can be seen from the chart, the kit includes models of media or worlds such as a crystal, models of objects such as a particle, and models of interactions such as a collision. The objects populate the media, and the interactions are, for example, between objects and media. In addition, there are commonplaces and conventional strategies for formulating and working on a problem, such as searching for equilibrium states and being on the lookout for pervasive analogies. The commonplaces and strategies might be called skills, but they are more often seen as tools.

Using a toolkit requires technical skill, for adept manipulation of mathematical and diagrammatic expressions. And it also requires judgment, for deciding which tool or model is appropriate to a situation and for assessing when a strategy is likely to be effective. The kit I describe here is suited for the paper-and-pencil conceptualizing, explanatory, and problem-solving work of a physicist. The toolkit is contemporary, oriented toward particle physics and field theory, and congenial with modern views of condensed matter. It is drawn from standard texts, examinations, and handbooks.

Mathematics is perhaps most apparent as a skill and a set of tools. I hazard a synoptic description of its scope in the physicist's context: Physicists have to be able to count and make approximations, and hence there are the tools of combinatorics, statistics, and asymptotics. They have to master patterns, and hence there is geometry and the calculus of variations, symmetry principles and conservation laws, and rules for the propagation of waves and for the influence of boundaries

(Green's functions). And given physicists' interest in marginalism and in adding up the world, they have to master the principles of linearity and limits and stability, in the calculus and in optimization procedures.

Built into this subset of mathematics are the deepest principles of the world as physicists understand it. And so characteristic features of the physical world might be employed to justify why the mathematics is useful. Physically, counting and approximation are often about an equilibrium or lowest-energy ground state, a state which may be shown to be vastly more likely than other nearby states. Patterns are about the restricted plenitude or variety of nature—not everything happens—and the classification of those restrictions, again as physicists concern themselves with nature. (Restrictions reflect the conservation laws evidenced in the patterns: What is not conserved is forbidden; and that forbiddenness makes for those patterns. Those conservation laws are in different degrees absolute, and the patterns are observed in different degrees of intensity and faithfulness. So sophisticated abstraction is required in order to see some of those patterns, and, for that matter, to identify the ground state or to find the regime when linearity applies.) Linearity and limits are about the fact that there is a discrete hierarchy of well-separated forces; namely, they are of very different strengths. As a consequence, there are stable objects which may be linearly perturbed or almost so. The methods of counting and approximation provide us with another way to account for the ground state's fluctuations and perturbations, which again are relatively small and marginal disturbances.

Of course, these justifications of mathematics' usefulness are circular. Any such justification will be about the mutual dependence of tool and world, and about the seemingly contingent fact that physicists restrict their concern to situations which are or may be set up to be patterned and marginal. That is what physicists do. Then they can go to work.

A second set of tools are diagrammatic or picturing tools, figures that represent the world and from which we may "read off" and "write down" the physics. These figures are either geometric and spatial, or algebraic and symbolically patterned. Vector diagrams, Feynman graphs ($\succ\!\!\sim\!\!\sim\!\!\prec$), and pictures of boundary conditions are of the first sort, while symmetric algebraic or "covariant" expressions and canonical forms of equations are of the second sort (for example, $\partial_\mu A_\mu = 0 \equiv \partial A_x/\partial x + \partial A_y/\partial y + \partial A_z/\partial z + \partial A_t/\partial t = 0$). Of course, diagrams have to be interpreted correctly. A symmetric equation of motion or a Lagrangian with a symmetric interaction energy can have an asymmetric ground state, as in the freezing of a liquid into an oriented crystalline solid. And parallelism on a sphere is not quite the same as parallelism on a plane.

Again assume that the physics itself might justify the diagrammatics. Diagrammatic expresses the fact that physics literally accounts for nexuses and flows, and so there could be conservation laws. Vectors and covariant expressions are means for displaying the flows and conservation laws more or less automatically. Now physics is also a story of symmetries and of systematic categories for organizing phenomena. As we noted when discussing patterns, the conservation laws and the symmetries are intimately connected; invariance under a group of transformations is equivalent to conservation and to symmetry. The various patterned symbolisms can be set up to express these invariances and symmetries, again automatically. Interestingly, the diagrammatic also recalls everyday images of plumbing and of symmetric ornamental patterns, to express the perhaps less manifest facts of conservation of flow and of balanced order.

THE ART OF ADDRESSING NATURE

The third skill is a mastery of the rhetorical or descriptive tools of the craft, namely, modeling—what might be called the art of addressing nature. The tools here are the models invoked when we encounter a situation, models that make nature something we can then work on and talk about. They include the models of media, objects, and interaction, as well as the commonplaces and the more explicit strategic skills, such as searching for conserved quantities.

What is distinctive about this mode of rhetoric or description is that the various media, objects, and interactions are nicely separable, and they may be combined in seemingly arbitrary ways—x medium with y object with z interaction mechanism. Nature for a physicist is modular. It comes in isolable yet combinable parts or individuals, individuals known by a small number of properties. There are distinct states of matter, separated by sharp phase transitions; continua are remarkably smooth, so they may be defined by a small number of parameters; particles have well-defined properties and boundaries; and there is a hierarchy of fundamental interactions.

When physicists approach a situation as physicists they immediately take it as a physical world or a *medium*. The media include the spacetime vacuum; an atom or a solar system; an orderly crystalline solid; continuous elastic media, including liquid drops and drum surfaces; and fluids and gases.

The media are often treated as sequences tending to greater un-biasedness or symmetry and higher temperature, for example, solid/liquid/gas or atom/nucleus/quark. As the temperature rises each medium melts into the next one, and so unfreezes some degrees of freedom. In each of these media there are fluctuations. And, generally, high fluctuation, and susceptibility to external influence at melting or phase transition, alternates with the smooth and highly damped stable states.

While settling on the medium the physicist immediately identifies the things in that medium, such as particles. Let us call these things *objects*. What seems crucial about objects is that each object is individual, well separated from the rest of the world, and characterized by its own properties—even if the object itself is made up of much more complicated stuff. And its properties are addable to the properties of other objects, something like a linear superposition or an arithmetic. Objects are demographic. The total effect of such a group of demographic objects is a matter of adding up their individual and presumably marginal effects. Often there are conservation or invariance rules, so that it does not matter how we do the adding up. If it proves impossible at first to do such demographic addition, then, as we have seen in earlier chapters, one looks for objects that will nicely add up, such as normal modes, eigenstates, and quasi-particles. Or one develops suitable correction factors, such as curvatures and binding energies, to account for the differences from straightforward arithmetic addition due to nonlinearity, interaction, and composition. For example, when elementary particles compose an atom, or atoms compose crystals, such composition is usually neither linear nor homogeneous nor marginal.

As objects, there seem to be particles, oscillators, and fields and waves. Conspicuous in their absence are actual structures, such as levers and beams. Their substantiality and extension delegate them to the realm of engineering, where the inevitable effects of scale and nonlinearity are taken into account.

Characteristically, this rhetoric may invoke itself. A medium can be taken as an object in another medium, so a gas of electrons can fill a crystal. And there are modes of transformation among the objects. A particle can come to be seen as a wave; or a wave becomes an oscillator; or an oscillator becomes a particle. For example, a vibrating crystal lattice may be seen as a vacuum populated by particles such as phonons which represent its vibrations, in effect a many-body symmetric field. These transformations or rhetorical tropes are not only at a single scale, as are metaphors; they are also between scales, as are synec-doches. And so an atomic hypothesis advises us to look more closely.

This description of the toolkit is schematic, but in actual usage tools are taken quite specifically. A crystalline solid has a particular conventional symmetry, an atom will be the hydrogen atom, a gas will be ideal or van der Waals, a field will be Maxwell's electromagnetic one, and an interaction may be inverse square. Not only is the number of tools not large, the variety of specific instances or forms of those tools is also quite limited. Still, we may cover a wide range of situations. That is what a toolkit must do.

Media and objects *interact,* perhaps eventually being transformed into something other than what they were initially. Interaction requires actors, means, and resolution. As actors, we may have objects interacting with each other in a medium, such as two electrons in a vacuum. That vacuum might be spacetime, or the well-evacuated beampipe of a particle accelerator, or a crystal. Or an object may interact with a medium in which it is embedded, as does an electron within a crystal. Or an object may interact with a medium taken as an object, for example, an electron bouncing off a crystal, both in an evacuated chamber. As for means of interaction, they may be expressed as forces and influences—in contact, propagated through a medium, or at a distance; as exchanges of information; as energies or potentials; or as probing feelers and responses in a polarizable medium. Eventually interaction may be seen to have expended itself and be resolved. The now-interacted and perhaps transformed objects and medium may once more go along independently—until the next episode of interaction.

Formally, interaction is expressed through a variety of conceptual means that convey the objects toward each other in the medium, and eventually free them from each other. The scattering matrix of quantum mechanics brings together well-defined initial states; preserves constants of the motion such as energy and angular momentum; and produces well-defined nicely separated final states, states which represent the sum of most of the interactions. Differential equations move objects around or push them forward in time. Symmetry groups properly combine them. Correlation or transfer functions relate what happens in one part of a medium to another. Quantities such as energy, momentum, or angular momentum lead to translation operators (e^{-iHt}, e^{-ipx}, $e^{-iJ\phi}$) that take a world into a similar world at a different time, place, or orientation. If the conceptual means of interaction are expressed as linear operators, they may be combined to get nature going, much as objects are more generally combined to make up nature. But the space that these conceptual objects occupy is explicitly mathematical or formal.

Populating a medium with interacting objects brings the necessary rhetorical tools to bear on a situation. Of course, we shall also need to bring in the mathematical and diagrammatic tools and skills. Yet even with all this apparatus, a physical explanation still requires using those tools effectively. One needs a mode of addressing nature.

There are a number of such *strategies* of address. Perhaps the most crucial is to find a good equilibrium, or ground state, or vacuum, each taken as a medium to be populated by suitable objects: the crystal lattice taken as a vacuum, to be populated by collective excitations and quasi-particles; the physical spacetime vacuum, to be populated by elementary particles; Cooper pairs of electrons in a Bardeen-Cooper-Schrieffer (BCS) superconducting ground state in matter, to be eventually populated by thermal excitations; a singlet S-state hydrogen atom, to be populated by more highly excited states; or an ideal gas, at uniform temperature, pressure, and composition, to be populated by thermodynamic and hydrodynamic excitations. A study of the ground state's perturbations or excitations—namely, those objects that populate it—describes how it interacts with the world, and that proves fruitful for finding out about its structure. It may be possible to find conservative potentials, as in thermodynamics, which characterize how the ground state changes quasi-statically. We may invent new quantities and particles, such as entropy and the neutrino, to achieve such potentials and conservation.

Once we have a good ground state, the toolkit now becomes applicable and we can go to work. For the tools are designed to work on marginally changing situations; and the alterations of the ground state that preoccupy physicists are in fact marginal.

Two other strategies might be mentioned. The first is that of analogy and heuristic. The same equations have the same solutions, and there are physical analogies behind this. And if we can get away with treating a blackbody as an ideal gas, or light as a particle, or nuclear forces as potential forces, we should do it. Eventually we'll figure out why we could get away with it.

Another strategy, one we have referred to already, concerns what might be called the plenitude of nature: Everything that can happen will happen. Two consequences follow from this principle. If something does not happen, it must be forbidden, and we should find out why. And, second, when we address nature, we should not be surprised if a good stable world is not the best of all possible worlds, but rather the one that is most popular or orderly. Statistically, equilibria have vastly many more macroscopically-equivalent microscopic states than do other configurations. Combinatorially, some structures are vastly more stable, substantially more invariant to interchanges of their components, and more self-reinforcing than are most others. Equilibrium in gases, general equilibrium of markets in economics, and the macroscopic inverse square law are often shown to be products of the plenitude of nature, whether it be through the maximizing of entropy or through the Invisible Hand. A sign of plenitude is that while we might expect $N \times N$ different cases for N objects interacting with N others, we often end up with $N \log N$, much less than N^2. In the physical world, it seems that for any given set of components there are many configurations which are quite similar in their form and consequences.

We might summarize the strategies as follows: Get ahold of something that will mostly stay put and that will allow for simple and marginal investigation. Use all you know about one situation to investigate another that seems to be like it. Assume that the world is tractable, one way or another, to your understanding. And believe that nature is designed or patterned or hierarchical, and that it is robust, remarkably invariant to interchanges among its components. Of course, we might say that if it weren't so stable, probeable, and robust, and subject to analogy and pattern, we could not get ahold of it by the means that physicists employ. That may well be true. What is rather more significant is that there is lots of the world that fits these substantive criteria, lots of the world that may be worked on with a physicist's toolkit.

The structure of this toolkit is actually quite conventional. For it is drawn from descriptions of classical rhetoric, taken as the art of address. Media correspond to genres, objects to tropes, interaction to plot, strategies to modes of address, and standard methods to commonplaces. So it is perhaps not so surprising that such a kit might work, once we are willing to acknowledge that doing science is a human cultural activity as well as a craft. Scientific explanation is rhetorical. For in addressing nature we are as well producing persuasive demonstrations, for ourselves and for others.

This schematic toolkit slights some crucial tools. Diagrams are often of pieces of apparatus rather than vectors or algebra. Thermodynamics conceived of in terms of heat engines, electricity in terms of resistors and capacitors, and optics in terms of mirrors, lenses, and light rays may be fit into this kit, but they do not quite belong. In part, the kit concentrates on the microscopic world. And in part this toolkit and the set of skills and strategies for employing it are concerned with paper-and-pencil problem-solving activities.

When the problems are derived more directly from experiment and empirical investigation, we might imagine additions to the kit. There would be both tools of inquiry and tools of recognition. For inquiry, there are logical tools, such as "electronics" or filters, for picking out events; amplifiers for making them more prominent; and stimulators or probes, to search for and bring out the cases of interest. For recognition there are tools and skills of simulation or empathy, say in order to figure out how an electron might act in an apparatus; tools to manage dissimulation, for dealing with how chance and fakery produce what appear as valid data or good events; and tools for emulation, to set up situations so that they are sufficiently the same, so as to provide for reproducibility and stable outputs, namely, data. In a good toolkit the problem-solving and the experimental tools are intimately connected, so that a particle had better be a probe, and filters and amplifiers had better be interaction mechanisms.

The nature that is available to us through this kit of tools and skills is remarkably additive, smooth, and dumb or deanimated. Here nature is a sum of its parts. The parts interact smoothly as in the calculus, and discontinuities may be shown to disappear in a higher dimension or be the limiting consequence of a very large number of smooth interactions. And the tools are objective and independent of context, having no memory or will of their own. The modularity of the toolkit mirrors images of modern society or economy as composed of alienated individuals.

Physics, taken as a craft possessing a toolkit, is true because the toolkit works and leads to interesting work. And how it works may be justified internally, in physical terms. The kit focuses the craftsperson's effort on reproducible and explainable phenomena, within a historical tradition which gives the craftsperson a standard of what it means to work and to be interesting. When the toolkit does not work or becomes of limited interest, new tools and practices need to be invented and new probes, filters, and models created. The new tools may be seen as adaptations of the old, even if they are used rather differently. So, for example, modern electro-weak theory, the "standard model" of particle physics, is taken as just another step in the tradition of Maxwell's equations for electromagnetism.

One of the interesting developments in physics in the last few decades has been the large bureaucratized research team, and the concomitant rise in the use of standardized instruments, detectors, and computer programs. We return to a highly articulated division of labor—instrument making crafts and performer or user crafts—in the doing of physics. Also, much of what was once crafted is now manufactured. How does the work of science change in the age of mechanical reproduction? What is the fate of the sacred and of aura in modern industrial society?

CHAPTER EIGHT

The Possibility of Doom

Despite the fact that we may take the world toolishly; that we may make the world smooth and marginal, and so add it up or analyze its components; and that every surprise seems to have the silver lining of an explanation—the world remains discontinuous and resistant. There are big decisions and stickinesses, and parts of the world resist our conceptual entreaties. It is in the realm of the sacred that such discontinuity and resistance is most fully realized and justified. And we have no choice but to take sacredness seriously, for it won't go away. Even so-called rational scientific endeavors, such as planning and policy analysis, are rife with transcendent concerns which deeply influence their practice and outcomes.

We seem to require both the sacred and the mundane, and at the same time. Doomsday is surely a sacred event, and analyses which treat it as one event in a probabilistic universe (as I shall describe) do not capture the moral dilemmas it presents for us. Conversely, natural environments are a matter of our invention and designation, and of deliberate sacralizing and purification rituals—and if we treat those environments only as God-given, again we find ourselves mistaking their nature. Sacred places have rather more mundane and dubious histories to which we must reconcile ourselves.

Doom is both a transcendent moment and an ordinary event. Nature is sublime and biological. And built environments are both integrated wholes and historical artifacts of human device and action. We want to get a feel for the both-and quality of the world, what is sometimes called its transitionality, its two-in-oneness. And a feel for the kinds of policy arguments we can make given this duality.

In order to do so, we might examine the interplay of history and policy. In particular, what does a description of the various horrible ends of the world, such as plague, war, and famine, tell us about how we ought live now? And if historical accounts of earlier dooms, natural disasters, or urban decline are meant to be monitory, supposed to tell us something, rarely is it clear what their lesson is. In part, accounts of past sacrifice and discontinuity do not readily mix with the more gentle and everyday stories we tell ourselves in the present, stories which are about what we would otherwise take as prospectively likely and marginally different from where we are now. And how should those accounts affect our assessment of the likelihood of future discontinuous transformations? How might we generalize from individual "unique" past events and histories, so that we have a universe of them and thereby can be probabilistic, or we have representative archetypes and can be paradigmatic? These are, of course, standard historiographical questions. Here their answers affect the claims we can make about the possibility of doom.

Historical study shows that crisis and rapid discontinuous change, even if self-limiting, surely do occur. They affect us deeply, for worse and better, and we might barely control such changes, if at all. As we have seen repeatedly, such crisis and change may be a combinatorial consequence of rather more smooth marginal processes or be modeled by phenomenological archetypes of discontinuity. So we might well take historical accounts and then generalize from them, in terms of mechanisms and archetypes, and so speak of the possibility of future great transformations.

In reconciling the apocalyptic and moral with the practical and the particular, again the lessons of history are never so easily drawn. Stories of past famine, war, and devastation may scare us, and even convince us that those catastrophes will recur in our lives. Yet the stories may also give us confidence that we might be able to avoid such horrors given our current modes of government and technology. Our pride is to believe in either the exact recurrence of history or its avoidance. The horrors recur, but in their own way. Cautions cannot be absolutely monitory, for incautiousness is a source of invention and reformation.

More generally, historical accounts will not give us a justification for Providence: why our current state seems to us all but inevitable. Rather, insofar as we take our current state as inevitable, such historical accounts of origins may be demystifying, allowing us to conceive of alternatives to the present.

These various philosophic considerations will deeply affect the kinds of practical advice we give about potential catastrophe and doom. My purpose here is to sketch the prerequisites for such a reasonable account of the possibility of doom.

DOOMSDAY IS JUDGMENT DAY. Stories of doom are moral descriptions, judgments of how we live now and claims about how we ought live.

They are motivated by what seems least under our control and is most frightening, and they are meant to warn us of our wayward paths and to influence what we might do next. As worst-case scenarios, we pay attention to them not because they are likely but because the untoward consequences they describe are so very great.

Science has perhaps succeeded religion and theology as the source of the most authoritative stories of doom, and consequently the credibility of these stories depends more on rational and empirical argument than on scripture or priestly authority. Poetic and rhetorical devices drawn from imaginative literature must be supported by rather less dramatic analyses of contingencies and calculations of reaction rates and probabilities. "Nuclear winter" is a powerful image, winter being the archetypal time of irony and reversal. Yet within months, that image of the environmental effects of an exchange of nuclear weapons yielded to detailed calculations of atmospheric flows and resource disruptions.

The stories need not be perfect. Their admonitions are likely to be in the form of if-then-otherwise, since our predictive capacities are modest, and we are both resilient to catastrophe and responsive to warnings. But given these inherent limitations, we will want to place our bets rationally or to plan sensibly.

A reasonable doomsday story needs to be credible, and as we shall see it is likely to feature catastrophe, curse, and contingency. It will sketch a plausible and to some extent probable picture of the road to doom. The potential harm will usually vastly outweigh the costs of avoiding that harm; otherwise not only are we doomed, but there is nothing sensible we might do about it. The story will often feature a breakdown of the social order, or disease, or counterintuitive response to our actions, or large fluctuations. So it may show how we will still be surprised or overtaken by the oncoming doom, even if we are warned by the story.

Moreover, the role of the storyteller or the doomsayer affects the story's content and claims, for the doomsayer is no ordinary narrator. Doomsayings almost surely influence the plot and are heard by its characters.

It turns out to be quite difficult to tell reasonable stories of doom. Crucially, stories of doom are about a judgment we mundane persons could not make. More poignantly, practicality supersedes judgment: We know that there are terrible catastrophes. We may be able to sketch the downward spiral that leads to them. So, for example, famines occur, and we know how they occur, and how governmental actions may encourage or prevent their worst consequences. We may then even make moral judgments of such actions. But given such an account, we are pushed into the realm of policy and practical action and away from the realm of judgment and transcendence. The possibility of doom or salvation yields to the possibility of saving particular people. The "end of the world" is an entirely different phenomenon than the particular historical and analytical problem we face just now. And insofar as we get ahold of our situation in these latter terms we are no longer telling a doomsday story, but rather a practical one about what we must do next.

The lessons we draw from historical accounts of catastrophe may be about how we shall eventually and inevitably be doomed. Or such a catastrophe is just one more event in a universe of such catastrophes, its mechanism to be decoded and its lessons to be generalized from. We are drawn to both lessons, the sacred and the mundane, the discontinuous and the marginal. Neither is a safe harbor for pessimism or optimism, although nowadays the sacred has a reputation for pessimism and the mundane for optimism. Rather, our continuing problem is to draw the lessons most appropriate for our particular situation.

THE STORY

A prediction of catastrophe may be treated as a story, a narrative told by a storyteller to an audience. Such a predictive story is a realistic picture of what might happen, formulated as a linked sequence of prospective events in the context of a society and government. In a story of doom, the catastrophe is very grave indeed, and its impact is not only as an event but as a moral description. Whatever else, the story must provide a plausible sequence of events leading up to the catastrophe. In a plausible story the details of how we are affected by difficulties and crises should correspond to what one could reasonably expect persons to do. Our inventiveness in responding to the difficulties should be assumed to be about the same as it always has been, unless good reasons are given. And the abstractions we make in telling the story should not themselves be the source of the predicted crisis.

In a plausible story people are not totally complacent when things become problematic, even if they do have a tendency to ignore warning signals. They can be and are technologically and socially quite inventive. That they (and we) cannot now conceive of an appropriate invention to solve a future problem does not imply that none will come along. Yet some future problems will not be solved by an invention, if they are solved at all.

A plausible story must also hold up to criticism of its structure. So the abstractions and limitations built into the mathematical or historical model we use to think about ourselves, abstractions that help us work out the model's consequences, may not be realized in our society. If the predicted catastrophe in the model is due to these abstractions, we had better be sure that they apply to us.

Worst-case stories will stretch all of these requirements, but at a cost of becoming less believable. But that is what a worst-case story must do. Still, a doomsday story will be more convincing if warning signals are not completely ignored, if invention is not completely dead, and if people do not always act individualistically and mechanistically in the face of difficulty, but may act solidarily. Even those storytellers who are especially concerned with survival and extreme situations must fulfill these requirements in their analyses, at least if they want to appeal to a wider audience.

The story must be probable as well as plausible. Only some stories are likely. Fluctuations cannot be too far out of normal range, or be too numerous, unless we are telling a worst-case story. If the story depends on a chain of independent improbable events, it will be quite unlikely as a whole. In general, the length of the sequence of events should be short, and each transition should be reasonably likely. Most predictions for the long term, say beyond thirty years, must be viewed quite skeptically—unless we have reason to believe that they represent very large-scale trends. The variance may still be substantial, but at least the prediction is not merely an accumulation of uncertainties and noise.

One way of finessing the problem of plausibility and probability is to sketch a seemingly innocent process that has as its result not-so-innocent effects. Thus, we would have no warning, and the process itself could be quite common. This has been done nicely in game theory and for voting paradoxes; and in the qualitative shift from parts to wholes exemplified in the market with its Invisible Hand, in bureaucracy, and in the Malthusian story of demographic instability. Reasonably common marginal processes, continuous or discrete, lead to and account for emergence and discontinuity. Also, such marginalism and locality may contribute to a decline of an overarching political consciousness, limiting the capacity to mobilize people for larger purposes, so making them even more vulnerable to untoward events.

The story must also be of substantial consequence. A titrational balance of the value of loss against the costs of avoidance, suitably weighted by probabilities, will nicely discriminate among different but comparable consequences. But in a story of doom the untoward consequences are very large and the probabilities can be quite small. Multiplying the two to get an expectation value is useful for comparable alternative dooms, but may seem absurd if $p = 10^{-6}$ and cost $= 10^6$ versus $p = 10^{-1}$ and cost $= 10$. Then we may need to take into account both the decreasing marginal utility of money, and the fact that the variance is likely to be much larger for the first case than for the second and that we tend to be somewhat risk averse. It may still be quite difficult to compare two dooms that happen to be on the same Dantean levels. For they are likely to have diverse sets of consequences, not easily put on a single scale. And if a worst case is being considered, the low probabilities cannot be used to easily diminish the significance of the untoward consequences, unless we are comparing worst consequences of roughly the same order.

Balanced against considerations of consequence will be the degree of undesirability of the needed readjustments if we are to avoid a projected disaster. If survival required that we give up justice or freedom, or that we sacrifice one part of the society such as the poor or the firstborn for the rest, we might have great difficulty in going along with an otherwise plausible story. We find it hard to treat these sacrifices as abstract and commensurable costs. They make sense only in terms of the larger meanings or purposes of the society. For then some value may be given up temporarily or be sacrificed for the sake of a deeper or more overarching value. Yet we might rather search for other more acceptable stories, responsive to the same insights and facts as the original one, but which require fairer adjustments in our lives.

Still, we may be attracted by cost-benefit, statistical decision theory approaches—even if we are concerned with extreme cases and fluctuations, where plausibility and probability are stretched, the costs may be substantial, and the variances are large.

Pascal's wager provides one exemplary case. We cannot know if God exists. If we act as if he does, the benefits of the consequent good behavior are very great, even if it turns out he does not. If we act as if he does not exist and we are wrong, the losses are very large indeed. We cannot afford to be wrong. Only if we are absolutely sure of the nonexistence of the afterlife and of God can we ignore the enormity of the stakes involved. Once we allow a bit of belief, then we seem to have to commit resources appropriate to the large or infinite benefits and expectation values involved in a Pascalian world, at least one without suitably decreasing marginal utilities. And the very large variances encountered when infinite payoff is multiplied by perhaps infinitesimal probability encourages the risk averse to go along with Pascal.

Still, believing that God exists if he does not may well be costly in terms of what we must do as believers. And Pascal may be wrong in arguing that these costs are comparatively small. So we might enumerate the costs of preparing for the afterlife and decide if they are worth it. It may not be the case that there are infinite net benefits to believing God exists if we are not sure that he does exist.

A Pascalian wager may be incoherent as well. The afterlife might be an unconvincing notion, and not only to a hard-nosed materialist. Just because we can conceive of something does not mean it exists or will happen. That concern for an afterlife may reflect present-worldly needs we might manage here and now. Then the issue will no longer be so clearly about probabilities, payoffs, and costs versus benefits. And even if the issue remains in the decision theoretic realm there may well be other Pascalian bets, with different but still infinitely costly consequences—unless we believed in something else, other than God, and followed a different path.

Pascal would reply that even if his account and warning were wrong, still it leads us to live a better life here and now. Or, more generally, even if a millennial prediction were not completely believable, the kind of life we lead taking it seriously can be more just and good than another. Hence, even if wrong, the prediction is useful and wise. Of course, Pascal still has to deal with alternative Pascalian predictions.

As I have suggested, when the probabilities are low and the costs are high, the resulting expectation values are hard to believe. At the least those expectation values need to be supplemented by measures of fluctuation and sensitivity. If the event is potentially extreme such as our extinction, and "one-time" so that there is no real universe of possibilities, we still might imagine a range of possibilities or harms so that the situation is no longer one-time. The estimates of probability may still be sensitive to the universe of possibilities we assume, but now we are comparing a graduated sequence of incrementally or marginally different alternatives and their variances. In so doing, the event is no longer unique and sacred. There is no longer the mixture of the infinite and the finite that is characteristic of Pascal's argument.

SOCIAL ORGANIZATION

A story that demands our attention and action—even a worst-case scenario—has to be plausible, probable, and consequential. It must balance survival against sacrifice, and harm against protective reorganization and disruption—none of which may be readily commensurable with each other. In stories of potential doomsday these factors are large, and they are often roughly equal, so that error and fluctuation are significant. Subtle factors of social organization are then quite critical in determining outcomes.

Societal survival strategies are aided by cooperation at moments of need, and an effective capacity to design and plan so as to achieve roughly what we intend. We also may need public ways of controlling disease and famine and their consequences, and an ability to withstand short-term limited disasters. A story of catastrophe will become more believable as a potential doom if it can rationally incorporate a breakdown of the social order; an exogenous disease or environmental change which acts independently of what we do, and which resists our protective actions; a series of systemic interconnections which cause our preventive actions to work against our intentions; or substantial fluctuations with disastrous consequences, over extensive spaces and times. If these fluctuations repeat close-by, and we cannot count on averaging or smoothing effects such as aid from neighbors who have not been devastated, then the story will be even more believable as a doomsday story.

Heilbroner has argued that the prospect of nuclear war becomes more likely unless we are committed to our traditions and to future generations, and so have a will to survive. Effective social institutions also give us the capacity and the will to shift resources and make investments, so as to provide for short-term hedges and long-term security. Were such institutions ineffective we would be less resilient and more subject to the devastations due to shocks.

Yet a partial breakdown of the social order and of its codes of obligation and behavior may be a good thing. For social institutions also restrict our actions, setting up conventional prohibitions and taboos. The conventions may prevent us from doing ourselves in, but they may also prevent us from acting inventively to save ourselves. Nuclear deterrence is seen by some as such a conventional taboo. In response, models of nuclear war fighting are offered, employing incremental steps or escalations, presumably to give us greater flexibility if deterrence were to be breached, along the way perhaps making the breach more likely.

So the breakdown of the social order is ambiguous, to be taken as anomic and liberating. It may mean a break with tradition that leads to a breakdown of our mutual commitments and so to annihilation, or a break that leads to flexibility, invention, and resilience—or both. A potential catastrophe might lead to doom but also to a vigorous response. And the now broken social order might be seen as an anachronism rather than a comforting tradition.

If disease and environmental change are external to the social order and not under its influence, their capacity to ravage might be very large indeed. If they are to doom us, the disease must be unresponsive to public health measures and the environmental changes be unresponsive to public protection or intervention. Moreover, we are further doomed if there is a series of compounding consequences, such as famine, to magnify the effects of disease and disaster.

Systemic analyses, whether of ecological or economic systems, often exhibit so-called counterintuitive behavior. Our good but naive intentions turn out to defeat us. But to be realistic these models need to incorporate a degree of stickiness and social convention, which in effect gums up their works and casts doubt on their conclusions. So, for example, if fertility is not directly connected to food supplies and is mediated by self-conscious social convention, then Malthusian mechanisms are not so ravaging as their reputation suggests. The models also must incorporate designers and planners about as able as we are. The designers can be self-conscious and aware of their society and the system. They appreciate the systemic problems and might design around them; or if defeated, they are defeated while fighting. A fault-tree analysis of the breakdown of a large mechanical system had better include the possibility of deliberate sabotage and of designed preventive moves, and also of quick fixes to limit the harm if the sabotage succeeds. Our systems are made up in part of designing self-conscious persons who belong to a society governed in small but real part by their knowledge and designs.

Finally, as I have already indicated, fluctuations can make a catastrophe much worse. Two or three bad years in a row, how improbable that may be, can be devastating, especially if repair mechanisms are quite limited and help from neighbors is precluded by space or culture. An isolated gambler may not only lose, but in a typical run may be ruined more or less permanently. On the other hand, a single quite catastrophic event may well inspire more flexible responses such as pooling resources and banking, so preventing a second catastrophic fluctuation from being as devastating as the first. If a form of catastrophe is regular, such as flood or disease, we tend to develop social institutions to take care of its effects, although we might well underinvest in those institutions.

SURPRISE

The doomsday story becomes even more convincing if it not only is plausible and features a breakdown in the social fabric, but also shows how we shall be surprised by the consequences of our sinfulness (even if we are told about them ahead of time, as in such a story), and so be incapable of responding and adapting fast enough to worsening circumstances.

We might distinguish two kinds of surprise. Some catastrophes occur very rapidly once a certain threshold is passed. Nuclear wars, as they were initially conceived, have this property. We lack an ability to control them beyond the threshold, and they can slip past it too quickly for us to act. Other catastrophes build up very slowly. They are surprising because we do not notice them at first, or their consequences may be hidden from us, or our knowledge may be defective about the meaning of their initial stages and so we misinterpret the signs of their development. Pollutants, poisons, and disease may sometimes work in this way.

Surprise would seem to be precluded by an absolutely complete story told to a rational audience. Being sensible they would act to save themselves, and the story would predict that they would act sensibly. But it is in the nature of stories that they are selective, and in the nature of people that their rationality is bounded by their interests and by tradition. So the audience will not always respond to sensible warnings, even to warnings that they will not respond to warnings. They may have Pascalian bets in their lives other than the one presented to them. And their own prudential considerations may give rather different weight to aspects of the story than was intended by the storyteller.

Now we might describe collective social effects that prevent our noticing indicators of catastrophe and our paying attention to stories about those indicators, or that cause us to misinterpret the indicators, or that make our combined responses counter to our best intentions even if we know about the strange effects of combined actions. For example, say that the structure of nuclear weaponry systems ensures an eventual rapid surprise unless there were reduced armaments. If we can show how reduction is precluded despite the best intentions of people, and despite their being told that reduction is precluded despite their best intentions, and they do not change the world so that their intentions could be more effective—we would have a powerful story. But this is a very tall order. Any chink in this narrative's armory destroys its apocalyptic character.

Such a story must show how we become more capable of ignoring precursors of catastrophe as the precursors become more insistent. Actually it need only show that by the time we wake up it will be too late to do much good or that the transformation required to avoid the catastrophe will be impossible. It need not prove that we shall be eternally blind to signals and precursors, only that we shall be too blind to save ourselves.

Of course, we need to be sure that there is such a point as too-late. Perhaps at almost any time we can design our way out of the morass and justify the sacrifices needed in terms of our eventual survival. Pascalians would argue that the cost of being wrong should make us want to avoid anything close to a too-late situation. Conceding this, we still need some rational idea of when it is too-late.

As I have indicated, an actual self-reinforcing blindness is hard to conceive. Malthus tried to draw one such picture for the poor, which depended on their not having a larger vision of their lives. And Marx drew another of bourgeois capitalists who, as long as they remained in that role, would systematically act in ways that would counter their own long-term interest. It is fair to argue that both Malthus's and Marx's models suffer from their abstractions. The models do not allow people to transcend their roles as the predictors defined them. Hence, while capitalists might not be able to see beyond their noses, the persons who enact the role of the capitalist might be otherwise capable of being more aware of their personal interest.

Actual histories of great catastrophe show how precursors are ignored and threats get out of hand. So we might recall these untoward and surprising events in arguing for the prospect of a particular catastrophe or doom. Yet those histories also sketch how we recovered from the catastrophe, despite the losses. It is not clear which lesson we are to draw, although a historical account can be extraordinarily suggestive of mechanisms and means through which we find ourselves in trouble and perhaps are even saved.

There are some stories which are effectively complete. We might argue that there are catastrophic situations which we cannot anticipate since we cannot conceive of them. Such stories are about the limits of our predictive, conceptual, and storytelling abilities. For example, an outsider who could not talk to ants might know of the coming demise of an anthill. The ants, correspondingly, might not be able to conceive of that possibility or rationally believe in the existence of the kind of outsider who might know about their future.

We, as ants, may be warned that we must act differently if we are to avoid one of these inconceivable catastrophes. Such a story will be more effective if the limits of our conceptual capacities are well described. We then might find the story sufficiently convincing to act in accord with its recommendations. But usually we have many conceivable and genuine problems which are pressing as well. We might be wrong in ignoring the inconceivable and so face ultimate tragedy eventually. But in general it is hard to follow the recommendations derived from a story of inconceivable and unarticulated catastrophe, no matter how frightening it is as a prospect.

One form of the inconceivable is a story about our not being able to adapt and to manage the complexities of our world, and hence we shall eventually be overwhelmed. Something will get out of control. The complexities may be due to organization, technology, or environmental pollutants. Now we need not control everything to manage in the world. Some aspects and species can be left alone to their own ways, and perhaps to be destroyed or to flourish. If we believe that we can avoid all threats to endangered species and all environmental despoliation, we are committing the equivalent of a sin of pride. Secularly put, we have no sense of our limitations and of the relative importance of our various activities.

Rarely do stories make such extreme and comprehensive claims. Rather, a story of our being overwhelmed by complexity must show how those complexities preclude our managing what is crucial to our lives. The story will incorporate a model of how we do control things and how we develop more comprehensive frameworks for thinking about and governing ourselves and our world. It will also incorporate reasonable expectations for our capacity to adapt to changed situations and some sense about what we might be able to ignore. Then we might show how, in worst cases at least, we could fail to develop such more comprehensive frameworks. The story might now begin to be frightening.

I should note that Pascal did offer a rational argument and a way of considering evidence concerning the afterlife, so his story is not about the inconceivable. Religious claims are rarely made without substantial empirical support, including miracles, historical precedents, stigmata, and natural occurrences. Abraham felt duty-bound to sacrifice Isaac within a well-founded belief in God's will and wisdom, at least to him and to his culture.

THE STORYTELLER

The story of catastrophe is told by a storyteller to an audience. Should storytellers tell everything that they know? What if one is wrong? And does it matter if a storyteller is a member of the community or not?

Predictors may act as scientific professionals ministering to a body politic. But if a prediction turns out to be incorrect, and perhaps is the result of poor judgment, we do not have recourse to insurance and to suits for professional malpractice.

Moreover, any estimate of the probability of a degree of catastrophe or of doom will have an error or variance attached to it. It may well be the case that the range of the probability reasonably extends from, say,

0.4 to 1.0, even if the best estimate of the probability is 0.99. To most hearers of such a prediction, the guidance provided by marginalist decision theory pales before the rather different strategies implicit in the two values of 0.4 and 1.0.

In giving a warning, or in making an account explicit and detailed and perhaps frightening, storytellers fashion the public possibilities for a society; the prediction may then attract attention and resources away from other areas. If the prediction proves wrong or its ambiguity is misleading, we cannot recover the large costs unnecessarily invested and the social and political opportunities lost. We will bear all the costs of error if we are misled. And if a storyteller cries wolf too often, not only are there losses due to false preparation, but the credibility of other storytellers is impugned.

On the other hand, should storytellers who can see or predict a catastrophe for their community, were it to continue in its current ways, always warn the community? Say that desirable long-term effects might ensue if they were quiet and the community experienced the catastrophe. What should they say? Rational community members, by definition, could balance short- and long-term consequences. To them the storytellers need only present the best evidence and estimates of effect. But even for rational community members it can be very difficult to decide explicitly to make sacrifices now for rewards in the future. Looking back, a community (which now consists of survivors) might even come to believe a catastrophe was a good thing when they consider their improved and recovered state. But it is risky and perhaps arrogant for someone who can predict a catastrophe to then use the possibility of positive retrospective judgment to justify their keeping quiet.

On a personal level, the choices are perhaps clearer. If we suspect that an attempt at suicide will lead a person to seek appropriate help were the suicide to fail, should we encourage, or at least not discourage, such an attempt? It might succeed. Now a physician's professional distance may allow for the deaths of some people because of limitations of time and resources. But physicians cannot so easily maintain that distance with their own family members.

If the predictor were Tiresias, and the notion of fate were accepted, there would be no problem. Speaking would not affect the future. But modern storytellers and their audiences tend to be less sure about fate and more willing to believe that our predictions and technologies can alter what will happen. Telling a story may change the world.

The situation is actually somewhat less subtle. Rarely is there a lone predictor possessing the truth about the future, wondering whether to release it. Others are likely to have come to similar conclusions. And there will be even others who find those conclusions concerning catastrophe to be suspect and overdrawn. Publicity about potential catastrophe, and argument among experts, is good newspaper material. So it is quite difficult to keep such a secret, for both practical and moral reasons.

Outsiders to a situation—later in time, in the role of an onlooker, or when the situation involves others whom we may treat as objects—will speak and act very differently than will insiders. Watching an anthill, outsiders might say what they believe, perhaps even without consideration for how the ants as insiders will respond. But should those insiders listen to outsiders, if they could hear them? How do the ants know that outsiders appreciate what is important to an ant? Does the outsider require the ants to sacrifice what is most dear to them, what is perhaps a matter of life and death? If the ants could believe an outsider is all-knowing then it would be straightforward. But that alternative is usually not available. The ant community must rationally assess the prediction in its own terms. On the other hand, a storyteller who is an insider is one of us. We more readily believe an ant might appreciate our interests, even if those interests are not exactly its own.

Now a scientific stance that presents itself as being objective and fair may be appealing, especially if the question of doom could be seen as essentially scientific by everyone who is involved. But insofar as scientists are usually in the position of being outsiders to the systems they study, and those systems are populated by persons or citizens not like them, their authority might well be questioned. And if the situation involves political and social interests, as it surely will, and so the story of doom is not straightforwardly scientific, then the objective stance is even less likely to be authoritative.

Keeping in mind that knowledge and sacrifice are the recurring themes in advice we give about potential dooms, we might answer the questions that began this section: Yes, we shall pay if the storytellers are wrong. They probably ought tell everything they know. And it surely does matter if they are outsiders; it seems preferable that the storyteller be one of us.

A good story of doomsday is a coherent narrative that connects the present with a potentially awful future. It touches the vulnerabilities of a society, and it plays on the society's capacity to be surprised. And it judges that society and finds it wanting. Ordinary catastrophes, such as flood or periodic disease, are sufficiently regular so that we may have developed social mechanisms for avoiding the worst cases and for helping each other, and for compensating unlucky rather than sinful losers. Yet there is still terrible famine, war, and industrial disaster. And these are potential doomsdays insofar as we have yet to incorporate into society the necessary capacity for informed choice and mutual caring. What is terrible can become devastating.

Scare stories are likely to divert our attention, at least for a while, from perhaps more worthy concerns. Yet a well-supported prediction of sufficiently horrible catastrophe would seem to demand that we act to avoid the catastrophe, no matter what the cost. But if there is more than one such doom story, with different sources and consequences, or if the support and quality of the story is flawed but the story is not false, or if the costs of avoidance are not readily acceptable, it becomes less clear what to do. It may even be argued that survival may not be worth it, if the society we would inherit is inhuman or evil or unjust. Except for millenarians, such an argument has never defeated hope and the desire to go on with everyday life.

These critical considerations about the quality of stories concerning potential catastrophe and doom are not meant to diminish the significance of famine, decimation, or devastation of property or the natural environment. Such substantial harms are catastrophic, likely to lead to an overturning of our ways of living, disturbing the seeming stability of our lives.

Nor are these considerations meant to make light of the moral critiques central to stories of doom. For insofar as the stories are meant to be moral critiques they can ignore probabilities and treat losses as being of infinite value, and so uninsurable and unacceptable. And they can take survival and transformation as their primary themes. For they are then eschatological stories that describe our ultimate fate. Their purpose is to give a sense of meaning and finiteness to our existences, by showing how our lives and society might work themselves out. One kind of eschatology involves our return to organic nature, an ecosystemic mode. Another involves the eternal cycles of nature and how we might avoid them, a Malthusian picture. And in a third, our final state is our being saved or redeemed in history through men and God and not Nature, a political transformation. But if doomsday stories are meant to help us rationally compare alternative actions, they will have to be reasonable narratives, suited to an actual society, told by authoritative storytellers. Then their warnings will be worthy of our attention.

CHAPTER NINE

Los Angeles and the Frontier

The myths of Los Angeles provide a lovely example of the play of mundane marginalist commerce and transcendent discontinuist ambition, one buying up or conversely blessing the other. What is striking is how historical artifacts become sacralized so that they are taken as matters pure and eternal.

PLACES BECOME ARCHETYPES OF their countries or regions, epitomizing larger themes and conflicts, mythifying a culture's obsessions and taboos. For the United States, the West has been such a place, an other place compared to the East and the Middle West. And Los Angeles has come to be the place in which that otherness is crystallized—whether it be tinseltown Hollywood, or multiethnic world-city Los Angeles. How might the myth of a place be related to the actualities of life around it? For a place is not just a set of properties, whether they be demographic, spatial, or economic. Rather, it is a mode of interpreting what is going on at that location. And a place is also a *topos,* a rhetorical topic around which discourse is organized.

This archetypal notion of place is nicely displayed in some recent evidence of Los Angeles' mythic power—the national fascination with the varied immigrations of people-of-color, mostly from Mexico, Central America, and Asia, to the Southern California region centered on Los Angeles. And the topos, the sense of Los Angeles' place, is violation and purification, which are pervasive notions in America's historiography.

Now migration itself must be a recurrent theme for such "virgin" land, as America came to be known—whether it be migration by nineteenth-century frontiersmen or 1930s Oakies. But such virginity is bought at a cost, namely, that of genocide and forgetting. There were natives here before; this virgin land had experience. And the putative white people even married into that native stock early on. Things were never so pure to start with.

Given such an actual history, there are some straightforward problems: How do you create a city of angels, pure white angels, when it has such a swarthy and checkered past? You will need to efface that past, have her possessed by true and virile and virtuous men, and so restore a prelapsarian Edenic air—where, as usual, virginity is defined in terms of the actions and perspective of males. The Edenic air is also the pre-smog era of the Los Angeles basin, and the restoration of clean air is again a matter of a constructed virginity.

There is as well a second question: Where do white people come from? How can their histories be sufficiently cleansed and be made legitimate? The answer, in part, is to stigmatize latecomers, hegemonically projecting one's own feared images of oneself onto those latecomers. This will eventually lead to a Freudian return of the repressed, but more generally it is about the Oedipus myth of successive violation and ultimate redemption.

White people are those who have been able to forget their histories, and to adopt a more legitimate American history of proper birth or confirmatory wealth. And they are then fascinated by and scared of the Others, the ethnics: their fruitfulness, their sexuality, their industry and sin. Whether it be myths of black sexuality and fructiferousness, Mexican laziness, Asian industriousness, or Jewish entrepreneurship and glamor (tinseltown, again)—there is always obsession, disgust, and desire. True men and refined ladies do not actively and overtly participate in any of these obsessions, or so it is made to seem. But they cannot help but notice them. It has not been long since they were on the other side of town.

Just when Los Angeles was about to settle down to being a white and pure city, the Watts rebellions of the 1960s having been forgotten, it became a world city. And a good part of its new energy comes from just those people who one might have thought of as Other, from the East—Eastern Europe, the Middle East, and the Far East. Effete and dark forces turn out to be potent and fertile. And they are salvific as well. They provide for industry and entrepreneurship. And how else is one to afford a housemaid, or operate a garment industry, or populate an engineering school? Just when an earlier generation of escapees seem to have legitimated their new home, they are reminded of their escape and dubious legitimacy. And they find that for their economy they need just those people who will remind them of their own pasts. Now schoolchildren are taught a more complex native and ethnic history, especially of the early days. But if they are putatively white, they themselves are to remain pure, remarkably untouched in their own personal histories by that history of the Others.

These are of course central themes in American history and historiography: virginity, virility, and purity. They compose the myths of white America, where white is not so much an absence of color as it is a state of mind available to anyone who can get away with it, whose skin is not too dark, whose features are not too pronounced, whose wealth is sufficient. These myths are active constructions and require lots of work if they are to be maintained. And these are the themes that are operative in the contemporary myth of Los Angeles—where legitimacy provided by hard work and sweat equity competes with the legitimacy provided by dealmaking and real estate speculation.

In 1893, at the Columbian Exhibition, the University of Wisconsin historian Frederick Jackson Turner suggested a connection between an expanding geographical frontier and the political culture of the United States. The Turner thesis could, on the one hand, speak of an open land, offering escape from the hierarchical and constrained East. This virgin land was a place for pioneering, freedom, and democracy. And on the other hand, the "closing of the frontier" presented America with the end of its Eden and its democracy. But, as Turner's successors have emphasized, virginity could be bought only at the cost of effacing the native Americans, killing them off as need be. For they were physical obstacles to this American way of life. If violence would redeem the land and regenerate the power of its new inhabitants, so creating true men tested by fire, it did so at great human cost. Now Turner's work represented a new scientific history, using demographic geography as part of its armamentarium. Not surprisingly for such methods, the horrors of violence tend to be muted by their mode of presentation.

The frontier was also the virile place, with none of the effete institutions of Europe and the East, institutions that maintained ascribed rather than achieved statuses. The West would be a place of merit and democracy, not of privilege. Pioneers demonstrated their potency in their actual lives, supposedly never having to rely on family connections or corrupt politics. Such pioneers were pure, cleansed by hard work—and genocide.

Virility requires that one stigmatize the effete and feminine and that one daringly excise those supposedly weak aspects of the self, deny any remnants, and be vigilant for any polluting female elements. Now unlike males, females need not be free of such pollutions. They retain their own integrity as long as they stay in their proper school-marm, married, or prostituted roles. What is crucial is a gender polar-ization, so that in such a fluid society there is a simulacrum of struc-ture and order. People-of-color are outside this order and are often treated as genderless, lacking in potency and generativity. They might well be a part of nature, to be cleared and consumed as need be.

There are problems with such a constructed virility, its construction being not only an artifice but one that is denied by manifest facts. In a society occupied mostly by males there will be homosexuality that is at least ambiguous in its meaning with respect to virility. And as I have already indicated, people-of-color are as likely as not to be actually quite fruitful and industrious. In response to these signs of impurity and productivity, which are then taken as rapaciousness, one may scapegoat and sacrifice a hapless male, Asian, or black.

As for purity, it is quite difficult to stay pure. For usually a very large number of rules are needed to delineate purity, and so there is likely to be violations. Consequently, one must have readily available purification rituals. To create whiteness or purity there needs to be means of legitimating past intermarriage with the natives, cleansing one's forebears and simplifying a complex and mixed heritage. There also needs to be a way of denying or forgetting the reasons for the original migrations, such as feuds over land or felonious criminality. Any corruption has to be something that happens elsewhere, namely, in the East: Far, Middle, or Coast.

Los Angeles is the place in the West which is perhaps most impure, most built out of crossed kinship lines and diverse traditions and eth-nicities. As is always the case, virginity is dubious, virility is founded on unvirtuous acts, and purity is a wondrous and shaky construction. Now what is interesting about Los Angeles and California is not the lack of violence as a means of regeneration and redemption. There is plenty of that, whether it be ethnic turf wars or labor conflict. Rather, as has been argued more generally for the history of capitalism, it is how often the gentle arts of commerce have performed the dirty work of cleaning things up. Those arts have allowed for the transmutation of rubbish into wealth, of pigment into whiteness, of shotgun marriage into pedigree. We have a remarkable alliance of imagination with dealmaking and moneymaking.

Los Angeles' downtown development, as in development more gen-

erally, has required an imaginative and institutional creation of speculative value—a vision of how rubbish land might be synergistically
transformed into future wealth, a vision supported by the institutions
of finance, state, and government. Such imaginative creation is a Los
Angeles specialty, whether it be the motion picture industry, water
projects and agriculture, or in architecture. It is a standard theme in
the historiography of California: the painting of rosy pictures to lure
settlers from the presumably inclement, inegalitarian, and less fertile
East. This is a pyramid scheme, the settled profiting off newcomers,
until depression recurrently if temporarily wrings out the market. Of
course, the Southern California military and aircraft industries are
large, have their own cycles, and are in many ways a replay of the
frontier theme and its morbid subtext.

Still, sweat equity competes quite successfully with speculation and
dealmaking as modes of pioneering. So-called white people now rely on
speculation to fabricate their wealth, whether it be through trading
up, building, or foreclosure, to use the relevant terms for real estate.
But people-of-color and poor immigrants more generally have traditionally been willing to work harder and to employ the whole family in
enterprise—at least in the first generation or so. And since Biblical
times the latter form of wealth and accumulation has been considered
more legitimate, and surely not so leechlike. If as pioneers the white
people once gained legitimacy through hard work and genocide, it is
now the people-of-color who have that legitimacy on their side, and
they need not kill anyone.

More poignantly, the system of virginity, virility, and purity depends on there being people who are other, to take out the garbage,
absorb the pollution, and do the rest of the dirty work. The devalued
people and rubbish that provides low cost labor and employs di-
lapidated housing stock is the source of the next generation's ro-
bustness and resilience. Rather than being arbitrarily other, many
such people proceed to be absolutely American, adopting and realizing
American ideals and dreams, and so transforming what it means to be
American. For to be American is otherness canonized.

That some of the Others do not become conventionally American is
sometimes employed to suggest racial inadequacy. But this defense
misses the pervasive consequence of the assimilation of the many
Others—that transformation of what it means to be American.

Those who claim to be pure want to label diversity and difference as
other, and as eliminable at least in principle. But we know sin through
our own sinfulness. And civilization is its discontents. It is the differences incorporated into oneself that then allow you to conceive of that

otherness, an otherness that you could then propose to efface. It is surely a diabolical temptation to try to wash off those spots that are the signs of one's identity.

What makes Los Angeles work and what makes the West work more generally are contradictory aspects in the dynamics of hierarchy and purity. Having sharply separated a secure core from a contingent periphery, whether it be a matter of primary and secondary economies as in economic dualism or of whites and people-of-color in racism, the separation is then breached to fulfill the needs of that seemingly self-sufficient and secure core. (Here we have a model of a Hegelian master-slave relationship.) The breach is enacted through processes of commerce and fantasy, sometimes gently, sometimes violently. So, for example, there is both a system of taboo and a system of ritual readjustment and relegitimation of the lines of division. Such a dual economy or racism allows the core or primary or white part to act as if it is natural and pure; its detritus is taken care of by the periphery or secondary or pigmented part. There are places other than Los Angeles in which a polluted virgin may be restored to purity through dowry, as well as through the blessings of ritual provided by public relations and advertising. But Los Angeles does so unashamedly, and with greater vigor than perhaps anyplace else.

Armchair pioneers may think Los Angeles is overdeveloped. But without the immigrants and the impurities, and their turbulence, Los Angeles would not be the world city it has become and of which those pioneers are often so proud. I have been harsh on the claimants to virginity, virility, and purity because they desire a history and society that would deny their own histories. And such a cleaned-up history would also deny just what it is that makes Los Angeles work.

While no one claims Los Angeles is Augustine's City of God, it is sometimes proclaimed on AM radio that Los Angeles is a Christian God's city. But most of its residents are not so sure. And easterners— east of the Rockies, west of Catalina, and all the way around the globe—seem more convinced of its unredeemable sinfulness. The motion picture industry, for example, is an invention of Jewish migrants to California. Although some Christians may still believe that it is the untrustworthiness of the Jews or other foreigners that makes the Others a corrupting force, the Jews and their more recent representatives from Asian, Islamic, and Hispanic countries like to think that they are exemplars of the American way of enterprise, thrift, and individualism.

Immigrants and migrants more generally, insofar as they are successful, must violate the prevailing system of purity and pollution. And it is in the nature of the market economies that such violations are possible. One becomes well off, and in the next generation one's children fit into a rather inhomogenous white world.

America is fascinated by Los Angeles because Los Angeles displays the country's history, especially the parts we might want to forget. And it displays the country's hopes, as well as the future consequences we might want to ignore. I am not sure there can be a frontier without violence. But ethnicity on the frontier may be more plural and less a matter of hierarchical domination than in more established places. And when ethnic consciousness returns to the fore, as it surely will in the second and third generations, it is in the context of the now transformed white world.

To an intellectual's sense of righteousness, I suspect that what is most disturbing about the combination of practical religiosity and pious commerce so characteristic of Los Angeles is that the combination is productive and lively and is as well a liberating force. Such an interplay of religion and commerce has traditionally made for an analytical handle on modern society, and for an engine for growth. Still, such a combination leaves behind those who cannot participate in that society, and they might well be annihilated. If we take Los Angeles as representing an epitome of Western modernization, the challenge facing Los Angeles is whether a place must regenerate itself through violence. Can civic plurality and comparative abundance be satisfying enough, so that those who are most powerful do not have to kill the Other?

Put differently, the insidious aspect of racism is not mainly its caricaturing of people, but its treating some people as positively and purely white, and the rest as negatively polluted and impure, a matter of domination and annihilation. True plurality and difference make racism somewhat less problematic and surely less sharply defined. Now Los Angeles might thrive much in the same way as a putatively white aggressive team is dominant; or it might also thrive much as a more mixed race, feisty but generous team is triumphant. (Here I am thinking, circa 1985, of the Boston Celtics basketball team under Larry Bird, in contrast to the University of Southern California's Women of Troy basketball team under Cheryl Miller.) Neither represents old money, ascribed status, or traditional institutions. What they do represent is different ways in which the West may be won—by domination or by plurality. And in Los Angeles, the game is on.

Bringing Up Baby

IF OUR WORLD IS marginal and may be added up, it is as well resistant to that strategy and is discontinuous, nonlinear, nonconservative, sacred, and historical. Even if Marshall was right in asserting that nature does not make jumps, notions of bigness, stickiness, fluctuation, perversion, and fetishism and taboo are not likely to be retired by smoothing out the world or by any straightforward reductionist program.

These seemingly contradictory features are equiprimordially present in our world. We find ourselves within a dialectic of marginalism and discontinuity, mechanism and design, object and anima, and tradition and invention. We need all the various accounts of ourselves, whether they be the marginalist models which are predictive, the discontinuist and sacred models which are retrospective, or the transitional models which are experientially verisimilitudinous.

Whether it be marginal or discontinuous, the world may be taken toolishly. As a practice toolishness allows us to be committed to a way of getting ahold of the world without ideologically or philosophically being forced to deny other ways. Our commitment is provisional. We may carry the various models over to other disciplines, accumulating new examples and then returning home, the models now transformed by their additional concrete uses. We are productive because we concentrate on functions and on how tools let us get at the world, rather than what the world is really like.

Now the provisional character of a radical toolishness is perhaps insufficiently dogmatic to be an avowed commitment for many people. Try this first, try that next—the resolutely toolish and perverted approach—seems a poor comfort, even if it may work. Surely people are toolish in their everyday practice, but it is restricted to a particular toolkit. Most people are quite conventional, picking just one dialectical pole or one kind of model, and then going to work quite fruitfully. In order to do any work at all, even the self-proclaimed toolish physicist must usually work within and master a particular tradition. And on the Sabbath physicists want to hear orthodox and systematic doctrine and homily.

Moreover, toolishness and provisionality are not always a virtue. Toolishness might not be attractive to the critic or to the political theorist who describes a good society, and in fact toolishness is often taken as destructive of such efforts. Toolishness's cheerful openness to their critical perspectives, as just another provision of the world, is not greeted with delight but rather as an attempt to coopt their radical stance.

More practically, toolishness may not always be a good strategy, especially if the situation is transitional and both-and. As indicated in the introduction, for bringing up baby, no tool just works. Rather than your taking on a provision of the world and then going to work, initially there are several provisions simultaneously and equally present. And the situation is also deeply and unavoidably historical.

For when my baby wakes in the late evening screaming and shuddering with fear, and not simply crying, I just expect we'll work it out together. There may be no answer, no tool, and no handle to grip. But we do know what to do.

For tonight's a new kind of upset, and he cannot put himself together as he ordinarily does. So my usual talents fail me, and so do his. We are lost, or so it seems. No policy works, and it is not clear what the issue is. Eventually we both are exhausted and fall asleep. But the next time, which otherwise seems the same as before, I turn on the light, we play while he sobs, and in two minutes he rubs his eyes and wants to go back to bed. We have invented a second goodnight. The issue is not how I manage him, or my being firm, or my giving in to him, as it is often portrayed in the baby books. Rather, how do both of us reconstitute ourselves so that we can go on? How are we to abide by and understand each other?

Here is a potentially not so toolish world. Baby's crying is not so easily managed or fixed or repaired. And baby is autonomous and inventive, and he does have the capacity to organize himself. So we try one thing, then another, and then another, and something finally works; and it is that sequence of failures and successes that matters and is said to work. That the last thing we do is what works says that history matters, and that what led up to the present prepares us for what we will do next. Here change is conversionary, our past preparing us for transformation.

Eliminating all or even most of the seemingly ineffective moves, the ones before the last one, is a lovely fantasy. But in conversion there is no way to avoid history. And practically, avoiding mistakes has only a little to do with what I must do this first night.

Although we'll eventually establish new effective patterns, no single fix works reliably, for it will not work in some slightly different contexts. And in sequentially trying out the various remedies I change my baby's mood and my own, perhaps exhausting myself and him along the way. And perhaps it might have worked just as well to have done nothing, but that null hypothesis is hard to take for being caring. Life is a contaminated experiment, and I will never know for sure which part of the sequence made the difference, and whether it is a part rather than that whole historical sequence which worked. None of this prevents my doing better, and my finding patterns of action that work well most of the time.

The desideratum, the requisite talent is to be able to recognize moves that are beginning to make a difference and to exploit them—while baby is still mostly screaming, both of us are exhausted, I am frustrated, and those same moves may not have worked minutes before. This time it is a lullaby, or perhaps television, or perhaps a bottle. And so I may capture the hysteria and allow it to be focused. Or perhaps he might cry for a minute or so, and then calm himself down.

In these contexts, good advice may be of three sorts: Try this, then try that, then try this, then take a break, ... The suggestions are provisional, offered nonjudgmentally, meant as reminders of what might work. They provide new avenues for action after you have exhausted your own list and yourself, and help to shake you out of your own traps. Even more useful is a theory about what baby is doing, feeling, and experiencing; and then practical suggestions for action based on that theory. If baby is taken as a soulful and self-disciplined creature with authentic motives, like you yourself, the theory will allow you to have a feeling for him which puts you in his place. If that theory is also about yourself and what you are experiencing, it will make even greater sense, giving you both courage and the comfort of recognition.

What works surely depends on past history, the moment, this baby's character—a situation that is fully loaded with meaning and is multiply meaningful. The artist Robert Irwin describes the relevant experience, but in parimutuel betting at the race track: "The thing about the race track is the incredibly wide range of information that has a bearing. If you're going to have a chance there, you have to achieve the discipline necessary for keeping track of all of it. The one thing more than anything else is learning to pay attention . . . and then *it's like you run your hand over the race.*" Here the metaphor is not tools, methods, and management, so much as witness, testimony, and care and devotion—Winnicott's good-enough mother. You meet the challenge of fortune with virtue, so that you and your baby make the best of what you have been given. Luckily the baby is a going concern, and is willing to train his parents to treat him in just the right way. All we need do is to pay attention to what is going on.

There will always be realms of experience that are stubbornly transitional, like bringing up baby. In practice, these realms are resistant to advice and action based on a dialectic of mechanism and holism, resistant even to toolishness itself. And yet it is just in this realm that new tools are invented, and very different ways of being are realized.

Notes

PREFACE AND INTRODUCTION
The emphasis on tools can be found in Heidegger, or Kuhn, or in contemporary work in artificial intelligence. Insofar as toolishness is a Kantian legacy, formalism and structuralism are its strengths and its weaknesses. Analogy tends to efface detail and history, no mean losses. Conversely, insofar as toolishness is a rhetoric, it is meant to challenge tradition and the sacred.

See Gould (1982), Mayr, and Lovejoy on saltationism in nature and on *Natura non facit saltum*. Evolutionary theory is a discipline in which gradualism versus saltationism or discontinuity, and the nature of individuals (genes, organisms, species), has been the subject of extraordinarily lively argument. It is not coincidental that these arguments mirror those concerning market economies. Darwin was quite aware of the Invisible Hand, as well as the Great Chain of Being (that then becomes a Marshallian gradation). See also Levins.

See Kuhn (1987) and I. B. Cohen for some argument on the historiographical problems associated with revolution.

The different signs in the Hamiltonian formulation of classical mechanics reflects the fact that it is set in a symplectic space, that is, a space in which there exists an oriented volume ($\vec{dq} \times \vec{dp}$), which in classical mechanics is conserved (Liouville's theorem). See Arnold on Hamiltonians and their geometry. Schackle discusses marginalism in economics. See Mirowski on the nineteenth-century origins of economics and marginalism in physics, and Stigler for some developments in statistics.

On the models of urban change, see Krieger (1971) and also Schelling. Note that explanations of racial spatial segregation between neighborhoods, ones that are made in terms of individual preferences and freely made moves, cannot afford to ignore discriminatory redlining by bankers and real estate agents, as well as generational instabilities due to the aging of an area's residents.

I suspect that treating trees or animals as persons only leads to an inappropriate respect for Nature, and perhaps even an "overpopulation"; and that a whole earth philosophy denies us the benefits of distant garbage disposal and so the control of disease. See Tribe for a criticism of my position on artifice. On religion, see Krieger (1987).

My naive nominalism in the description of how we use models and understand them is motivated by the observation that this is actually how it seems to most users of models. And that semblance influences how they act. See chapter 6, where I get into further trouble of this sort. See Hacking (1984).

The traditional arguments concerning the relationship of faith, conceived of as transcendent, to science, conceived of as rational and mundane, parallel the ones presented here. It is Luther's and Kant's achievements to have defined a mode of coexistence of the two. See Gerrish on Luther.

On methodological individualism, see Buchanan. Scarf describes the nature of the Invisible Hand in modern terms. General equilibrium is a matter of invariance to rearrangement and of fixed points in transformations. See Mendelsohn and Bochner for a history of smoothness and discontinuity. On conversion, see Freccero and Marris, as well as Kuhn.

I have chosen to feature phase transitions as models of discreteness and discontinuity rather than photons (light particles) or the discrete energy levels of atoms. Surely phase transitions are the most powerful yet familiar physical example of discreteness and discontinuity. Water freezes, and at roughly 32°F two phases coexist as in iced tea. And permanent magnets keep refrigerators closed. Also, we may avoid the veil of sensationalism surrounding photons and the quantum discontinuity, yet retain all the scientifically and intellectually interesting features of quantum theory, by concentrating on condensed matter.

In the case of phase transitions or the stability of particles, one obtains the possibility of discontinuity and a "freezing out" into discrete states, namely, a transition temperature, in part because of some boundary restriction— whether it be the infinite volume and continuum limits of statistical systems or the bound state of single atoms. Also, all these problems may be treated as many-body problems, whether they be about the statistical mechanics of phase transitions or the quantum field theory of particles and their interactions.

Winnicott describes transitionality, and Venturi is the source on both-and. I paraphrase and also quote phrases of Winnicott here.

CHAPTER ONE

The reduction of big to little is not a new development, and the classical modes of dialectic and rhetoric and the Hebraic modes of Talmudic exegesis and interpretation were ways that one could methodically get at big problems. But since early modern times the emphasis in getting at big problems has been less on discourse and exegesis and more on an arithmetic for putting things together.

Braybrooke distinguishes small and large changes in a somewhat different fashion than I do here.

For Darwinian evolution, a universal measure of value is provided by fitness. The process of exchange takes place in the zygote, or in populations among genes; variation is the randomizing work; and the Central Dogma of molecular genetics guarantees the independence of each gene from its environment, the notion of a gene being about (almost) independent units.

Simon (1957) emphasizes how satisficing and organizational strategies are about stability, equilibrium, and adaptation. They are more about averages than about marginal effects and optimization. Still, one can develop on a different level of aggregation an effective marginal calculus for these cases, as one does in thermodynamics. Mirowski indicates some of the difficulties of adapting the physics formalism to economics: What is conserved?

The process of tâtonnement or arbitrage, in coming to equilibrium in a market, is an example of building something up marginally—at least if one is close to equilibrium. And the renormalization group with its similarity transformations or its use of continuous dimensions, and the density functional theory of phase transitions (Haymet), are ways of making the development of a discontinuity marginal and smooth.

On gift relationships and the residuals of exchange, the classic source is Mauss. On Augustine, see Brown; and on early Christianity and conversion, see Macmullen. Kahrl describes the Owens Valley water project. I. B. Cohen gives a set of historiographic criteria for recognizing revolution, while Kuhn (1987) offers a set of cognitive and conceptual criteria.

As for public projects: "All the predictive mechanisms economists use are valid over short periods of time for small changes. Here [for a nuclear plant] we're talking big changes—$3 billion is a big shock—and over long periods. What that means is there is a very high level of intrinsic uncertainty in the predictive process. How are you going to grapple with that?" John Marburger, Chairman of the New York Governor's Commission on the Shoreham Nuclear Power Plant.

The Schumpeter quotation comes from Schumpeter (1934, p. 64).

I discuss conversion in Krieger (1981, pt. 2). See especially Freccero. The margin or "marge" is an inverted reflection of both the before and the after world, for which see Turner. Thompson is the source on rubbish. Goodman takes the Aristotelian tack on narrative.

Kuhn (1987) gives a vivid description of his own conversion experience, in his reading of Aristotle. His more general point is that a scientific theory is a confession, because it not only gives an account of the truth, but often gives an account of how that truth was missed in the predecessor "false" theory. Kuhn (1984, p. 236) argues that even if we report a revolutionary change, often the process is altogether more "continuous." "The stages that prepare the way to fundamental innovation are seen to be more numerous than they seemed before, but also individually smaller, more fully prepared, more obviously within the reach of an exceptionally capable person."

On random processes, see Arthur, J. Cohen, and Schelling. See Anderson (1984) for a lovely survey of the kinds of discontinuity and phase transition, including broken symmetry, nonlinearity, and percolation.

In physics, the great advance in understanding discontinuous changes such as the onset of the spontaneous magnetizability of an iron bar was a matter of finding new subparts and new modes of addition: namely, ways of forming nested blocks of molecules, and the so-called renormalization group to in effect perform the addition. The discontinuity then became the limit of a doable and continuous process. It is as well a fixed point of a transformation, and that is how it is marked off without explicitly talking about discontinuity. See Wilson (1975, 1979).

More generally, thermodynamics is a "limit" science. Quantities such as the free energy are defined in the limit of infinite volumes and infinite numbers of particles (N/V being held constant). And it is just in those limits that phase transitions are theoretically possible, since functions that are smooth and analytic can break down and exhibit discontinuity in the limit. We return to this in chapter 2.

Preemption and surprise is intrinsically historical and particular, and in everyday life we assume that how one does something should affect the outcome. Invariance and independence, like Heavenly eternity, are remarkable abstractions, and that they work at all is testimony to the peculiar character of parts of the microscopic world of physics and economics.

Consider the following example of oligopolistic competition. If each of the small number of producers in an industry assumes that the others are rational, yet is otherwise ignorant of their plans, there is an optimal smooth mode of growth of the industry. But if one producer clandestinely and irrationally decides to go for broke, defecting as in a prisoners' dilemma situation, the outcome is chancy—perhaps others will have decided to do so, too, and which of the others?—and not at all so predictable. *Marginalism adds up invariantly; discontinuity is historical.* See Porter for this example in greater detail.

The oppositions and mediations in this culture of decisionmaking are constructions and are surely not exact. The gap falls more naturally under taboo, while entrepreneurship falls more naturally under action—neither quite in the middle. But none of this is obvious or necessary, even if it is made to seem logical. It is derived from trying to account for what we do. The proof of the value of such a structure will lay in its organizing power.

See Scarf on the composition of markets. The problem of equilibrium concerns multi-market optimality as well as market clearing. Probabilistic decision theory need not find the best case if the shape of the universe is peculiar.

On skeptical doubt, see Clarke. On Mosaic leadership, see Walzer and Wildavsky. The planner Robert Moses is described by Caro as an actor, and so is Mulholland described by Kahrl. Caro's description reads as a dramatic cartoon.

The logical problems of decisionmaking are not restricted to the mundane world, but come up in the construction of the transcendent one as well. Another useful analogy is based on gender, where the genders are treated as if they were in opposition. So that actors are male and inseminating, but managers are female and housekeeping. The theological analogy reminds us that decisions are often made in the context of a concern for perfection, while the gender analogy reminds us of the concern for domination and purity. I am not unaware of the gender biases built into my descriptions of the culture, and I would maintain that those biases are reflected in conventional conceptions of the practices.

It is significant that pregnancy as a model for the gap is not conventionally treated as a form of action. It is not a matter of transcending the world, for it is taken as automatic. A less conventional view would speak of the world as animate, of action as cooperative, and of homemaking as Godly provision. But this unconventional world, and the roles it implies, is just what is often left out of the culture of decisionmaking (but see entrepreneurship). See Krieger (1988) on courage and analogies to sport.

On judgment, see Kant in *The Critique of Judgment;* and Arendt (1982) on Kant. Note that virtue is male and Fortuna is female, and that Fortuna and Clio are wily women yet to be tamed by men. See Pocock, Shklar, and Pitkin.

Action and judgment can become practices characteristic of a world rather than roles distinctive from it. If the rules of marginalism or taboo are followed, then action becomes incremental or traditional, and judgment becomes a titrational balancing (as in cost-benefit analysis) or legalistic.

Middles and mixtures are characteristic of big decisions. Big decisions are taken as outside an allocative and accounting economy. See chapter 5. They are the place where grace and bounty appear. For it is in the middle where value is created and maintained, where meaning is given, and where responsibility arises—through taboo, ambiguity, and choice, respectively. Actual history is the way middles are temporally resolved, and it is where will is expressed, where specific paths are realized, and where responsibility is made actual—where big decisions happen. See Bataille, Douglas, Douglas and Wildavsky, and Tigerman.

In my discussion of entrepreneurship, the working out of the notion of chance-taking and risk in part reflects the history of probability. Put differently but obviously, there is an intimate connection between social or economic organization and our conceptual notions of chance. More generally, the discussion concerns the relationship between rights, desert, and the possibility of attributing individual agency, characteristic of contemporary discussions of justice. Here we encounter the so-called Cambridge controversy: Can effects be localized and marginal and so be attributed to individuals, and in this manner be employed to establish ownership? See also Schumpeter on the entrepreneur.

I use *independence* in several ways in the text: statistical independence of random variables, linear independence of basis vectors, and path independence of properties.

Hill-climbing does not always work. There are discontinuities and boundaries for which the direction of approach in maximizing is crucial. But these are to be treated as special cases. There are as well interesting and important cases, such as in statistical search, in which how one gets there determines whether one will get to the topmost point. But usually satisficing strategies are sufficient. Wilson's "statistical continuum limit" (1975) is a way of saying how there is an invariance to the direction of approach to a continuum from a discrete lattice. See also Kirkpatrick.

On phase transitions as models, see Krieger (1971, 1981) and Henry Adams on "The Rule of Phase Applied to History," in which J. W. Gibbs is the featured player.

One might be tempted to try to find a set of rules for recognizing big decisions, say according to the quantity of resources employed, the momentousness of the transformation, or the degree of discontinuity, abruptness, and uniqueness. More likely, however, a decision is big because we can take it as big and act accordingly. We cannot surely know or recognize a big decision prospectively.

CHAPTER TWO

Wigner is the most popular reference for the trope concerning mathematics' utility. And, of course, there is Kant's account of the transcendental categories. See Restivo for a review of the why-mathematics-works literature. See also Aspray. Jaffe discusses the mutual adaption of mathematics and the way we set up the world. Other arguments suggest that since mathematics abstracts some of the most general of the world's patterns, its utility follows naturally. See MacLane and Steen.

Adding up the world is often an ironic enterprise. The basic theme goes back at least to Adam Smith and Hegel, that the Invisible Hand or the Cunning of Reason is such that our individual motivations may not have the effects and meanings we originally thought they would, yet the world is orderly and our individual actions are efficient nonetheless. So-called counterintuitive results are a matter of our not appreciating the wisdom of Providence, namely, the emergent systematic order of the world. See also Levins on Cartesianism.

We often find little pieces by tweaking the world and seeing if it responds in an incremental way. Shock a crystal and see how it vibrates. Now a tweak could completely transform an object, causing a phase transition or a revolution. But some of the time tweaking stimulates the appearance of (pseudo-) individuals, such as the phonons of the crystal's vibrating atomic lattice.

In a metal the interactions of the electrons with each other should be quite substantial, and we should not be able to disentangle them in any simple way. There might well be no well-defined little effects. But it turns out that for tweaks that are not too large (a region of some interest), the crystal looks as if it is inhabited by particles behaving almost like electrons, with roughly the same properties. These quasi-particles (or elementary excitations) move freely through the crystal, although we know that the actual electrons do not. See Anderson (1984) for a lovely exposition.

One other example. The nucleus is filled with strongly interacting neutrons and protons. We should not be able to disentangle their interactions or even observe discrete particles in that nuclear soup. But some of the time we can, for two reasons. First, the fundamental forces have a particular (anti-)symmetry since the particles are fermions. Consequently, there is subgrouping or shell-model effects that cancel out many of the interactions, leaving some particles comparatively free. Second, when the nucleons interact strongly, they form collective excitations, such as vibrations of the whole nucleus, each mode of which looks like a simple free particle.

On smoothness, see Wilson (1975, 1979) on "the search for analyticity," continuum limits, and the $4 - \epsilon$ expansion in the theory of phase transitions. Wilson's procedure makes explicit use of the hierarchies of forces to tame problems. At every stage or strength of force one tries to deal with only those degrees of freedom "relevant" to that stage. Maxwell's construction in thermodynamics uses a more commodious space to achieve smoothness and continuity.

On versatility, I follow Hacking (1983), who equates versatility with realness.

Derivatives provide for a nice algebra (the derivative of f times g is defined, for example), but given the size of a function its derivative remains unbounded. In contrast, integrals are good for estimating sizes, but are not so nicely algebraic (the integral of f times g is not readily defined in terms of the integrals of f and of g). Derivatives define good objects which then may be added up by the integral. This is not a tautology or an identity, but rather it is practical guidance. To find the length of a path, the prescription is to find the velocities or marginals or derivatives, and add them up.

On oriented addition: Each bit of volume or surface or distance can have a sign or vector associated with it reflecting its direction or orientation. And effects of different sign or charge can cancel each other. As indicated earlier in the notes, in Hamiltonian dynamics the Liouville conservation of volume in phase space means that the volume element must be antisymmetric (which, as $\overrightarrow{dq} \times \overrightarrow{dp}$, it surely is), for the same reason. Given such an oriented addition, we may then have a Fundamental Theorem of the calculus, including Stokes theorem, and we can write conservation laws. See Misner.

Nonlinear systems may exhibit addable and superposable objects—such as solitons, most elementary particles, or the polarization vector for electric polarizability in bulk matter.

Lebesgue integration gets around "unimportant" unsmoothnesses and discontinuity.

Steering is exemplified in LOGO, with its comfortableness with line integrals and differential geometry. See Abelson and diSessa. The relationship of local to global will have some problems if there are multiple maxima.

The addition rules may seem otherwise curious, reflecting perhaps deeper linearities. So in adding independent random variables, we add their variances. The Poincaré spacetime symmetry of special relativity leads to the Lorentz rules for the addition of velocities and other non-four-vectors. And as we shall see, we may find ourselves performing what seems like conventional addition, but it is represented as phase integrals or sums ($\Sigma_j\, e^{i\theta_j}$), when we add up electromagnetic field strengths in optics, quantum mechanical amplitudes, and steps in a random walk.

One does not immediately add amplitudes in harmonic or springlike systems, even given that such systems are at equilibrium, if correlation among the modes of vibration is substantial. One must first find the uncorrelated amplitudes, measures of the normal modes, before doing that addition. Then one may add excitation amplitudes for each mode in a nicely vectorial fashion. And then one may add the squares of those amplitudes, the energies of all the modes, arithmetically.

As in general equilibrium in a market economy, or equilibrium in a mechanical system, a global optimization rule for a sum may have an equivalent surrogate local rule for each of its summands—the sum being of local quantitites, such as costs or energies—even if there are additive constraints such as on the total energy. What is optimal for any single individual, given that it is part of the system, will be optimal for the whole. See also chapter 1.

See Feynman (1964) on $\delta \int L \, dt = 0$ implies $\delta L = 0$ along the path. Feynman often shows how the interference of some relevant phases is coherent along an extremal path.

Concerning integrating factors, there is the more general story of gauges and homologies. Path dependence is also expressed by non-zero Poisson brackets or commutators. These latter make for interesting action integrals, and so in a profound sense they make for physics.

On hierarchies of collected objects, see Kitcher.

On the method of steepest descent in computing the partition function of statistical mechanics, see Fowler; and also Huang on the Darwin-Fowler method.

As indicated in the text, nice well-defined classical notions are the consequence of sharp identities of the mean and the mode, as expressed in the interference of phases in quantum mechanics, in the notion of a temperature (in the Darwin-Fowler derivation of the partition function), or in diffusion as a consequence of Brownian motion. In the latter case the large variance for any single random walk is relatively narrowed by the very large number of particles participating in the diffusion process.

As mentioned earlier, we compute the electrostatic energy of a crystal by forming superlattices, each cell of which is electrically neutral (Ewald sums). Or we may divide the spins in a ferromagnet into blocks, assigning a summary spin to each block. As we scale up, we can use the self-similarity (rather than a length scale or linearization, as in perturbation expansions) to more or less completely take account of the interconnections among pieces, and so "thin out the degrees of freedom" (Wilson, 1975).

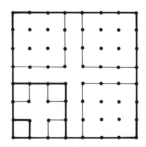

(So one also defines new scaling variables which are smooth and subject to the calculus.) Interaction and correlation between a part of a sublattice and a part of another sublattice or superlattice are either small (that is, like the triangular leftover parts in Riemann sums, with their unimportance in the limit) or at least we can get a handle onto them in some tractable analytic way. This mode of grouping can handle sub- to superlattice correlation and interaction; it is meant to do so. Wilson (1975) discusses the enumeration of the various leftover interactions. The form of addition here is a semigroup, and the limit is called the statistical continuum limit. See Wilson (1975, 1979).

Wilson (1975, pp. 773–774) is worth careful reading concerning the philosophy of continuum limits. If Nature is described locally, then the local equations require continuum limits, namely, a derivative; and associated with such a derivative is a characteristic length over which the system may be treated as if it is linear. But if one is concerned with statistical averages or going from a lattice to a continuum, as modes of approximation, then as we have mentioned there is another limit, the statistical continuum limit. For if the quantities of concern are to be defined locally one has a problem; there is no well-defined length scale. Instead one discovers there is a something like a scaling variable, the exponent μ in t^{μ}, which surrogates for a length scale. The linearity of the derivative becomes the similarity in a renormalization transformation.

Anderson (1984, pp. 213–214) argues for "an attempt to look at larger and larger groupings of animals, people, or whatever, as averages or distributions over their internal degrees of freedom, and then to allow the larger groupings to interact. . . ."

See Anderson (1984, pp. 49–51) on rigidity and infinite volume limits. Macroscopic rigidity is quite remarkable from a microscopic point of view and reflects the appearance of an order parameter at phase transition.

On patterns of fluctuations, see Kac and Mandelbrot.

On adding up in computation, "Progress in computer science comes from putting things together. Progress in physics comes from taking them apart" (Hillis). One can imagine a physics that is not about the Fundamental Theorem, but is rather about general properties of algorithms and recursive functions.

Linear excitations are a way of getting at the derivative. They also explore the degeneracies or symmetries of the ground state.

The ground state may be said to hide the complex interactional processes that added up one way or another to produce it—whether that state is a market, an individual atom or particle, or a crystal. We cannot go back on the addition process; we have a semigroup property. In effect there is a cognitive and literal shield provided by a surface, or equilibrium, or the infinite volume limit. What we do see are the marginal leftovers: individual marginal transactions in a market and elementary and collective excitations of a crystal. As indicated earlier, tweaking or plucking gently to get an excitation, in effect taking derivatives, turns out to produce and characterize well-defined states or particles, where the derivatives' values are measures of the states' properties. And the interactions of these leftovers with the external world is linear, a charge times a field, for example.

The quotation on perturbation theory comes from Bender and Orszag (p. 319). The perturbation expansion is only in the spirit of the Fundamental

Theorem, since it is actually an asymptotic expansion that will eventually blow up. What is crucial if the method is to be useful is that there be a qualitative demarcation between the ground state and the perturbed one: a degenerate ground state atom versus its excitations, such as without and then with an external magnetic field; an isolated equilibrium state versus external interactions; or a cold crystal versus its thermal or phonon excitations.

"The way one identifies the states of the system usually relies very much on the success of the perturbation theory: one starts with a zeroth order approximation to the theory in which the states are easily recognized. The full theory is recovered by adding a small perturbation to the idealized zeroth order theory. Then the effects of this *small* perturbation on the idealized zeroth order states are computed. These steps are possible only when one can recognize the full theory in terms of a small perturbation on a simple system and, having done that, calculate corrections to the idealized zeroth order states. As an example of this procedure, consider quantum electrodynamics QED where a small parameter α, roughly equal to 1/137, is easily recognized. Then the zeroth order theory is that for which $\alpha = 0$. It is easily identified in terms of *idealized* photon and electron (or muon, tau, quark, . . .) states. The effect of the interaction is then computed on these states and their interactions order by order in α. After some trickery (that is, renormalization theory), these corrections are found to yield physical electron and photon states and their interactions. The point of this discussion is to emphasize the reliance of the success of QED on our ability to recognize the emergence of idealized electron- and photon-like states in a zeroth order theory. This procedure was made possible because α is a *small* number, otherwise such a recognition could not have been made" (Ramond, pp. 88–89).

On Leibniz, see Edwards (p. 232).

On the doability of the various phase integrals, see, for example, Feynman and Hibbs, where it is a recurrent concern.

See Creutz, Brush (1961), Feynman and Hibbs, and Glimm and Jaffe on the phase integral analogies, analogies pursued at the levels of differential equations, propagators or Green's functions, and as sums over states. It should be noted that the Gaussian (Feynman-Kac) and Poisson (Gibbs) processes are quite different even if they are formally similar. These formal similarities may lead to modes of asymptotic approximation, such as methods of stationary phase and steepest descent. The existence of a diffusion constant for a gas or a propagation direction for light, as well as the Darwin-Fowler method for deriving a notion of temperature (and the canonical ensemble) in statistical mechanics, are all about coherent addition or a pole in an integral (and the sharp identity of mean and mode), as indicated earlier.

In the Darwin-Fowler method, the fact that the temperature is well defined for the system means that one never need actually do the integral, for most quantities of interest are functionals of the integral—and the integral factors out.

In paying attention to different measurements and physical variables, scaling also led to the block spin transformation ideas of Leo Kadanoff. It also led to new algorithmic procedures for doing the sums of the partition function, and to Kenneth Wilson renormalization group formulation of the problem and to his and Fisher's work on dimensionality as a variable. See Brush for a brief history. What was once a problem in the theory of complex variables has become a computational and combinatoric one about "managing" a lattice.

On integration by parts, see Edwards (p. 244); Feynman (1964, II-19-5). As for quadratures and tangents, see Edwards (p. 247) on Leibnitz: a quadrature, $\int_a^b y\, dx = (\int_a^b z\, dx + xy_a^b)/2$, where $z = y - x\, dy/dx$, a tangent line. Substituting z in the above formula gives integration by parts. See Feynman (1981) on gauge theories in two-plus-one dimensions, on how A_μ and $\partial A_\mu/\partial t$ are connected, and on how variations in one affect variations in the other. See Misner for the relationship of fields, sources, and potentials, "wiring up the field," and the constraints this induces. See Bender (chap. 6.3) for more on how one arranges constraints so that integration by parts may be used.

Note that if $D = d/dx$, then the commutator $[D, x] = 1$, an operator equality (which is also the definition of quantum mechanical momentum and position), is a restatement of integration by parts. Again, the definition of the derivative (D) and its inverse (the antiderivative or the indefinite integral) implies integration by parts.

On economics and marginalism, see Schackle and Mirowski. Schackle points out that the human psychology implicit in marginalism says that what counts are differences, and indifferences. He also argues that the calculus is secondary to the simultaneous equations aspects of economics, that is, general equilibrium. See M. Schabas in *Isis* 80:60–73.

A case can be made that the employment of the calculus is actually a ritual—a practical procedure meant to have transcendent effects, here mathematical manipulations meant to lead to truth about the world. The crucial fact is that rituals must give an account of when they do not work or other rituals may well displace them. See Evans-Pritchard and Sahlins. A ritual "works" in the context of a particular historical circumstance which also delineates acceptable alterations, ones that do not invalidate the ritual, alterations both in our goals and in the ritual's operation.

To be a scientist is to master the received tradition of a particular science so as to perform its practices appropriately and to provide the correct justifications for one's practice. To say that a tool works is to say that it is effective in the appropriate way in particular circumstances. An apprentice may at first perform the rituals thoughtlessly, and only later come to understand the doctrinal and theoretical justification. A new tool such as the calculus or quantum theory is used at first because it works—it successfully takes on prevailing problems, although its principles are only dimly understood by most adopters. Only later are the principles appreciated more fully by the journeyman user.

As a rather different example, consider early commitments to Christianity, many of which were based on miraculous healings. The consequent professions of conversion to Christianity meant neither articulated doctrinal commitment nor the exclusion of other religions. Only in subsequent generations does Christianity become an orthodoxy. See Macmullen.

The play of history and structure is, of course, a pervasive contemporary theme. Kripke emphasizes the relationship of scientific findings to our philosophic notions; Hacking (1983) shows that *how* we discover what things are is about *what* they really are; and Sahlins, reversing the usual anthropology of taboos, argues that the performative creates the prescriptive, the tools create the categories.

Kitcher argues, ". . . we might consider arithmetic to be true in virtue not of what *we can do* to the world, but rather of what *the world* will let us do *to it* . . . arithmetic describes those structural features of the world in virtue of which we are able to segregate and recombine objects" (p. 108); ". . . *To collect is to achieve* a certain type of representation, and, when we perform higher-order collectings, representations achieved in previous collecting may be used as materials out of which a new representation is generated" (p. 129). This suggests that the calculus is something the world allows, and the crucial features the calculus exhibits might be said to be arithmetic.

Marshall's Preface is a paean to a Principle of Continuity.

CHAPTER THREE

I should note that much of what I say here is drawn directly from Keller, Arthur, and J. Cohen, both in specifics and in tone.

The quotation on islands comes from MacArthur (p. 94).

Lynch has a beautiful survey of theories of city form and reasons given for centralization. Webber is the standard source on aspatial urban life.

My notions on the various stochastic models are taken from Arthur, Cohen, Schelling, and Krieger (1971). See Feller (vol. 1, chap. 3) on fluctuations in random walks. Keller (1985) presents a dissection of the problems associated with the allegiance to centralization; I draw directly from her work on the slime mold. Kubler discusses "prime works." On surprise, see Thompson and Tayler.

On Ising models, see, for example, Wilson (1979).

Foucault gives a description of authorship, a standard problem in humanistic work. The idea that there is a center is called "phallocentrism" by contemporary French thinkers. Schulman describes how galaxies are formed through percolation mechanisms. Pratt suggests how fluctuations might be tamed; E. O. Wilson, in his epilog, presses his commitment to explaining complex processes in terms of interacting individuals; and my remarks on polycentricity and this paper itself were triggered by reading Gordon.

On dynamical systems theory, see Schöner. On there being just a few relevant variables in complex systems, see Weinberg, who is quite eloquent on this point. See also Wilson (1979) on "irrelevant" and "relevant" variables, the relevant ones being those that survive scaling transformations and are not averaged out. See Anderson's exposition on "rigidity" (1984) for a generic discussion of the consequences of broken symmetry, and of the kinds of centralization that ensue.

See Viner on God, Providence, and mechanism.

See Krieger (1973) on plastic trees and the creation of value. I have not discussed some of the problems associated with sacred centers. For example, were one to try to explain Jesus of Nazareth as Christ, one might examine other Judaic sects in Roman times and messianic candidates of other periods. But in general, sacred centers, including the failed pretenders, are thought to be of a distinctly different character than mundane centers. So comparative analysis may not be relevant.

Einstein, in 1905, showed the connection between fluctuation and diffusion. See Pais. Cellular automata provide a nice example of a centralized coding system with very substantial power. See Wolfram.

Planners sometimes act as if their plans were "genetic," projects merely being realizations of the master plan, with, of course, the inevitable political influences of the environment on the original plan. The modes of reading off the code, namely, practice, and its origin are of some current research interest.

It has been suggested that the central molecule is not DNA but RNA, since the latter not only encodes information but also possesses enzymatic activity. This displacement of the center does not, it seems, deny the fact of centralization; it merely changes its locus.

CHAPTER FOUR

Feynman (1964, I-46) shows how a ratchet and pawl only works if the ambient temperature is low enough to limit thermal excitations that might allow the pawl to loosen its grip and so allowing the mechanism to go backward. He also connects the mechanism's unidirectionality with the arrow of time and the increase of entropy. The asymmetricality of stickiness depends on the mean energy or excitation being low enough, and that there be memory or historical time. As indicated in the text, stickiness makes sense in a macroscopic and historical world.

A sphere falling in a fluid feels a viscous force of $6\pi\mu a v_a$ (Stokes Law), where μ is the viscosity, a is the sphere's radius, and v_a is the drift velocity.

On stickiness, see Kuran and Schelling (1978). On hysteresis and non-conservative systems, see Elster (1976). On Schumpeter, see Elster (1983). The quotations are from Schumpeter (1934, p. 64, and 1942, p. 139). See Keynes (chaps. 1, 18). On gift and ritual, see Mauss, van Gennep, Turner, and Sahlins.

On conversion, the *locus classicus* is Augustine in his *Confessions;* see also Kuhn (1970) and Krieger (1981, pt. 2). I am thinking here of Kuhn's account (1987) of the moment when he understood that Aristotle's physics made very good sense in its own terms. On Christianity, see Macmullen. On continuity, see Mendelsohn and Lovejoy.

Concerning oligopolistic competition, see Porter and these notes to chapter 1. The Metropolis algorithm shakes a system out of stickiness by giving it the equivalent of thermal fluctuations. See Kirkpatrick. On implicit contracts, see Schultze; on transaction costs, see Alchian. Solow discusses stickiness and asymmetry in the context of growth theory. Hirschman (1970) describes market entry, and Hirschman (1977) shows how in the history of modern economies gentle smooth commerce proved preferable to discontinuous homicidal passion. On evolution, see Gould (1980, chaps. 1–3).

On tradition, see Shils; on cultural lag, see Ogburn and Rogers. On first order transitions, see Haymet. More generally, we have a story of the relative balance of two forces or energies and of the different modes of organization of the two states: for example, volume versus surface energies, or the free energy of expansion or contraction of a uniform liquid versus the free energy for setting up density modulations that define a crystal. See Landau (pp. 471ff.) on fluctuations and metastability. See Wilson (1979) on second order phase transitions.

Percolation is another model of phase transitions. See Stauffer. At the threshold of percolation, the "infinite" size connected sublattice or cluster is charactered by its having many dead ends. It is a product of the linking up of a large number of small clusters. See the comments of Anderson (1979, pp. 162–163) on the paradigmatic revolution in condensed matter physics, concerning percolation and localization.

Einstein, in 1905, showed the relationship of fluctuations to diffusion and to dissipation, for which see Pais.

On walks subject to springlike forces, see Kac. Say there were another, external force on the particles, now roughly proportional to the distance from equilibrium, as in a spring. Then as a particle moves away from the zero or equilibrium the restoring force grows. So we have in effect given each individual particle information about the zero point. If a particle is far from equilibrium, now it will be drawn back to the origin. And that return will be more rapid than would be the case in a random walk or diffusion without a restoring force, namely, somewhat faster than N^2 moves. Of course, in the purely random case the diffusion is equally likely away from the origin as well as toward it, while in the harmonic case, with a restoring force that grows with distance, motion will more likely be toward the zero. See Kac also for a discussion of irreversibility as modeled by the elastically bound walk.

On Polya urn processes and their application, see Arthur.

Computation may provide some interesting models of stickiness, the stickiness or rigidity here being modeled by the rate at which a computation terminates, and whether it does so at all. The path from problem statement, say a program, toward a stopping point might wander forever, or wander and then home in on a stopping point, or just smoothly "converge." Techniques of probabilistic solution, or those that employ generic schemata, may exhibit behavior not unlike that of a physical system (statistical mechanical annealing, for example, for which see Kirkpatrick). This world of "NP-completeness" may well reproduce the phenomena of stickiness I have mentioned.

On solidarity and stickiness, see Piore (1973).

CHAPTER FIVE

The economist Robert Solow said about being lured away from MIT, "A man would have to be a fool to go somewhere just for money when instead he could sit and talk with Paul Samuelson every day." See E. Marshall.

Levins, drawing from biology and evolution rather than economy and sexuality, provides an elegant discussion of "Cartesian" individualism, and proposes something like perversion as an alternative. Here there is a convergence of nineteenth-century thought about biology, economics, society, and sexuality.

Sexual perversion might be analogized to the ancient economy. For both are mixtures, denying any single universal value. Economy may then possess that universality through the price system, as does conventional sexuality (heterosexual intercourse in marriage, carried to completion) through a fetishism of male and female roles. The virtue of the more usual sexual fetishes is that they challenge the conventional hierarchies, as the economic orders challenge the market.

In the text I make use of the homonymy between properness, property, and properties, analogizing formally correct behavior, ownership, and qualities. My argument will stress how all three are intimately connected in economy and radically challenged in perversion.

We might attribute suitable prices to statuses, high transaction costs to change, and so forth, converting order-like behavior into rational economic behavior. This kind of post-hoc economizing may well work, since there is little canonical constraint on the kinds of transaction costs that may be imputed. (Physicists also invent particles to preserve conservation laws, but the particles must then be found. Are well-established particles ontologically different than conventional transaction costs?) Economists may show that there are prices even for the incommensurable or the tabooed, or at least there are mechanisms that justify that absence of exchange. Exchange need not require money, but for my purposes it is convenient and not problematic to assume their equivalence.

On the value of economy over passion, see Hirschman (1977) and Pocock. On the retention of status, or not, during the transformation to economy and on economy's power to challenge an icon, see Stone; and on the way violations rearrange the boundaries, see Sahlins.

The identity of dynamics and classification naturally follows if you believe: (a) Dynamics is determined by classification. Everything happens or occurs unless it is forbidden. Lovejoy speaks of the "principle of plenitude." There is a "fullness of the realization of conceptual possibility in actuality" (p. 52). (b) And if two things act differently they are different; and if they have different properties they must act differently. Names may be made nondegenerate. (The trick here is to make precise the notion of differences-that-matter, and so the notions of symmetry and invariance, and so what is conserved.) Given plenitude and nondegeneracy, one may probe a structure by trying to violate the rules, and seeing what you can get away with.

Adam Smith argued that the process of exchange would lead to the division of labor implied by classification. Of course, his actors are inventive creatures.

Mauss describes gift systems in which there always are leftovers, stickinesses, and historical residues, and where exchange does not lead to equilibrium but to further unending exchanges.

Economy denies the idea of an incommensurable excellence. Here quality is to be treated as a matter of maximizing a variety of properties on a few mutually commensurable scales of value. And so we might ascribe a series of qualities to a great work of art, and add them up to estimate the work's quality. Actual quality does not seem to be measurable in such an additive fashion. Rather, each work has its own integrity, its own great qualities—whose meaning and excellence are only convincing because those qualities are present in the way they are in this work. But see Meehl on situations in medical diagnosis when one may well be better off in using the economic strategy. Note that in multi-attribute mathematical programming there are multiple alternative solutions, with different qualities, none of which solutions is dominated on all qualities by any other solution.

The term "nonconservative" comes from the description of mechanical systems which dissipate energy. After returning to their "original" state they are not the same. See Elster (1976).

As described by Bataille, perversion is a "sovereign" expending, a cultic ecstasy, a feeling of community, a universal sharing and binding, a connection between death and continuity.

On need, see Ignatieff. On Neurath, see Quine.

The computation of development, rather than its actual simulation, may not be practically possible—unless we have a schema suggesting its general format ahead of time or a capacity to abstract crucial features, again a schema.

"Deferent" comes from my reading in Jacques Derrida's work; and the relationship of gender to metaphor comes from an article, which I cannot now locate, by S. Felman.

Some remarks by Ruben Miller suggested the example of mixed meals.

As for goodness, Sacks argues that illness is not a defective version of goodness or health, not health minus a bad heart or leg. It is another state, one which is not-whole, not repairable in any spare-parts way. Illness is a mediating state. And when things are good again, they are good in a new way.

See Marx on "The Jewish Question" and Arendt on "The Jew as Pariah."

See Sabel on choice of a political economy.

On confinement into well-defined particles, the efforts of physicists to confine quarks are perhaps instructive. The problem was to preserve the quarks' naked properties even when they are bound into a particle—hence the notion of "asymptotic freedom," quarks being more bound and affected by their binding as one tries harder to pull them apart from each other, and more (or asymptotically) free when they are bound in the particle. As for handles and a small number of variables, see Weinberg on the renormalization group.

The McClintock quotation comes from Keller (1983, p. 179).

The wonder that convinces us there is something real to what we are up to is that our breakfast-to-supper everyday work, and the jerry-built stuff we make then, seems to persist and be more useful than we could have imagined. Something invented to do one job becomes with subtle modification a universal tool. The secret is that what is not so versatile or so modified is forgotten, to be succeeded by something more versatile. See Geertz and Hacking (1983).

Among the chapters I will have sketched three accounts of fruitfulness: things are discarded unless they are versatile; the world is archetypally patterned, and once we tap into these patterns we are so to speak in business; and anima. What is perhaps most interesting is our choice of account: historiographic, cosmological, or biological.

In thinking in terms of anima we might be accused of anthropomorphism or of one of the "fallacies" popularized by the New Critics. Such an accusation is, of course, to be affirmed. See Fish on what he calls affective stylistics.

An individual may be defined in statistical physics by its prospectively occupying a region of phase space (momenta, positions, spins) for a very long time, "irreversibly." For example, a crystal is not only a solid, but its axis of symmetry is frozen, fixed along a particular direction. Given our time scales, the individual is for our purposes well defined, even if it may well—with probability $e^{-1,000,000,000,000}$, according to Anderson (1984, p. 29)—mosey over to another region. But that original region, or that orientation defined by the direction of its symmetry axis, is quite arbitrary. We can demonstrate how there can be such order without a directing soul—which is just the purpose of statistical mechanics or of a central limit theorem in probability. As are markets or ecologies, this is the grammar of dumbness exemplified.

Now if we heat up the world, individuals would not be so well defined. Formerly well-separated regions of phase space now overlap and the fluctuations are larger. So individuals won't stay separate, potent, and unto themselves. The grammar of dumbness changes. Far from equilibrium there are seemingly stable individuals such as animals. But they require continuous flows of energy to remain whole and functioning.

A truly dumb world (à la Leibniz) would be one in which the "arbitrary" restrictions—our particular temperature and chemical composition—were also one of its dumb features, say a random chance. Yet, and this is the countertheme to dumbness, we would not be around to appreciate the world's dumbness if the Earth's temperature or water salinities were very different than they have been—for human biology would be impossible. Dyson (1979) describes what would be minimally necessary for such a biology.

Not even the size and commodiousness of phase space, its dimensionality and connectedness, are arbitrary in their implications. And fluctuations and chaos may have their own symmetries and order. So the effects of randomness are not at all arbitrary. *Our* dumb phenomena are perhaps just some particular, predictable, fully meaningful phenomena in the range of the world's possibilities. What we take as an unmarked dumb phase space is actually of a rather canonical, particular, significant form—once we see its features at a high enough level of generality. What we take as dumbness is actually a tight and fortuitous fit. Or so it can be made to seem.

CHAPTER SIX
As indicated in the preface, my discussion here is not meant to directly address the conventional philosophic questions, as presented in something like Aspray. Most of the literature on the philosophy of mathematics (for example, as in Benacerraf and Putnam's collection) is not concerned with the practice of mathematics, especially as would be recognized as verisimilitudinous by mathematicians. Partial exceptions are due to Hadamard, Polya, Lakatos, and Livingston. See Bloor for a review of Livingston, in which it is argued that Wittgenstein's contributions need further acknowledgment.

My concern in this chapter is not so much psychological, methodological, or philosophical. Rather, can we provide a description that would be true to the experience of a working mathematician (at least to some of them), and craftspersons more generally.

My description of "it must be true" deliberately pays less than usual attention to error and mistake. Surely mathematicians are misled, but what concerns me here is how they are led.

On toolmaking, see Dupree. The quotation is from Feynman (1985, p. 224). Milton speaks of justifying the ways of God to man. So application justifies the ways of theory. See also, on mathematical practice, MacLane (chap. 12) and Steen, in which the notion of pattern receives great emphasis. As indicated in the text, what is interesting to me here is not so much the account we give of the unreasonable effectiveness of mathematics, as the experience we have of that surprising fruitfulness. See Daston in Aspray on "mixed" mathematics.

CHAPTER SEVEN
This material was first presented at the Boston Colloquium for the Philosophy of Science.

In a private communication, Steven Woolgar emphasizes to me how unsociological is my account of a toolkit. I conflate the way people talk with the way the world is. I accept the speakers at face value when they use the word "tool," not asking what such a usage might hide. Of course, my purpose here is to describe how that world is talked about and show its congruence with the talk.

On uncovering Nature's secrets, see Keller (1985) on Bacon. On the relationship of physics to meals, see the quotation in Geertz (p. 163). Of course, prandial discussion is often noted as being crucial to the endeavor, and postprandial returns to work are not uncommon. On the sacred in science, Merton provides a nice description. The issues of the relationship of the sacred to the mundane arise in many professions. So, for example, priestly practice is often quite mundane, between breakfast and supper, and so forth.

On tools, see Kuhn, Ravetz, Heidegger, and Polanyi. Heidegger employs tool-using as a central image in his work. Wittgenstein uses craft practice as exemplary in the initial parts of the *Philosophical Investigations*. Tools and craft are the metaphors of a philosophy concerned with function versus essence, with practice versus ideas, with technology versus nature.

Any toolkit actually varies among different institutions and nations and eras, and tools enter and leave the kit. Coaching styles vary, and masters pick their own disciples in varying ways. Different examples and counterexamples are brought up when a point needs to be made, and error and surprise are variously treated.

Hacking talks of tools that have to be used to manipulate the world. On particle physics, see Pickering, Cushing, and Brown and Christ. See Harwit, Price, Latour, Garfinkel, Galison, and Traweek on instruments, as well as Kuhn, Ravetz, and Dupree. Heidegger and Luria discuss the hiddenness of tools behind practice. See Harris for an anthropological perspective on tools. On Feynman, see Feynman (1985) and Dyson (1979). On Fermi, see H. Anderson. Kubler describes how certain practices are successful and come to dominate a craft.

One should keep in mind that tools are not restricted to carpentry or physics. Tools in computer science include "software tools" which are used to build and organize large programs, and recursion and data structures (say as embodied in LISP); literary studies use classical rhetoric and deconstructionist strategies; and lawyers and physicians will speak of professional skills and tools. But not all fields lay claim to their tools as tools. Much of political theory and the humanities see themselves as in opposition to tools or methods. See Wolin.

Sociologists distinguish professions from guilds. My concern here is to emphasize the craft character of professional work.

The Darwin-Fowler method and statistical mechanics in general depend on equilibrium being much more likely than any other state. And in quantum theory, à la Feynman, one might show that the ground state is the most coherent superposition of contributing amplitudes. See also Feynman (1965) on invariance principles.

On physicists and tools, see Purcell, James, Holton, Pais, Livanova, Peierls, Cronin, Dyson (1970), and Feynman (1965), as well as Migdal and Wilson (1983). Anderson (1984, p. 2) characterizes Landau as "less formal, logically more complete," not unlike characterizations of Fermi. Migdal's methods is the source of the "Commonplaces" in the chart, and they reflect a situation in which computers are comparatively unavailable.

S. S. Schweber argues in a forthcoming work that the style of American post–World War II physics reflects the support of the defense community, and this style includes what I call its toolish character.

On diagrammatic and flows, see Misner, in which the geometric, algebraic, and analytic formulations are nicely unified. On the art of addressing nature, see Rabi.

Strictly speaking, my description is of second order phase transitions between the media. This heuristic picture of media is inspired by current models of the early universe and of elementary particles, as well as those of condensed matter.

Feynman (1965) discusses the use of similar equations. Just because two systems have the same equations does not mean that they are the same—the approximations used in getting those equations may be different. Lovejoy discusses the history of plenitude, and Simon and Kirkpatrick discuss cases of $N \log N$. More generally, these $N \log N$ issues arise in sorting.

As for $\log N$: Perhaps the world is hierarchized, so that N objects divide into $\log N$ subgroups, much as the number N requires about $\log_{10} N$ places in a decimal representation. Or perhaps the multiplicity or degeneracy of equivalent states is exponential, so that $N = e^{S/k}$, where S is the entropy, a macroscopic state variable. So, again, the interesting observable number is $\log N$.

Plenitude is crucial. If in a binary representation of our objects, they were only allowed to be represented by 1, 10, 100, 1000, . . ., then for N objects we would need N places (and 2^N would be the largest number). Usually all we need is $\log N$ places (N being the largest number), at least if there is plenitude and all possibilities are allowed and realized (1, 10, 11, 100, . . .).

On strategies for working, see Polya; and Mosteller on J. Savage, for which see the quotation in Krieger (1988) on writing.

See Hacking for a discussion of representing and intervening with tools. The rational economic man in neoclassical microeconomics is smooth, addable, and objective, as Marshall argued.

Another example of making the world suit the physicist is the recent interest in "chaos." It is a way of studying aspects of formerly intractable nonlinear phenomena, in a form a physicist can handle conventionally.

See Traweek for a comparison of training styles in the United States and in Japan, and Bosk and Peierls (1979) for a discussion of error and surprise. On mechanical reproduction, see Benjamin. Dupree articulates the different types of crafts.

Galison (pp. 23–27) discusses Maxwell's division (1876) of instrumental functions into sources of energy, transporters of energy, and measurements of effects, with which the experimental toolkit I suggest has some affinity. In terms of linear systems theory, one has inputs, transfer functions, and outputs.

CHAPTER EIGHT

This chapter originally grew out of an earlier paper (Krieger 1973), "What's Wrong with Plastic Trees?" See also Krieger (1987).

On nuclear war, see Heilbroner, Greenwood, Ikle, Brams, Peattie, and Platt. On risk and rare events, see Douglas and Wildavsky (1982), Mosteller, Pratt, and Machina. The low-probability high-payoff problem is exemplified by the St. Petersburg paradox, and for a history see Jorland. On Pascal, see Hacking (1975). On population, see Ridker. Hollings is illuminating on resilience. On the breakdown of the social order, see Sahlins, and also chapter 5 here. On transitionality and both-and, see Winnicott (1971) and Venturi, respectively, and also Arendt (1978) on the two-in-one. On the lessons of history, see Sabel, and Neustadt.

Dubins recommends a "bold" strategy of betting all in order to achieve unlikely but large returns. If you must gamble, go for broke.

Sharples and Davis provide particularly clear examples of arguments concerning the possibility of doom, in the case of genetically engineered organisms. Are various untoward events near-catastrophes on the way to becoming dooms, or are they signs of our capacities to be responsive to problematic situations?

Environmental changes may be external yet under our influence, as in the greenhouse effect and the decrease in the ozone layer. The crucial question is how reversible is the situation. And how might we design earlier warning mechanisms that give greater weight to dubious evidence if the effects are global? On warning the community and telling the truth, see Bok on lying.

For potential dooms which have long incubation periods and hidden precursors, at least at first, the best current model is AIDS, for which see Lui for some estimates of incubation times. It has been "too late" for some seropositive individuals (the numbers of 0.99, 0.4, and 1.0 I use in the text come from Lui). But drug therapies are likely to alter these numbers or at least the prognosis of AIDS, so in effect it will not be too late for many seropositive individuals. The public health message is that it is surely not too late for the society as a whole. Without diminishing the societal devastation brought by AIDS, it does seem that mundane dooms, even the worst ones imaginable, respond well to invention and prophylaxis.

Obviously, much of what I say about probability, feedback, and information might be expressed in terms of control theory. An alternative formulation might be in terms of ecological systems and predator-prey models. This was suggested to me in conversation by Robert Solow.

There is an interesting application of the Kolmogorov zero-or-one law in probability, to computing the probability of doom. See Feller (vol. 2, pp. 123–124). The Kolmogorov law considers an infinite sequence of independent random variables and defines a "tail event" as one that is expressed in terms of those variables, but is independent of any finite set of them. So doom depends on an infinite sequence (let us say) of moves and countermoves, each of which might be considered to be an independent random variable (a very strong claim). If we believe that there can always be saving moves, that it is never too late, *and* that we are never fully safe from disaster, then doom is such a tail event. No finite set of moves tells us whether doom will happen, if it hasn't already. Doom is a limit, and its nature may well be very different from its precursor events. The theorem then says that if A is a tail event, then the probability of A is either 0 or 1. The probability of doom is zero or one.

Put differently, if we are neither apocalypticists nor marginalists, and we believe doom is to occur through a sequence of moves rather than by an arbitrary divine choice, then doom is either impossible or a certainty. But if we are apocalypticists, then we are likely to believe doom is all but certain; and if we are marginalists, we are likely to believe doom is all but impossible. So for "all" cases doom is either certain or impossible.

The law does not apply to the text of this chapter. There we implicitly assume that there will be just a finite series of moves and they may well not be independent. For example, there could be planning. So despite such a proof, people will still assign a probability to the possibility of doom. They may well feel that doom could occur in a finite number of moves, that is, in historical time, and so we can well be too late. And even if they accepted the condition of an infinite sequence of moves, they still might assign and bet on subjective probabilities. Perhaps the condition is wrong—laws and abstractions are one thing; life and invention are another.

When one examines the proof of the zero-or-one law, it is seen that what is crucial besides independence of the variables is the belief in a path to doom—that is, doom is approximated by a sequence of moves. The demand for a path places Kolmogorov in the historian's realm, but the infinity of the sequence places him in the theological realm.

CHAPTER NINE

On Turner and his thesis, see Billington. Fredrickson provides a review of the subsequent arguments about regeneration through violence. Bellah reviews what it might mean to be American. On otherness and stereotyping, see Gilman. Piore, in Berger (1980) discusses primary and secondary labor markets, and dualism more generally. On immigrants, see Piore (1979) and Glazer. And on the power of commerce to transform absolute values, see Hirschman (1977), Pocock, Sahlins, Thompson, and Turner; and on religion and commerce, see Marx and Weber.

Starr records some of the more violent and impure stories of Southern California's past. On purity in the anthropological realm, see Douglas (1966).

EPILOG

Of late, toolishness and a craft model of design have reemerged as a picture of professional practice. Capacities for observation, assessment, and judgment are encouraged. And many of the new tools reflect a concern with design, holism, purpose, choice, emergentism, anima, history, and discontinuity. If we are still drawn to a story of parts and mechanisms, now the parts are algorithms, automata, and computers that may exhibit memory and purpose rather than clockworks, rational economic men, and atoms. Even more remarkably, synoptic design, represented by the Anthropic Principle, is in fashion. See Gale, and Barrow. And the Great Chain of Being as described by Lovejoy, the world reproducing itself at all scales, is mirrored in modern pictures of phase transitions. See Wilson (1975, 1979) and Mandelbrot.

None of the professions is so sure of what should be in a toolkit. Recently the Association of American Medical Colleges (1983) tried to say just what should be included in a medical education, and implicitly the kit for physicians, with the usual concern about craft and skill. The anatomists believe that the most humanistic of educational experiences is several students, an instructor, and a cadaver. Others recommend Shakespeare.

Payne and Schön discuss the emerging character of the professions. On discipline, see Hearne. My description of the baby as a "going concern" comes from Winnicott, as does the notion of transitionality and good-enough more generally. See Leach as well. See also Krieger (1988) on the inner game of writing and its relationship to transitionality and being a good-enough mother. On deliberate choice, see Sabel and Hirschman (1977). On computation as composed of parts, see Abelson and Sussman.

The quotation from Irwin is in Weschler (pp. 140–141). As for toolishness, Wolin describes why method itself is destructive of thought.

Bibliography

Abelson, H., and A. diSessa. *Turtle Geometry*. Cambridge, MA: MIT Press, 1980.

Abelson, H., and G. Sussman. *Structure and Interpretation of Computer Programs*. Cambridge, MA: MIT Press, 1984.

Adams, H. "The Rule of Phase Applied to History" (1908). In E. Stevenson, ed. *A Henry Adams Reader*. Garden City, NY: Anchor, 1958.

Alchian, A. A., and S. Woodward. "The Firm Is Dead, Long Live the Firm." *Journal of Economic Literature* 26 (March 1988):65–79.

Anderson, H. L., ed. *Physics Vade Mecum*. New York: American Institute of Physics, 1981.

Anderson, P. W. "Lectures on Amorphous Systems." In R. Balian, R. Maynard, and G. Toulouse. *Ill-Condensed Matter*. Amsterdam: North Holland, 1979.

———. *Basic Notions of Condensed Matter Physics*. Menlo Park, CA: Benjamin/Cummings, 1984.

Arendt, H. *The Jew as Pariah*. New York: Grove Press, 1978.

———. *Thinking. The Life of the Mind*. Vol. 1. New York: Harcourt Brace Jovanovich, 1978.

———. *Lectures on Kant's Political Philosophy*. Chicago: University of Chicago Press, 1982.

Arnold, V. I. *Mathematical Methods of Classical Mechanics*. New York: Springer, 1978.

Arthur, W. B. "Competing Technologies and Lock-in by Historical Small Events: The Dynamics of Allocation Under Increasing Returns." Manuscript, Center for Economic Policy Research, Stanford University, 1985.

———, Yu. M. Ermoliev, and Yu. M. Kaniovski. "Path Dependent Processes and the Emergence of Macrostructure." *European Journal of Operations Research* 30 (1987):294–303.

Ashcroft, N., and D. Mermin. *Solid State Physics*. New York: Holt, Rinehart & Winston, 1976.

Aspray, W., and P. Kitcher, eds. *History and Philosophy of Modern Mathematics*. Minnesota Studies in the Philosophy of Science 11. Minneapolis: University of Minnesota Press, 1988.

Association of American Medical Colleges. *Summaries of Reports* . . . Washington, DC: Association of American Medical Colleges, 1983.

———. "Physicians for the Twentieth Century." *Journal of Medical Education* 59, no. 11, pt. 2 (1984):1–208.

Barrow, J. D., and F. Tipler. *The Anthropic Cosmological Principle*. Oxford: Clarendon, 1986.

Bataille, G. *Death and Sensuality*. New York: Arno, 1977.

Bellah, R. N.; R. Madsen; W. M. Sullivan; A. Swidler; and S. M. Tipton. *Habits of the Heart*. Berkeley: University of California Press, 1985.

Benacerraf, P., and H. Putnam. *Philosophy of Mathematics*. New York: Cambridge University Press, 1983.

Bender, C., and S. Orszag. *Advanced Mathematical Methods for Scientists and Engineers*. New York: McGraw-Hill, 1978.

Benjamin, W. *Illuminations*. New York: Schocken Books, 1969.

Berger, S., and M. J. Piore. *Dualism and Discontinuity in Industrial Societies*. Cambridge: Cambridge University Press, 1980.

Billington, R. A. *Fredrick Jackson Turner*. New York: Oxford University Press, 1973.

Bloor, D. "The Living Foundations of Mathematics." *Social Studies of Science* 17 (1987):337–357.

Bochner, S. "Continuity and Discontinuity in Nature and Knowledge." In P. Wiener, ed. *Dictionary of the History of Ideas*, vol. 1. New York: Scribner, 1973.

Bok, S. *Lying*. New York: Vintage, 1979.

Bosk, C. *Forgive and Remember*. Chicago: University of Chicago Press, 1979.

Brams, S. *Biblical Games*. Cambridge, MA: MIT Press, 1980.

Braybrooke, D., and C. Lindblom. *A Strategy of Decision*. New York: Free Press, 1963.

Brown, N. R., and N. H. Christ. "Parallel Supercomputers for Lattice Gauge Theory." *Science* (March 18, 1988):1393–1400.

Brown, P. *Augustine of Hippo*. Berkeley: University of California Press, 1982.

Brush, S. G. "Functional Integrals and Statistical Physics." *Reviews of Modern Physics* 33 (1961):79.

———. *Statistical Physics and the Atomic Theory of Matter*. Princeton, NJ: Princeton University Press, 1983.

Buchanan, J. M. "The Constitution of Economic Policy." *Science* (June 12, 1987):1433–1436.

Caro, R. *The Power Broker*. New York: Vintage, 1975.

Chandler, A. B. *Strategy and Structure*. Garden City, NY: Doubleday, 1966.

Clarke, T. "The Legacy of Skepticism." *Journal of Philosophy* 69 (1972):754–769.

Cohen, I. B. *Revolution in Science*. Cambridge, MA: Harvard University Press, 1985.

Cohen, J. "How Is the Past Related to the Future." *Annual Report*. Stanford: Center for Advanced Study in the Behavioral Sciences, 1982.

Creutz, M. *Quarks, Gluons, and Lattices*. Cambridge: Cambridge University Press, 1983.

Cronin, J. A.; D. F. Greenberg; and V. L. Telegdi, eds. *University of Chicago Graduate Problems in Physics with Solutions*. Reading, MA: Addison-Wesley, 1967.

Cushing, J. T. "Models and Methodologies in Current Theoretical High Energy Physics." *Synthese* 50 (1982):5–101.

Davis, B. D. "Bacterial Domestication: Underlying Assumptions." *Science* (March 13, 1987):1329–1335.

deNeufville, J. I. "Symbol and Myth in Land Policy." In *Values, Ethics, and the Practice of Policy Analysis*. Lexington, MA: Lexington Books, 1983, chap. 12.

Dickson, D. "Science and Political Hegemony in the 17th Century." *Radical Science Journal* 8 (1979):7–37.

Douglas, M. *Purity and Danger*. Baltimore: Penguin, 1966.

———. *The World of Goods*. New York: Basic Books, 1979.

———, and A. Wildavsky. *Risk and Culture*. Berkeley: University of California Press, 1982.

Dubins, L. E., and L. J. Savage. *Inequalities for Stochastic Processes*. New York: Dover, 1976.

Dupree, A. H., and H. W. Dupree. "Performer Crafts and Instrument Maker Crafts: The Persistence of Craft Traditions in Industrial Transformation." Mimeographed, May 7, 1979.

Dyson, F. "The Future of Physics." *Physics Today* 23 (September 1970):23–28.

———. *Disturbing the Universe*. New York: Harper & Row, 1979.

———. "The End of Time." *Reviews of Modern Physics* 51 (1979):447–460.

Edwards, C. H., Jr. *The Historical Development of the Calculus*. New York: Springer, 1979.

Elster, J. "A Note on Hysteresis in the Social Sciences." *Synthese* 33 (1976):371–391.

———. *Explaining Technical Change*. Cambridge: Cambridge University Press, 1983.

Evans-Pritchard, E. E. *Witchcraft, Oracles, and Magic Among the Azande*. Oxford: Clarendon Press, 1937.

Feller, W. *An Introduction to Probability Theory and Its Applications*, vols. 1 and 2. New York: Wiley, 1968, 1971.

Feynman, R. P. *The Character of Physical Law*. Cambridge, MA: MIT Press, 1965.

———. "The Qualitative Behavior of Yang-Mills Theory in $2+1$ Dimensions." *Nuclear Physics* B188 (1981):479–512.

———. *Surely You're Joking, Mr. Feynman*. New York: Norton, 1985.

———, and A. R. Hibbs. *Quantum Mechanics and Path Integrals*. New York: McGraw-Hill, 1965.

Feynman, R. P.; R. B. Leighton; and M. Sands. *The Feynman Lectures in Physics*. Reading, MA.: Addison-Wesley, 1964.

Finley, M. *The Ancient Economy*. Berkeley: University of California Press, 1973.

Fish, S. *Is There a Text in This Class?* Cambridge, MA: Harvard University Press, 1980.

Foucault, M. "What Is an Author?" In P. Rabinow, ed. *Foucault Reader*. New York: Pantheon, 1984.

Fowler, R. H. *Statistical Mechanics*. Cambridge: Cambridge University Press, 1936, 1955.

Freccero, J. *Dante: The Poetics of Conversion*. Cambridge, MA: Harvard University Press, 1986.

Fredrickson, G. "Redemption Through Violence." *New York Review of Books,* November 21, 1985, pp. 38–42.

Gale, G. "The Anthropic Principle." *Scientific American* (December 1981): 154.

Galison, P. *How Experiments End*. Chicago: University of Chicago Press, 1988.

Garfinkel, H.; M. Lynch; and E. Livingston. "The Work of the Discovering Sciences Construed with Materials from the Optically Discovered Pulsar." *Philosophy of the Social Sciences* 11 (1981):137.

Geertz, C. *Local Knowledge*. New York: Basic Books, 1983.

Gerrish, B. *Grace and Reason*. Oxford: Clarendon, 1962.

Gilman, S. *Difference and Pathology*. Ithaca, NY: Cornell University Press, 1985.

Glazer, N. "The Schools of the Minor Professions." *Minerva* 12 (1974):346.

———, and D. P. Moynihan. *Beyond the Melting Pot*. Cambridge, MA: MIT Press, 1963.

Glimm, J., and A. Jaffe. *Quantum Physics: A Functional Integral Point of View*. New York: Springer, 1981.

Goodman, P. *The Structure of Literature*. Chicago: Phoenix, 1964.

Gordon, P.; H. Richardson; and H. L. Wong. "The Distribution of Population and Employment in a Polycentric City: The Case of Los Angeles." *Environment and Planning A* 18 (1986):161–173.

Gould, S. J. *The Panda's Thumb*. New York: Norton, 1980, chaps. 1–3.

———. "Darwinism and the Expansion of Evolutionary Theory." *Science* (April 23, 1982):380–387.

Greenwood, T., and M. L. Nacht. "The New Nuclear Debate: Sense or Nonsense." *Foreign Affairs* 52 (July 1974):761.

Hacking, I. *The Emergence of Probability*. Cambridge: Cambridge University Press, 1975.

———. *Representing and Intervening*. Cambridge: Cambridge University Press, 1983.

———. "Five Parables." In R. Rorty, J. B. Schneewind, and Q. Skinner, eds. *Philosophy in History*. Cambridge: Cambridge University Press, 1984.

Hadamard, J. *The Psychology of Invention in the Mathematical Field*. New York: Dover, 1945, 1954.

Harris, M. *Culture, People, and Nature*. New York: Harper & Row, 1980.

Harwit, M. *Cosmic Discovery*. New York: Basic Books, 1982.

Haymet, A. D. J. "Freezing." *Science* (May 29, 1987):1076–1080.

Hearne, V. *Adam's Task*. New York: Knopf, 1986.

Heidegger, M. *Being and Time*. New York: Harper & Row, 1962.

Heilbroner, R. *An Inquiry into the Human Prospect*. New York: Norton, 1980.

Hessen, B. "The Social and Economic Roots of Newton's 'Principia'." In *Science at the Cross Roads,* 2nd ed. London: Cass, 1971.

Hillis, W. D. "New Computer Architectures and Their Relationship to Physics." *International Journal of Theoretical Physics* 21 (April 1982):255–262.

Hirschman, A. *Exit, Voice, and Loyalty.* Cambridge, MA: Harvard University Press, 1970.

———. *The Passions and the Interests.* Princeton, NJ: Princeton University Press, 1977.

Hollings, C. S. "Resilience and Stability of Ecological Systems." *Annual Review of Ecology and Systematics* 4 (1973).

Holton, G. *The Scientific Imagination.* Cambridge: Cambridge University Press, 1978.

Huang, K. *Statistical Mechanics.* New York: Wiley, 1963.

Ignatieff, M. *The Needs of Strangers.* New York: Viking, 1985.

Ikle, F. "Can Nuclear Deterrence Last Out the Century." *Foreign Affairs* 51 (January 1973):267.

Jaffe, A. "Ordering the Universe, The Role of Mathematics." In *Renewing U.S. Mathematics.* Washington, DC: National Academy Press, 1984.

James, P. B., and J. S. Rigden. "Editorial: The Back of the Envelope." *American Journal of Physics* 50 (December 1982):1069.

Jorland, G. "The St. Petersburg Paradox 1713–1937." In L. Krüger. *The Probabilistic Revolution,* vol 1. Cambridge, MA: MIT Press, 1987.

Kac, M. "Random Walk and the Theory of Brownian Motion." *American Mathematical Monthly* 54 (September 1947):369–391.

Kahrl, W. L. *Water and Power.* Berkeley: University of California Press, 1982.

Kant, I. *The Critique of Judgment.* Oxford: Clarendon, 1952.

———. *The Critique of Pure Reason.* Trans. N. K. Smith. London: Macmillan, 1963.

Keller, E. F. *A Feeling for the Organism.* San Francisco: Freeman, 1983.

———. *Reflections on Gender and Science.* New Haven: Yale University Press, 1985.

Keynes, J. M. *The General Theory of Employment, Interest, and Money.* New York: Harcourt, Brace, 1936.

Kirkpatrick, S.; C. D. Gellatt, Jr.; and M. P. Vecchi. "Optimization by Simulated Annealing." *Science* (May 13, 1983):671–680.

Kitcher, P. *The Nature of Mathematical Knowledge.* New York: Oxford University Press, 1983.

Krieger, M. H. "Modeling Urban Change." *Socio-Economic Planning Sciences* 5 (1971):41–55.

———. "What's Wrong with Plastic Trees?" *Science* (February 2, 1973): 446–455.

———. *Advice and Planning.* Philadelphia: Temple University Press, 1981.

———. "Phenomenological and Many-Body Models in Natural Science and Social Research." *fundamenta scientiae* 2, nos. 3–4 (1981):425–431.

———. "Planning and Design as Theological and Religious Activities." *Environment and Planning* B14 (1987):5–13.

———. "Courage and Character in Planning." *Journal of Planning Education and Research* 7, no. 3 (1988):191–194.

————. "The Inner Game of Writing." *Journal of Policy Analysis and Management* 7 (1988):406–416.

Kripke, S. *Naming and Necessity.* Cambridge, MA: Harvard University Press, 1980.

Kubler, G. *The Shape of Time.* New Haven: Yale University Press, 1962.

Kuhn, T. S. *The Structure of Scientific Revolutions.* Chicago: University of Chicago Press, 1970.

————. "Revisiting Planck." *Historical Studies in the Physical Sciences* 14, no. 2 (1984):231–252.

————. "What Are Scientific Revolutions?" In L. Krüger. *The Probabilistic Revolution,* vol 1. Cambridge, MA: MIT Press, 1987.

Kuran, T. "Preference Falsification, Policy Continuity, and Collective Conservatism." *Economics Journal* 97 (September 1987):642–665.

————. "The Tenacious Past: Theories of Personal and Collective Conservatism." *Journal of Economic Behavior and Organization* 10 (September 1988):143–172.

Lakatos, I. *Proofs and Refutations.* Cambridge: Cambridge University Press, 1976.

Landau, L. D., and E. M. Lifshitz. *Statistical Physics.* Reading, MA: Addison-Wesley, 1958.

Larson, M. *The Rise of Professionalism.* Berkeley: University of California Press, 1977.

Latour, B., and S. Woolgar. *Laboratory Life.* Beverly Hills: Sage, 1979.

Leach, P. *Your Baby and Child.* New York: Knopf, 1979.

Levins, R., and R. Lewontin. *The Dialectical Biologist.* Cambridge, MA: Harvard University Press, 1985.

Lévi-Strauss, C. *The Elementary Structures of Kinship.* Boston: Beacon Press, 1969.

Livanova, A. *Landau: A Great Physicist and Teacher.* Elmsford, NY: Pergamon, 1980.

Livingston, E. *The Ethnomethodological Foundations of Mathematics.* London: Routledge & Kegan Paul, 1986.

Lovejoy, A. O. *The Great Chain of Being.* Cambridge, MA: Harvard University Press, 1936.

Lui, K-J.; W. W. Darrow; and G. W. Rutherford III. "A Model-Based Estimate for the Mean Incubation Period for AIDS in Homosexual Men." *Science* (June 3, 1988):1333–1335.

Luria, A. R. *Cognitive Development: Its Cultural and Social Foundation.* Cambridge, MA: Harvard University Press, 1976.

Lynch, K. *Good City Form.* Cambridge, MA: MIT Press, 1984.

MacArthur, R. H., and E. O. Wilson. *The Theory of Island Biogeography.* Princeton, NJ: Princeton University Press, 1967.

Machina, M. J. "Decision-Making in the Presence of Risk." *Science,* May 1, 1987, pp. 537–543.

MacLane, S. *Mathematics Form and Function.* New York: Springer, 1986.

Macmullen, R. *Christianizing the Roman Empire*. New Haven: Yale University Press, 1985.

Mandelbrot, B. *The Fractal Geometry of Nature*. San Francisco: Freeman, 1982.

Marris, P. *Loss and Change*. Henley-on-Thames: Routledge & Kegan Paul, 1974.

Marshall, A. *The Principles of Economics*. New York: Macmillan, 1920 [1890].

Marshall, E. "Nobel Prize for Theory of Economic Growth." *Science,* November 6, 1987, pp. 754–755.

Marx, K. "On the Jewish Question." In R. C. Tucker, ed. *The Marx Engels Reader*. New York: Norton, 1972.

Mauss, M. *The Gift*. New York: Norton, 1967.

Meehl, P. E. *Psychodiagnosis*. New York: Norton, 1977.

Mellor, J. W., and S. Gavian. "Famine: Causes, Prevention, and Relief." *Science* (January 30, 1987):539–545.

Mendelsohn, E. "The Continuous and the Discrete in the History of Science." *Journal of Social Reconstruction* 1, no. 2 (April 1980):1–31.

Merton, R. K. *The Sociology of Science*. Chicago: University of Chicago Press, 1973.

Meyerson, E. *Identity and Reality*. New York: Dover, 1962 [1908, 1930].

Migdal, A. B. *Qualitative Methods in Quantum Theory*. Reading, MA: Benjamin, 1977.

Mirowski, P. "Shall I Compare Thee to a Minkowski-Ricardo-Leontief-Metzler Matrix of the Mosak-Hicks Type? Or, Rhetoric, Mathematics, and the Nature of Neoclassical Economic Theory." *Economics and Philosophy* 3 (1987):67–95.

Misner, C. W.; K. Thorne; and J. A. Wheeler. *Gravitation*. San Francisco: Freeman, 1973.

Mosteller, F. "Swine Flu: Quantifying the Possibility." *Science* (June 25, 1976):1286.

——. In *The Writings of Leonard Jimmie Savage: A Memorial Selection*. Washington, DC: American Statistical Association, 1981.

Neustadt, R., and E. May. *Thinking in Time*. New York: Free Press, 1986.

Newhouse, J. *The Sporty Game*. New York: Knopf, 1982.

Ogburn, W. F. *Social Change*. Gloucester, MA: Peter Smith, 1964.

O'Hara, F. *The Collected Poems of Frank O'Hara*. New York: Knopf, 1972.

Pais, A. *"Subtle Is the Lord . . .": The Science and Life of Albert Einstein*. New York: Oxford University Press, 1982.

Payne, B. "Contexts and Epiphanies: Policy Analysis and the Humanities." *Journal of Policy Analysis and Management* 4, no. 1 (1984):92–111.

Peattie, L. "Normalizing the Unthinkable." *Bulletin of the Atomic Scientists* 40 (March 1984):32–36.

Peierls, R. *Surprises in Theoretical Physics*. Princeton, NJ: Princeton University Press, 1979.

——. "Model Making in Physics." *Contemporary Physics* 21 (1980):3–17.

————. "Models, Hypotheses, and Approximations." In N. Metropolis, D. M. Kerr, and G. C. Rota, eds. *New Directions in Physics.* Boston: Academic Press, 1987.

Pickering, A. *Constructing Quarks.* Chicago: University of Chicago Press, 1984.

Piore, M. J. "Fragments of a 'Sociological' Theory of Wages." *American Economic Review* 63 (1973):377.

————. *Birds of Passage.* Cambridge: Cambridge University Press, 1979.

Pitkin, H. *Fortune Is a Woman.* Berkeley: University of California Press, 1984.

Platt, J. "Movement for Survival." *Science,* May 11, 1973, p. 580.

Pocock, J. G. A. *The Machiavellian Moment.* Princeton, NJ: Princeton University Press, 1975.

Polanyi, M. *Personal Knowledge.* Chicago: University of Chicago Press, 1958.

Polya, G. *How to Solve It.* Princeton, NJ: Princeton University Press, 1957, 1971.

Porter, M. E., and A. M. Spence. "The Capacity Expansion Process in a Growing Oligopoly: The Case of Corn Wet Milling." In J. J. McCall, ed. *The Economics of Information and Uncertainty.* Chicago: National Bureau of Economic Research, University of Chicago Press, 1982.

Pratt, J. W., and R. Zeckhauser. "Inferences from Alarming Events." *Journal of Policy Analysis and Management* 1 (1982):371–385.

Price, D. D. "Of Sealing Wax and String." *Natural History* (January 1984):49–56.

Purcell, E. M. "The Back of the Envelope, Round Number Handbook of Physics." *American Journal of Physics* 51 (January 1983):11.

Quine, W. V. O. *Word and Object.* Cambridge, MA: MIT Press, 1960.

Rabi, I. I. *Columbia Today* (Winter 1977):6.

Ramond, P. *Field Theory.* Reading, MA: Benjamin/Cummings, 1981.

Ravetz, J. *Scientific Knowledge and Its Social Problems.* Oxford: Clarendon, 1971.

Restivo, S. *The Social Relations of Physics, Mysticism, and Mathematics.* Dordrecht: Reidel, 1983.

————. "Representations and the Sociology of Mathematical Knowledge." In C. Belisle and B. Schiele, eds. *Les Savoirs dans les Pratiques Quotidiennes.* Paris: CNRS, 1984.

Ridker, R. "Population and Pollution in the United States." *Science* (June 9, 1972):1085.

————. "To Grow or Not to Grow: That's Not the Relevant Question." *Science* (December 28, 1973):1315.

Rogers, E. M. *Diffusion of Innovation.* New York: Free Press, 1983.

Sabel, C. *Work and Politics.* New York: Cambridge University Press, 1982.

Sacks, O. *Awakenings.* New York: Dutton, 1983.

Sahlins, M. *Islands of History.* Chicago: University of Chicago Press, 1985.

Scarf, H., and T. Hansen. *The Computation of Economic Equilibria.* New Haven: Yale University Press, 1973.

Schackle, G. L. S. *Epistemics and Economics*. Cambridge: Cambridge University Press, 1972.

Schelling, T. C. *Micromotives and Macrobehavior*. New York: Norton, 1978.

Schön, D. *The Reflective Practitioner*. New York: Basic Books, 1984.

Schöner, G., and J. A. S. Kelson. "Dynamical Pattern Generation in Behavioral and Neural Systems." *Science* (March 25, 1988):1513–1520.

Schulman, L. S., and P. E. Seiden. "Percolation and Galaxies." *Science* (July 25, 1986):425–431.

Schultze, C. "Microeconomic Efficiency and Nominal Wage Stickiness." *American Economic Review* 75 (1985):1–15.

Schumpeter, J. A. *The Theory of Economic Development*. New York: Oxford University Press, 1934, 1961.

———. *Capitalism, Socialism, and Democracy*, 3rd ed. New York: Harper, 1942.

Sharples, F. E. "Regulation of Products from Biotechnology." *Science* (March 13, 1987):1329–1332.

Shils, E. *Tradition*. Chicago: University of Chicago Press, 1981.

Shklar, J. N. "Putting Cruelty First." *Daedalus* 111 (Summer 1982):17–27.

Simon, H. *Models of Man*. New York: Wiley, 1957.

———. *The Sciences of the Artificial*. Cambridge, MA: MIT Press, 1969.

Solow, R. M. "Growth Theory and After." *American Economic Review* 78 (June 1988):307–317.

Starr, K. *Inventing The Dream*. New York: Oxford University Press, 1985.

Stauffer, D. *Introduction to Percolation Theory*. London: Taylor & Francis, 1985.

Steen, L. A. "The Science of Patterns." *Science* (April 29, 1988):611–616.

Stigler, S. *The History of Statistics*. Cambridge, MA: Harvard University Press, 1986.

Stone, L. *The Crisis of the Aristocracy, 1558–1641*. Oxford: Clarendon, 1965.

Thompson, M. *Rubbish Theory*. Oxford: Oxford University Press, 1979.

———, and P. Tayler. *The Surprise Game: An Exploration of Constrained Relativism*. Manuscript, University of Aston, 1986.

Tigerman, S. *Versus*. New York: Rizzoli, 1982.

Traweek, S. *Beamtimes and Lifetimes: The World of High Energy Physicists*. Cambridge, MA: Harvard University Press, 1988.

Tribe, L. "Ways Not to Think About Plastic Trees: New Foundations for Environmental Law." *Yale Law Journal* 83 (June 1974):1315–1348.

Turner, V. *The Ritual Process*. Chicago: Aldine, 1969.

van Gennep, A. *Rites of Passage*. Trans. M. B. Vizedon and G. L. Caffee. Chicago: University of Chicago Press, 1961.

Venturi, R. *Complexity and Contradiction in Architecture*. New York: Museum of Modern Art, 1966.

Viner, J. *The Role of Providence in the Social Order*. Princeton, NJ: Princeton University Press, 1972.

Walzer, M. *Spheres of Justice*. New York: Basic Books, 1983.

Webber, M. "The Urban Place and the Nonplace Urban Realm." In M. M. Webber et al. *Explorations into Urban Structure*. Philadelphia: University of Pennsylvania Press, 1964.

Weber, M. *The Protestant Ethic and the Spirit of Capitalism*. New York: Scribner, 1976.

Weinberg, S. "Why the Renormalization Group Is a Good Thing." In A. H. Guth, K. Huang, and R. L. Jaffe, eds. *Asymptotic Realms of Physics*. Cambridge, MA: MIT Press, 1983.

————. "Calculation of Fine Structure Constants." In R. Jackiw, ed. *Shelter Island II*. Cambridge, MA: MIT Press, 1985.

Weschler, L. *Seeing Is Forgetting*. Berkeley: University of California Press, 1982.

Wigner, E. P. "The Unreasonable Effectiveness of Mathematics in the Natural Sciences." In *Symmetries and Reflections*. Cambridge, MA: MIT Press, 1970.

Wildavsky, A. *The Nursing Father*. University, AL: University of Alabama Press, 1984.

Wilson, E. O. *The Insect Societies*. Cambridge, MA: Harvard University Press, 1970.

Wilson, K. "The Renormalization Group: Critical Phenomena and the Kondo Problem." *Reviews of Modern Physics* 47 (October 1975):773.

————. "Problems in Physics with Many Scales of Length." *Scientific American* (August 1979):158–179.

————. "Theoretical Science and the Future of Large Scale Computing." *CERN Courier* 23 (June 1983):172–177.

Winnicott, D. W. *The Child, the Family, and the Outside World*. Baltimore: Penguin, 1964.

————. *Playing and Reality*. London: Tavistock, 1971.

Wittgenstein, L. *Philosophical Investigations*. New York: Macmillan, 1958.

Wolfram, S. *Theory and Applications of Cellular Automata*. Singapore: World Scientific, 1986.

Wolin, S. "Political Theory as a Vocation." *American Political Science Review* 63 (1969):1062.

Index

Note: Major themes are indicated in boldface type, and are provided with more extensive cross references: **Discontinuity, Horizon, Marginalism, Middles and mixtures, Tools, Tool and toolkit.**

A

Abstraction. *See* Dumbness
Action, and actor, 14
Adding up the world, 4; computation and, 149
Addition: discrete pieces, 29–31; smooth pieces, 23–29. *See also* Oriented addition
Advice, 139
Alienation: in economy, 62; and fetishism, 77–78; and perversion, 74
American, ideal of being, 133
Analogy, ix; in physicist's toolkit, 108; and unity of mathematical world, 90
Analysis, in fetishism, 79
Anderson, P. W., on societal models, 149
Anima, 157; and fetishism, 77, 78, 79
Animation, 79–80
Anthropology, stickiness in, 53–54
Application, and mathematics, 87, 94. *See also* Horizon, Versatility
Argument from design, 157, xiv
Arithmetic, xx, 23–24, 152
Arthur, W. B., 59, 154
Aspectival variations, 90. *See also* Horizon
Augustine of Hippo: City of God, 134; on conversion, 5, 8; *Confessions,* 6
Authority, in perversion, 75
Autonomy of mathematical objects, 89, 90

B

Benjamin, W., 111
Big and little: defined, 6; relationship of, 3, 21–23
Big decisions, 3–17; recognizing, 145
Boltzmann, on adding up in a gas, 29
Boston Celtics, 135

Boundaries, and perversion, 68
Breakdown: of Ancient modes, 63; of social order, 120

C

Cage, J., 78
Calculation, and observation, 33–34
Calculus, xi, 20, 24–29; in adding up, 31; and marginalism, xiv, 17; as a technology, 32. *See also* Fundamental Theorem
Cambridge controversy, 145
Capitalism, and its modes of transformation, 132. *See also* Alienation
Cartesian individualism, 155
Catastrophe, 125
Causality, and centers, 46
Center: defined, 37, 45; setting up a, xxi; at X, 47
Centralization, 37–50
Chance, institutions for, 145
Christianity, and conversion, 151–152
Cities, as centers, 39
Classification, xxii; and dynamics, 155; and exchange, 66; and representation, 74
Coaching, in doing physics, 102
Collective excitations, 146. *See also* Quasi-particles
Collective action and blindness, 122. *See also* Invisible Hand
Command, and marginalism, 16–17
Commensurability, 22. *See also* Incommensurability
Commodity fetish. *See* Fetish, Economy
Community, and perversion, 71
Complexity, and doom, 124
Componential, vs. marginal, 7
Composition, and fetishism, 77–78

175